LE CORBUSIER & PIERRE JEANNERET

RESTORATION OF THE CLARTÉ BUILDING, GENEVA

BIRKHÄUSER BASEL

OFFICE DU PATRIMOINE ET DES SITES, GENÈVE

17 **Preface**
Jean-Pierre Duport

19 **Introduction**
Sabine Nemec-Piguet

22 **THE CLARTE BUILDING REFLECTIONS ON THE HISTORICAL CONTEXT**

24 **The historical context of the Clarté site – Le Corbusier and Pierre Jeanneret**
Catherine Courtiau

32 **"A milestone of modern architecture …" The Clarté building in the creations of Le Corbusier and Pierre Jeanneret**
Arthur Rüegg

42 **THE RESTORATION IN QUESTION**

44 **Lessons of a rehabilitation**
Bernard Zumthor

49 **The restoration of the Clarté building, an introduction**
Jacques-Louis de Chambrier

52 **BUILDING PLANS HISTORICAL PLANS RESTORATION PLANS**

74 **THE RESTORATION OF 2007–2011 AT THE HEART OF THE WORKS**
Sabine Nemec-Piguet, Marielle Savoyat

76 **Introduction**
78 **The site installation**
82 **The roof**
90 **The balconies**
100 **The metal facades and windows**
110 **The roller blinds and their enclosures**
116 **Masonry and reinforced concrete**
118 **Travertine cladding**
120 **The glass bricks**
124 **The technical services**
128 **The communal areas**
138 **Colours**

150 **ANNEXES**

152 **Chronology**
155 **Regulations for co-owners 2008**
158 **Excerpts from the Inventory undertaken by the firm of architects Laurent Chenu**
160 **Principles for conservation of interior areas – rules of intervention for the owner's attention**
163 **Construction of 1931–1932**
164 **Restoration project of 2007–2011**
165 **Biographical notes**
171 **Select bibliography and sources**

175 Acknowledgements
176 Credits

pp. 1–4 and 8–11
Collection of colour photos taken after building restoration.

p. 5
5-roomed full-depth apartment, south side, eighth floor of No. 4, belonging to Robert (brother of Pierre) and Paulette Jeanneret, parents of Jacqueline. Behind the balcony's round table, Pierre and Jacqueline Jeanneret. In the foreground, Francis Quétant and a 1931 Werner Max Moser chair. Photo delivered 12 June 1933, by Boissonnas.

p. 6
View of the roof terrace. On the left, Madame Quétant, to the right, her sister. Photo dated 19 October 1932, courtesy of Boissonnas.

p. 7
View of Francis Quétant's apartment, in the "wagon". Photo dated 19 October 1932, courtesy of Boissonnas. – Caption taken from "La maison de Verre", in *L'Art en Suisse,* Geneva, No. 45, April-May 1933: "G.A. Hufschmid, arch. dec. [architect decorator] Studio of Mr. Quétant, Metal furnishings manufactured by Wanner & Cie. Trimmings and fabrics: G.u.R. Desponds, upholsterers. Walls: wallpapers Le Corbusier (Salubra) pale blue and dark red."

Preface

Jean-Pierre Duport

President of the Fondation Le Corbusier from January 2003 to December 2012

After completion in 2010, following a long programme of works, the "House of glass" has recovered its transparency, its lightness, and its colour. The only building realized by Le Corbusier and Pierre Jeanneret in Geneva (in collaboration with Edmond Wanner) has regained its presence in the city. The Clarté building assumes its full meaning in the context of works by the architect.

The scope of the Clarté building restoration bears witness to the new approach to today's heritage adopted by governments, experts, and building owners. This is especially true of work by Le Corbusier. Over the past decade we have been lucky to witness the rescue of abandoned buildings designed by him, like the Jeanneret-Perret House at La Chaux-de-Fonds, allowing a rediscovery of work often overlooked by the public and critics. Simultaneously, other renovation projects have started, notably in Germany and France, often motivated by the need to maintain structures that are fragile, principally due to their experimental nature.

It should also be welcomed that these projects have all been undertaken with the greatest respect for the original. They have benefited from methods that today permit an understanding of the history and better knowledge of the materials used. The extent of work undertaken during a restoration such as Clarté represents a unique opportunity to "X-ray" all elements of a building, analyse the materials, and document its many layers. These studies enrich the original documentation and contribute to the theoretical and aesthetic knowledge of Le Corbusier's creations. Dissemination of this knowledge benefits the entire network of property owners and managers confronted by the same questions in different contexts.

The rebirth of Clarté required substantial scientific, technical, and financial resources, which contribute to the long-term preservation of the building. I would like to thank all those who, over recent years, have fought to prevent this building from falling into oblivion, and who have campaigned to ensure its exemplary restoration. The State of Geneva and the Federal Office of Culture have made available all their skills to ensure full scientific support of the project. They have financially supported the efforts of the community of owners, favouring the realisation of particularly complex and expensive work. I also salute the commitment of the project manager, Jacques-Louis de Chambrier, and that of his colleagues, who bravely decided to set up their workshop at the heart of the worksite, thereby sharing the daily challenges of the team.

This groundswell, which today benefits many of Le Corbusier's built projects, will allow us to reassess and revisit other more or less well-known buildings in years to come, thus providing their residents with a better appreciation of them. We must hope that, encouraged by these examples, new restorations will be undertaken, consolidating the experience and allowing the understanding of this legacy to prosper. This is also the approach taken by the seven countries that are committed to the addition of Le Corbusier's architectural work to the list of UNESCO World Heritage sites. Beyond the recognition of the universality of such work, it is a question of obtaining long-term commitment to preserve this exceptional heritage from the regions, communities, and other concerned partners. The re-birth of Clarté will undoubtedly help convince them.

Introduction

Sabine Nemec-Piguet

Director general, cantonal conservator of monuments, State of Geneva. Office of Heritage Buildings and Sites

In Volume 2 of his complete works published in 1935, Le Corbusier asked: "What did we achieve in those years from 1929 to 1934? First, some buildings, then many large urban studies. These buildings have served as laboratories. We wanted each element built during those years to provide the experimental evidence that would allow us to confidently take indispensable initiatives in urban planning." [1]

The Clarté building was not conceived as a simple apartment block[2]. At the architectural level it embodied a new urban construction project, where the construction of multiple housing units was only made possible by a revolution in the art of building and lifestyle. The model for implementation was to be sought in the production methods of heavy industry, with its processes of standardisation, prefabrication, and its rational economic logic.

The story of the Clarté building demonstrates how difficult it is to concretise totally innovative ideas, and to have them recognised. The construction of this building remained an isolated event, despite a development plan that targeted the future growth of the district, including replacement of the existing small houses, workshops, and warehouses. Today, eighty years later, the district remains chaotic: the few high buildings, erected in the years 1960–1980, form the western front of the Adrien-Lachenal road and dominate what remains of the old suburban fabric of Terrassière. In 1965, the year Le Corbusier died, the Geneva section of the Swiss Federation of Architects (FAS) applied to the cantonal government for classification of the Clarté building as a historic monument, but this was not successful. Four years later, when the company that owned the property wished to demolish the building, a petition relaunched the application for classification, while the FAS organised a bid to purchase shares of the property company Clarté AG, and thus save from demolition the only Geneva building designed by the famous architect. In 1985, another petition, this time aiming at thwarting the development of the Villereuse triangle before the Clarté preservation initiative, finally resulted in the protection of this historic monument[3].

The restoration of Clarté was also a long process. Having escaped demolition, the building underwent its first major renovation from 1975 to 1977. Over the next thirty years, no renovation fund having been established, the building deteriorated heavily in the absence of maintenance. In 1975, nearly half of the apartments (44 per cent) were sold to individuals to finance the renovation, while the majority of the building (56 per cent) remained in the hands of the company Clarté AG. When this company went bankrupt in the early 2000s, its holding, mortgaged to the Geneva Cantonal Bank (BCG), was repossessed by the BCG's Asset Valuation Foundation. In 2003, the State Council, based on the legal obligation for maintenance of listed buildings, interceded with the owners, and particularly with the majority owner, the BCG's Asset Valuation Foundation, brandishing the threat of mandatory works as required by law[4]. Conscious that the recovery of its investment would be helped by improvement of the building, the BCG's foundation decided to undertake the rehabilitation of the building envelope and the communal areas prior to the sale of lots in its possession. The Foundation received the unanimous support of the residents' association in September 2003 and the restoration project could be launched.

Protecting the heritage of the XX century, as recommended by the Council of Europe, must comply with specific rules[5], which complement those of the Venice Charter. The Federal Commission for historical monuments visited the building on 21 October 2003 and emphasised that its restoration must be of exemplary quality[6]. Furthermore, in December 2004, the Clarté building, recognised as a significant architectural monument of European culture, was proposed for inclusion on the UNESCO World Heritage list. Given the now national and international value of the building, the Federal Office of Culture delegated a federal expert to oversee the work. The Fondation Le Corbusier was also associated with the project's development. An architectural firm was commissioned by the majority owner, the BCG's Asset Valuation Foundation, to develop a restoration project under the supervision of the team of experts with the scientific support of the Office of Heritage Buildings and Sites. The building permit was issued on 24 June 2005. On 15 March 2007, the general meeting of the property's owners unanimously accepted the budget submitted. The project could then enter its implementation phase and construction started on site on 11 June.

A few months later, the Swiss section of ICOMOS organised a major symposium that took place at the Clarté site, with each trade presenting its planned interventions[7].

Preparatory work revealed that the building's original materials had survived remarkably well, the absence of maintenance funds having at least had the advantage of avoiding destructive work. The initial objective of restoring the building envelope and communal areas perfectly targeted the maximum preservation and repair of all original construction elements still in place. Nonetheless, after three-quarters of a century, material wear and tear, accelerated by chronic lack of maintenance, dictated a different approach. The advanced state of deterioration of the roofs and facades imposed a strategy for the replacement of these external components with identical or similar materials. To verify the restoration hypotheses, a prototype facade panel was realised and validated in late 2005 to early 2006, on a small south-facing duplex apartment. A balcony prototype was executed in January 2007. Elsewhere, part of the facade of a south-facing studio from the first to the fourth floor (three storeys), and a section of glass bricks with associated metalwork on the ground floor, were preserved in their original state for reference.

As an inhabited monument, the Clarté building cannot be treated as a simple artwork for which museum values prevail. By maintaining its use as collective housing, a necessary condition for preservation, it differs from other XX century architecture monuments that became museums open to visitors, as has been the case with iconic homes designed by great architects of the Modern Movement, such as Adolf Loos, Frank Lloyd Wright, Gerrit Rietveld, Mies van der Rohe, and Le Corbusier.

The essential features of the building, a "machine for living", must be guaranteed while meeting the current requirements for stability, sealing, security, heating, ventilation, water supply, and electricity. The necessary modernisation of these technical systems and the installation of devices for fire prevention were carried out with great care, respecting the architecture of the building, but nonetheless introducing new materials and construction elements such as doors, fire-resistant ceilings and walls, silicone seals, insulating glass, and multi-component paints.

As the work proceeded, a complete record of each apartment was established, detailing all changes made since the building's construction[8]. The state of conservation of the building's interiors was also found to be remarkable, except for the disappearance of the original Salubra wallpapers, removed between 1975 and 1977[9]. Only a few rare modifications had altered the original plan of the housing units. Therefore, it appeared essential to rigorously maintain the types of apartments, excluding demolition of any internal walls, with one exception, the enlargement potential for the kitchen by including its

(6.40 m^2) adjoining room. The residents' association incorporated the principles of conservation and intervention, developed by the Office of Heritage Buildings and Sites, in the building's Rules of Administration and Use[10].

Investigations conducted before and during construction have enhanced knowledge of the building. It has unfortunately not been possible to correct some earlier changes, such as the layout of the restaurant or the privatisation of the roof area. Regarding colour[11], however, the restoration of the original colours, identified by a methodical and scientifically conducted campaign of stratigraphy, has highlighted the extraordinary architectural coherence that, with alteration over time, had become lost to memory. Clarté has always embodied a functionalist, rationalist approach, the model that was to inspire the "ville radieuse", the perfect architecture for an ideal city. This restoration has revealed its poetic dimension, an expression of great formal mastery, a demonstration of magisterial architecture, a true artistic achievement. We dream of one day being able to rediscover the jubilant facade effect of the vibrant interior colours of each apartment and the collection of transparent fabrics behind the smooth wall of glass, both desired by Le Corbusier and initially imposed upon the building's tenants.

With the concept of "immeubles-villas" imperfectly realised in his eyes by Clarté, Le Corbusier was seeking an architectural and urban style for single-family city housing units. He sought a style opening perspectives other than neighbourhoods of detached homes, a conception issuing from a simplistic transplant of mono-functional land occupation, and resulting in excessive ground consumption devoid of urban advantages. This problematic remains relevant today.

Thanks to this remarkable restoration, Clarté, which has lost none of its innovative character eighty years after its construction and instead enjoys a new-found allure, should entice and inspire property investors and their architects in search of an exemplary urban habitat, following in the footsteps of Edmond Wanner and Le Corbusier.

1 Le Corbusier and Pierre Jeanneret, *Œuvre complète de 1929–1934*, Zurich: Girsberger, 1935 and 1964, 11.

2 Siegfried Giedion, Preface, ibid.

3 Protection order adopted by the State Council on 12 November 1986 (MS-c 219).

4 Law on the protection of monuments, nature and sites (LPMNS) of 4 June 1976, Article 19, Obligations of the owner: "The listed buildings must be maintained by the owner. If necessary, the competent authority shall set a reasonable time for the owner to carry out the necessary maintenance work. If he does not comply, the competent authority shall carry out the work at the owner's expense."

5 Recommendation No. R (91) 13 on the protection of architectural heritage of the twentieth century, adopted by the Council of Europe Committee of Ministers on 9 September 1991.

6 Federal Commission on Historic Monuments, Geneva, Clarté building, position taken on 16 December 2003.

7 Seminar entitled *"Enhancement of the built heritage"*, on 2 and 3 November 2007, organised by ICOMOS Switzerland (International Council on Monuments and Sites) with the participation of DOCOMOMO Switzerland (Foundation for the Documentation and Conservation of Buildings of the Modern Movement).

8 Inventory and record of apartments built between 2003 and 2006. Scale: 1:100. Architect: Laurent Chenu. Mandate of the Office of Heritage Buildings and Sites of the canton of Geneva.

9 See page 139, illustration No. 2, pieces of Salubra wallpaper.

10 Principles of conservation of interior spaces, intervention rules to the attention of the owners, Office of Heritage Buildings and Sites, 18 January 2008. See extracts drawn from the Rules of Administration and Use, attached as an appendix.

11 See the table on page 144.

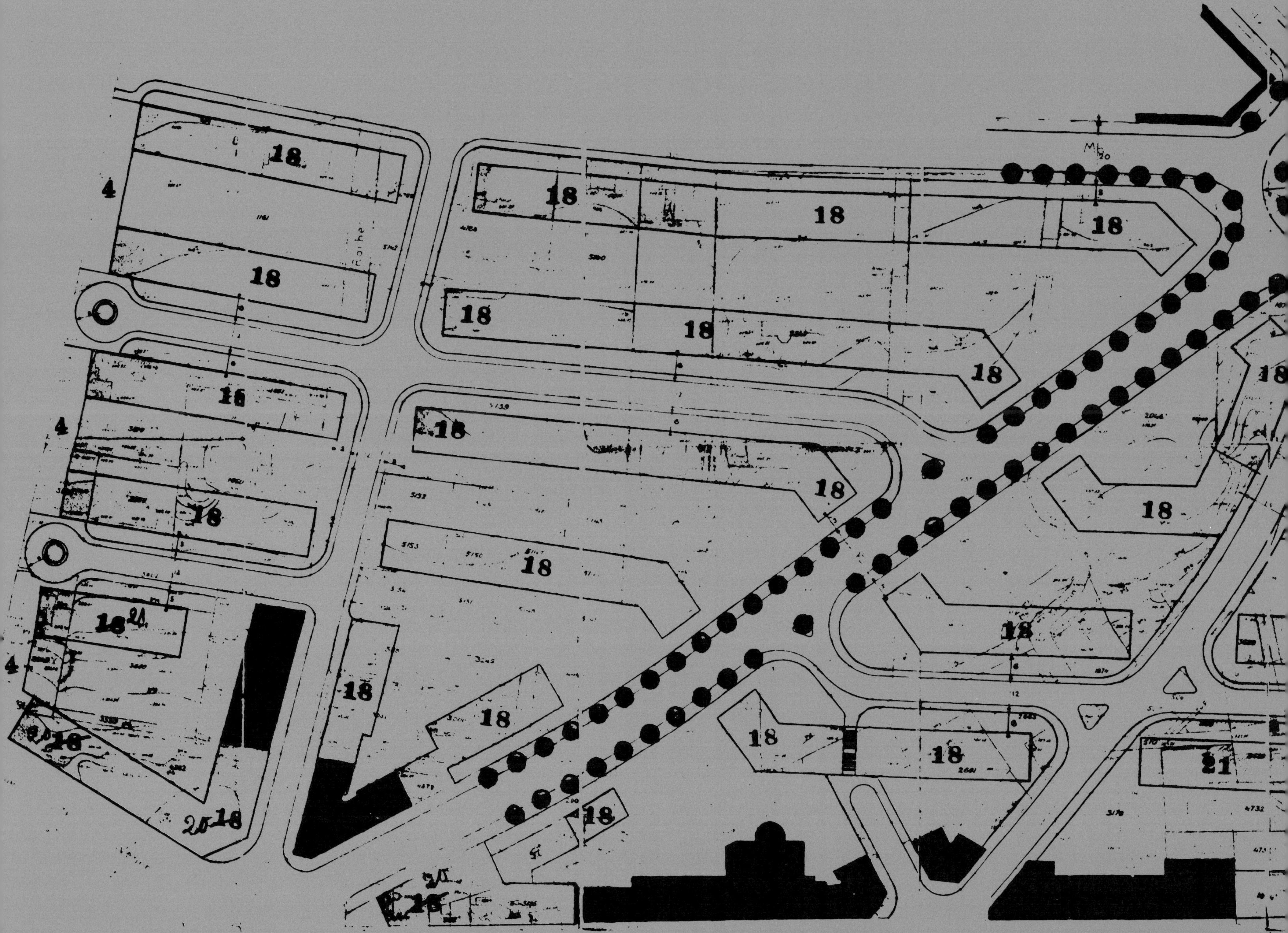

4
18
21

THE CLARTE BUILDING REFLECTIONS ON THE HISTORICAL CONTEXT

The historical context of the Clarté site – Le Corbusier and Pierre Jeanneret

Catherine Courtiau

Geneva under full expansion

Between the two world wars Geneva underwent extensive development, deploying great energy and imagination to rise to its new status as an international city, as designated by the Treaty of Versailles in 1919. The city quickly built its first airport at Cointrin, recognised in 1920 by the Federal Air Office, and planned the Palais des Nations, constructed between 1929 and 1936.

The law of 9 March 1929 on the extension of transportation routes and neighbourhood development, initiated by Camille Martin, director of the expansion plan, sparked the launching of many urban development projects.

Despite the crisis following the 1929 stock market crash, Geneva saw the renovation of its dilapidated 1858 railway station between 1927 and 1932, the construction of several housing ensembles in 1931–32, and the building of the Hôtel Cornavin and Hôtel Richemond, as well as the Disarmament Pavilion behind the Palais Wilson, a project that at the time was in competition with the Clarté site regarding construction methods and speed[1].

Developed by the contractor and landowner Edmond Wanner, the Clarté building remains the only witness to the extensive development planned for the Terrassière neighbourhood, where Le Corbusier and Pierre Jeanneret initially envisioned an ensemble of detached houses. Originally, the Clarté was meant to be located on rue de l'Athénée, near Parc Bertrand, and then parallel to rue de la Terrassière, a thoroughfare travelled since 1864 by the legendary number 12 tram line. This area, the former suburb Villereuse, was part of the Eaux-Vives district that merged with the City of Geneva in 1931, the year that the construction of the Clarté began.

The Clarté building was Le Corbusier and Pierre Jeanneret's sole built project in Geneva. However, they worked on many other projects in the city: the transmutation of the universalist ideals of Paul Otlet into a vast architectural programme called the Mundaneum or World Museum (1928), then the Cité mondiale (1929), the Wanner projects on the rue de l'Athénée (1928–29), the extraordinary Palais des Nations (from the 1926 design competition to a second accusation of plagiarism in 1931), and

p. 23
Development plan No 1137 / 68 of the Terrassière neighbourhood, adopted by the State Council on 2 June 1931.

1

the development of the right bank in Saint-Gervais (1933)[2]. There was also the Villa Ruf built in 1929 in Grand-Saconnex, for which the architects had drawn up preliminary sketches and plans. The design for the Villa Ruf was completed by Francis Quétant, a member of the GANG (New Architecture Group in Geneva); a Wanner employee, he was responsible for the studies and costings for the Clarté building.

This group, created in 1931, brought together Frédéric Gampert, Alberto Sartoris, Marc Joseph Saugey, Jean-Henri Schürch, and René Schwertz, along with two major actors in the construction of Clarté, Boris Nazarieff and Quétant. The GANG, impressed by the 1929 International Modern Architecture Congress (CIAM)[3] in Frankfurt, organized an exhibition entitled "New Frankfurt" in April 1931 at the School of Industrial Arts of Geneva on the theme of "minimum housing", and invited Ernst May, social housing architect and designer.

1
Disarmament Pavilion by the architect Adolphe Guyonnet and the engineer Louis Perrin, at the completion of works in 1932. In the background, the National hotel (Palais Wilson).

2
Geneva, rue Saint-Laurent, Clarté building (metallic structure), south side, 1932. Assembly of the welded-in-place metal framework, Solomite, etc., commencing the realisation of habitation units from top to bottom, method proposed by Edmond Wanner, then abandoned after an accident on site. Crane on rails by Wanner & Company.

3
Villa Ruf under construction at 12, chemin des Manons, Grand-Saconnex (Geneva), in May 1929; constructed by Francis Quétant, following the plans of Le Corbusier, at the instigation of Edmond Wanner. Metallic Structure by the Sécheron ateliers, prior to placing walls made of Solomite.

4
Clarté building, Geneva. View of the north facade showing the advertisement of an exhibition of modern buildings, 4 June 1932.

2

3

4

5

The prolific activities of Le Corbusier and Jeanneret in the 1920s and '30s

Painting and furniture

During the years of preliminary studies and particularly during the construction of the Clarté, from 1928 to 1932, Le Corbusier devoted himself to painting and the design of furniture and interiors. The young interior designer Charlotte Perriand[4], who began working with Le Corbusier and Jeanneret shortly after the 1927 Salon d'Automne, presented several pieces of furniture (including an easy chair) in Paris during the 1929 Salon d'Automne, while Le Corbusier was on a lecture tour in South America.

In 1930, during the first exhibition of the Union of Modern Artists (UAM) at the Pavillon de Marsan at the Louvre in Paris, Perriand, a member of the UAM, presented, among other work, the famous rocking chair chaise longue the three had designed.[5]

Concepts – publications and exhibitions

Under the Esprit Nouveau imprint that Le Corbusier launched in Paris in 1920 with his friend the painter Amédée Ozenfant, he published several books explaining, sometimes in conjunction with Jeanneret, his concepts and positions (standardisation, the rationalisation and industrialisation of construction, mass-produced housing, and modular housing, Dom-Ino, Monol, Citrohan, etc.): *Vers une architecture* (1923), *Urbanisme* (1925), *Almanach d'architecture moderne* (1926), *Une maison – un palais* (1928), *Précisions sur un état présent de l'architecture et de l'urbanisme* (1930), and *La Ville radieuse* (1935).

The concept of "lotissements fermés à alvéoles" or "immeubles-villas"[6] – although not concretized in the first of the rue de l'Athénée projects, nor those on the rue de la Terrassière – had been developed by Le Corbusier at the Salon d'Automne in 1922 and published the following year in *Vers une architecture,* included in *Urbanisme,* and described as follows in l'*Almanach*[7] in 1926: *"The IMMEUBLE-VILLAS is not a simple rental apartment block. It brings about complete independence for each owner and includes this important new element: a garden of 70 m², onto which the main rooms of each 'villa' open. The IMMEUBLE-VILLAS is a new form of urban housing."*

5
Geneva: Wanner Buildings. First of the Athénée projects. Perspectives of the immeubles-villas for construction at the Athénée.

In 1925, the printed invitations to the Modern Decorative and Industrial Exposition in Paris described the New Spirit Pavilion of Le Corbusier and Jeanneret as "dedicated to the reform of housing (the transformation of the layout, standardisation and industrial construction). It includes an entire cell of 'immeuble-villas' with a hanging garden." It was at this event that the two architects probably first met Edmond Wanner; the jury awarded him the first prize with distinction for his work in decorative ironwork.

On the occasion of the Weissenhofsiedlung exhibition held in 1927 by the Deutscher Werkbund at Stuttgart, Le Corbusier and Jeanneret designed two houses and announced the "five points of a new architecture" (pilotis[8], roof terrace, open plan, broad windows, open facade) in a book by the Zurich architect Alfred Roth, who was responsible for the Stuttgart[9] construction. Four of these five points (roof terrace, open plan, broad windows, open facade) were applied to the Clarté building.

Finally, in 1931, Le Corbusier created his first "clavier de couleurs"[10] or colour chart, at the request of Salubra, the Bâloise wallpaper factory, whose extensive range was used in the Clarté building.

6
Two residential houses by Le Corbusier and Pierre Jeanneret at Weissenhofsiedlung, Stuttgart, 1927. Photo Dr Lossen & Co.
7
Clarté building, Geneva. View of the roof terrace, showing the radio antenna above the skylight. Photo dated 19 October 1932, courtesy of Boissonnas.

7

8

9

10

8
Geneva, rue Saint-Laurent, Clarté building. Rear facade on the ruelle du Couchant. Plunging view from the Adrien-Lachenal road, 4 June 1932.
9
Clarté building, view of the south and west facades. Photo by Boissonnas, dated 12 June 1933.
10
Clarté building, view from the entrance hall of No 4. Photo by Boissonnas, dated 19 October 1932.

Urban planning and architecture

During this particularly prolific period, Le Corbusier, together with Jeanneret, conceived many large-scale urban development and architectural projects[11]: the South American sketches of 1929, the Ville radieuse in 1930, the Plan Obus for the renovation of the city of Algiers in 1931, the development of Porte Maillot in Paris, the Loucheur houses, and the Palace of Soviets in Moscow and Centrosoyus, which took from 1928 to 1934 to build because of the many proposed designs required and the construction difficulties that had to be resolved.

During this period Le Corbusier and Jeanneret designed several historically significant buildings: the villa at Carthage in Tunisia (1929), the Savoye villa at Poissy (1928–31), the Helen de Mandrot villa at Pradet near Toulon (1929), the Cité de Refuge for the Salvation Army in Paris (1929–33), the installation of a triplex penthouse apartment in an old building on the Champs-Elysées for Charles Beistegui (1930–1931), and the Swiss pavilion at the Cité universitaire in Paris (1931–33), for which Charlotte Perriand fitted out the student rooms and the library. Finally, Le Corbusier refurbished his own duplex apartment in the building he had had built on rue Nungesser-et-Coli in Paris between 1931 and 1934.

Voyages and lectures

Despite these many commitments Le Corbusier undertook long voyages: Prague in 1928, Moscow in 1928, 1929, and 1930, South America in 1929, Spain in 1930, Sweden, Norway, England, Morocco, and Algeria in 1931, Holland in 1932, lectures in Zurich in 1932, and Stockholm, Oslo, Goteborg, and Antwerp in 1933.

There were also trips for congresses and exhibitions, notably the CIAM[12], launched at the initiative of Le Corbusier, Gabriel Guevrekian, Sigfried Giedion, and members of the Swiss Werkbund. The first CIAM was held in 1928, at the La Sarraz castle, home of Hélène de Mandrot, patron and fervent admirer of Le Corbusier, who had supported him throughout his troubles associated with the Palais des Nations competition in Geneva.

This first congress was followed by the second CIAM in Frankfurt in 1929, the third CIAM in Brussels in 1930, the Congress of the CIRPAC (International Committee for the Realization of Contemporary Architectural Problems) in Barcelona in 1931, and the fourth CIAM in Athens in 1933. The presentations at this last congress were the basis for Le Corbusier's *La Charte d'Athènes,* not published until 1942.

11

11
CIAM, June 1928 at La Sarraz (Canton of Vaud, Switzerland). From left to right, standing: Mart Stam, Pierre Chareau, Victor Bourgeois, Max Haefeli, Pierre Jeanneret, Gerrit Rietveld, Rudolf Steiger, Ernst May (face half hidden), Alberto Sartoris, Gabriel Guevrekian, Hans Schmidt, Hugo Häring, Juan Zavala, Lucienne Florentin, Le Corbusier, Paul Artaria, Hélène de Mandrot, Friedrich T. Gubler, Charles Rochat, André Lurçat, Henri-Robert Von der Mühll, Gino Maggioni, Huib Hoste, Sigfried Giedion, Werner Max Moser, Josef Frank. From left to right, seated: Fernando Garcia Mercadal, Molly Weber, Christophore Tadevossian. (Photography Emile Gos, Lausanne, Elysée Museum)

Consequently, Le Corbusier had little time for frequent travel to Geneva to supervise the construction of the Clarté building. Jeanneret, however, did go there more often, both as chief architect of the Paris agency and as a Geneva native. Oversight was provided by the developer and owner Wanner; John Torcapel[13], the on-site architect; Quétant[14], the architect responsible for costings, employed by Wanner; and the foreman Boris Nazarieff[15], Quétant's brother-in-law.

1 Construction of the Disarmament Pavilion under the architect Adolphe Guyonnet and the engineer Louis Perrin. Unlike the Clarté building, its metal structure was bolted. The pavilion was destroyed by fire on 1 August 1987.

2 Publication series, *Le Corbusier à Genève 1922–1932. Projets et réalisations,* Lausanne: 1987.

3 Twenty-eight established European architects, including Le Corbusier and Jeanneret, decided in 1929 to found the International Congress of Modern Architecture (CIAM) to focus on architecture and functional planning. These congresses were interrupted after the tenth and last meeting in 1959 at Otterlo (Netherlands). Some members continued to meet under the name of Team 10. See also, "Voyages and lectures" below.

4 Charlotte Perriand (1903–1999), interior designer, associated with Le Corbusier and Jeanneret from 1927 to 1937. See Arthur Rüegg, Charlotte Perriand. *Logbook 1928–1933,* Golion/Basel: Infolio Editions/Birkhäuser Verlag, 2004.

5 *UAM,* first association newsletter, Paris: Editions Charles Moreau, 1930, plate 19.

6 The concepts "lotissements fermés à alvéoles" and "immeuble-villas", literally a "closed-cell housing group" and "house buildings" invoke a compact form of urban dwelling where the individual "villas" are grouped together in one building.

7 Works of Le Corbusier appearing in Paris in the series *La Nouvelle Esprit, Vers une architecture,* 1923, pp. 206–222; *Urbanisme,* 1925, pp. 205–219; *Almanach d'architecture moderne,* 1926, pp. 121–128 and, at the end of the volume, on non-numbered pages.

8 Pilotis are ground floor columns that replace the supporting walls.

9 Alfred Roth, *Zwei Wohnhäuser* von *Le Corbusier* und *Pierre Jeanneret. Fünf Punkte zu einer neuen Architektur,* Akad. Verlag Dr. Fr. Wedekind & Co., Stuttgart, 1927.

10 Arthur Rüegg (ed.), *Polychromic architecture. The Claviers de Couleur by Le Corbusier from 1931 and from 1959,* (three volumes, including the two-volume *Salubra claviers de couleur),* Basel: Birkhäuser-Verlag,1997.

11 "Le Corbusier & P. Jeanneret", *L'architecture d'aujourd'hui,* October 1933, Paris. 1933. *Das Werk,* 21/9, September 1934, essential publication devoted to Le Corbusier and Pierre Jeanneret, focusing on the Clarté building and the Swiss pavilion of the Cité Universitaire in Paris. *Today,* 9/51, November 1965, special edition consecrated to the work of Le Corbusier and Jeanneret.

12 Congrès International d'Architecture Moderne.

13 John Torcapel (1881–1965).

14 Francis Quétant (1905–1953).

15 Boris Nazarieff (1908–1979).

"A milestone of modern architecture …"
The Clarté building in the creations of Le Corbusier and Pierre Jeanneret

Arthur Rüegg

Le Corbusier never succeeded in transposing the "Ville contemporaine" (1922) or the "Ville radieuse" (1930) to a grand scale in cities such as Paris or Moscow. Only a few individual buildings enabled him to illustrate, with pertinence, the impact of his ideas on the practice of urbanism. Constructed in Geneva from 1931 to 1932, the Clarté residential complex is one of the steps along the route leading to the "Ville radieuse".

Through this building, realised in collaboration with Pierre Jeanneret, Le Corbusier managed to design an urban fragment which, inserted in a historic town, embodied in an exemplary manner the various aspects of a new housing concept. In the words of the two architects, the Clarté building was a "milestone of modern architecture in an outdated environment" of which they did not fail to emphasize the qualities: "Clarté embodies: a) the reform of the apartment; b) the transformation of construction methods; c) the elements of a new aesthetic." [1]

Inhabiting the "Ville radieuse"

From 1925, the Geneva metalwork entrepreneur Edmond Wanner sent objects of his creation destined to be presented at the International Exhibition of Modern Industrial and Decorative Arts in Paris. It is doubtless on this occasion that he discovered the "Pavillon de l'Esprit Nouveau" [2], where Le Corbusier presented his conception of a habitation module in his project "Ville contemporaine". Half of the pavilion was occupied by a cubic habitation unit arranged as a duplex. All rooms looked onto a large covered terrace, also integrated within the unit's volume. This box-shaped habitation unit, tailored according to the needs of an enlightened bourgeoisie, was designed as a freely positioned and stackable element of the "immeuble-villas", through which Le Corbusier proposed in 1925 to revolutionize the living quarters of a large town [3]. Following his visit to the City of Weissenhof exhibition (Weissenhofsiedlung) at Stuttgart in 1927, Wanner commissioned Le Corbusier and Pierre Jeanneret,

1
Le Corbusier and Pierre Jeanneret, "A part of the Ville Radieuse residence", 1935, taken from: *Le Corbusier & Pierre Jeanneret, Complete works 1934–1938,* Max Bill (ed.), Girsberger, Zurich, 1939, p. 35.

1

probably in the same year, to undertake the large development project in the Athénée neighbourhood of Geneva. This project was to comprise four orthogonal elements, each one composed of standard duplex habitation units, following the "immeuble-villas" model[4]. Contrary to this undertaking, known as the Wanner project, the Clarté building, also realised for Wanner but at another site – namely in the suburb of Eaux-Vives – is not composed of standardised habitation units.

Circa 1929/30 Le Corbusier's interest was in minimal dwellings. This study led to a subdivision of habitation units based on an open-plan principle. In the regimented closed-cell subdivisions of the "Ville radieuse", the subdivisions were devised to be occupied by variable-sized habitation units, tailored to the occupants' needs. Charlotte Perriand was charged with designing floor plans having a surface limited to 14 square metres per person. In order to economise on space while satisfying the different night- and daytime functions she arrived at a flexible solution[5]. Thanks to such "machines for living", Le Corbusier sought to transpose the Taylorist industrial model to the field of minimal housing.

2
Le Corbusier, Pierre Jeanneret and Pierre Scheidegger, "La Maison de verre. Immeubles Clarté", ***Art in Switzerland,*** **Geneva, 1933. Cover of the French edition.**
3
Le Corbusier and Pierre Jeanneret, "A façade of the 'immeuble-villas' concept", 1922. Vertical Organisation of Apartments, taken from: Le Corbusier, ***Almanach of modern architecture,*** **Crès, Paris, 1926, p. 128.**
4
Charlotte Perriand, design of an apartment for nine to sixteen people for the "Ville radieuse", 1930. Horizontal organisation of transformable apartments, taken from: Arthur Rüegg, ***Charlotte Perriand. Livre de bord 1928–1933,*** **Infolio, Gollion, 2004, p. 56.**

2

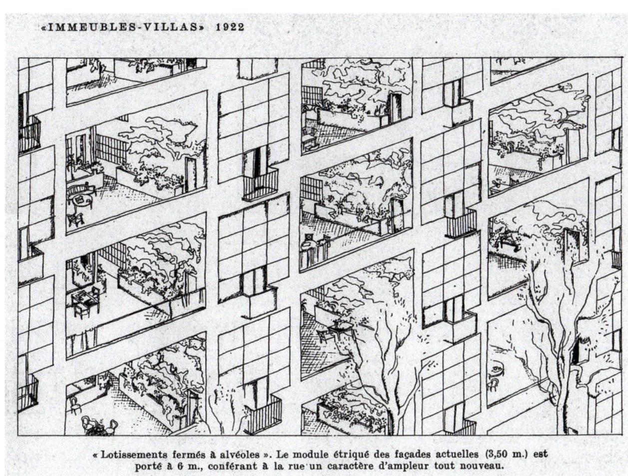

3

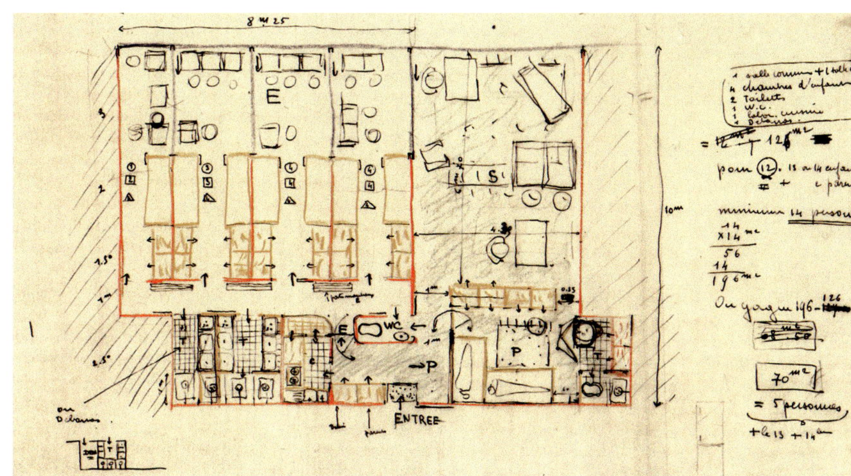

4

5

If the Clarté building is also composed of living spaces of varying size and shape, it is nonetheless neither reduced to a strict minimum, nor liberally subdivided horizontally on an open-plan principle[6]. Moreover, the subdivision was not done, as in other Le Corbusier projects, by open walkways or "corridor-roads", but by means of generous stairwells. Veritable wells of coloured light, the latter allow at-a-glance perception of the building throughout its entire height. The forty-five closely grouped habitation units are, for the most part, organised as duplexes and constitute detached houses in many ways[7]. Juxtaposed according to precise rules, these duplexes constitute a palette of ten units of varying sizes; from studio to nine-roomed town house, including a single-level four-room apartment. Le Corbusier and Pierre Jeanneret have thereby tested, in this first apartment building, the diversity of their theoretical housing ideas as formulated in the framework of the "Ville contemporaine" and the "Ville radieuse". They abandoned the homogeneous typology in favour of real data and the demands of the developer. Like the buildings in Doldertal at Zurich or the Parkhaus Zossen at Basel, they managed to demonstrate, with inimitable precision, the benefits of "modern duplex apartments with the features of a detached house."[8]

Surprisingly, the architects gave up implementing their own "équipement de l'habitation" of which the most recent example, developed in collaboration with Charlotte Perriand, had been presented in an installation that aroused great interest at the 1929 Salon d'Automne. Among the new tubular steel furnishings, only the famous rocking chaise longue was displayed in the Clarté building on the occasion of a private exhibition organised by the firm Wohnbedarf SA of Zurich. This company's programme, established for the most part by Sigfried Giedion – the general secretary of the Congrès internationaux d'architecture moderne (CIAM) – significantly reflected the international movement regarding modern furniture design. The Geneva public's taste, however, more attuned to a refined "Art Deco" style – particularly that of Gustavus Adolphus Hufschmid or Else Hamann – led to the closure, in 1933, of the Wohnbedarf showroom installed on the ground floor of the Clarté building[9].

5
Clarté, five-room apartment model furnished by Wohnbedarf Zurich, with a tilting chaise longue by Le Corbusier, Pierre Jeanneret, Charlotte Perriand, June 1932, taken from: Friederike Mehlau, Arthur Rüegg, Ruggero Tropeano, *Schweizer Typenmöbel 1925–1935. Sigfried Giedion and Wohnbedarf AG,* gta Verlag, Zurich, 1989, p. 45.

Dry Construction

Within the framework of a refinement process, it was also a question of: acknowledging modern construction techniques, the accuracy and realisation of construction details, a contemporary infrastructure, and adequate interior design. Of these issues, Le Corbusier and Pierre Jeanneret had broad contemporary knowledge and much practical experience. Notwithstanding, they were impressed when Wanner, this metalwork entrepreneur eager for innovation, opened new paths for the development of their ideas.

Free subdivision of the different building storeys, as practised with the "lotissements à alvéoles" and partially in the case of the Clarté building, depends on the distinction between load-bearing elements and partitions. Le Corbusier had, from the outset, laid the foundation for this fundamental distinction in modern architecture. Shortly after the outbreak of the First World War, in order to speed reconstruction, he gave up the traditional bases and vaulted elements of the era and drew up a basic system consisting of columns and concrete slabs – the system "Dom-Ino". To subdivide the framework, Le Corbusier initially resorted to masonry partition walls, then he experimented with membranes of concrete sprayed onto formwork. It was only with the aid of forms developed in the purist painting movement that he succeeded in separating and freeing the partitions from the supporting structure. Thus he knew in depth how to aesthetically exploit a simple concrete frame [10].

The development of Solomite, a material commercialised in 1923 and presented in the form of composite panels composed of compressed straw reinforced by galvanised steel wires bound together by cement or plaster, was to improve the construction procedure. These panels, which could measure up to four metres long for a thickness of five centimetres, also provided thermal and acoustic insulation. Installed in a concrete frame,

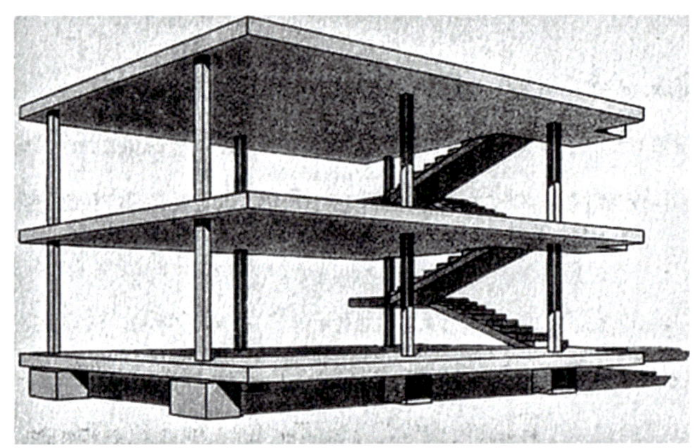

6

they could then be covered with a layer of sprayed concrete[11]. In 1925, Le Corbusier and Pierre Jeanneret used Solomite panels to form the walls within the concrete frame of the "Pavillon de l'Esprit Nouveau". However, they limited themselves to a single panel in place of the two originally specified (thereby leaving a concrete finish visible on one face of the wall). The layer of concrete was also placed by hand rather than by the usual spray application.

Edmond Wanner, a man fond of innovations, acquired the rights to manufacture Solomite panels and created his own production company[12]. This material, insulating and lightweight, seemed ideally suited to form the walls of the steel structures that Wanner hoped to develop in the future. This explains why the "projet Wanner", designed in 1928 by Le Corbusier and Pierre Jeanneret, specified a steel frame infilled with Solomite panels. This was at the root of a decisive period that influenced the realisation of the majority of Le Corbusier's important buildings of the 1930s: "The 'immeubles-villas' of 1922/25 thus found favour in Geneva, thanks to the shrewd initiative of an industrialist constructor of steel-framed buildings. The project, destined until then to be constructed of reinforced concrete, was changed to have a steel-framed structure following the latest design trend, that of the 'maison à sec'"[13].

Outside of large residential buildings Wanner was also interested in detached houses and mansions. To this end he developed the Citrohan housing style, organised on two storeys, that he'd discovered in Stuttgart, and ventured to realise such a construction – the Villa Ruf – based on a welded steel frame with partitions of composite coated straw panels. During the design process Le Corbusier and Pierre Jeanneret abandoned the project. It was thus the architect Francis Quétant, employed by Wanner, who designed and constructed the villa Ruf at Grand-Saconnex[14]. Given that the Disarmament Pavilion, constructed using the same techniques in 1932 close to the Palais Wilson, was destroyed by fire in 1987, the Villa Ruf remains the unique example of this important contribution to the development of dry construction or "construction à sec".

7

8

6–8
Le Corbusier, the Dom-Ino system. Construction at "la cité ouvrière de Liège"; "The cement gun prepares and applies an adherent mortar, waterproof and inexpensive", taken from: Brian Brace Taylor, *Le Corbusier and Pessac, 1914–1928,* Le Corbusier Foundation/Harvard University, 1972. Photo Hans Finsler.

9
Francis Quétant, Villa Ruf, Grand-Saconnex, 1928/29. Infilling the metallic structure with "Solomite", unknown photographer (Jean Ruf?).
10
Adolphe Guyonnet, Pavilion of the Disarmament Conference, Geneva, 1932. Application of the metallic framed Solomite system. The cement gun in action, taken from: *Schweizerische Bauzeitung,* 1931, vol. 38, p. 297.
11
The first "Le Corbusier" Salubra collection, autumn 1931. The volume contains: 43 sheets of plain colours, 1 sheet of diamond motifs, 18 sheets of polka dot motifs. The volume also includes a fold-out with 12 colour keyboards and a pocket containing two cardboard cursors, for use with them.

9

10

By comparison, and with a generally similar approach, construction of the Clarté building is both more refined and more pragmatic. Solomite panels have only been used as insulation in the ceilings, roofs, and facade elements. The internal partitions are light timber frames covered with plasterboard. As for the gable ends, they are of masonry construction. A modular steel frame welded on site by the Secheron Workshop – a first in Geneva – as well as numerous prefabricated elements (notably Wanner's spiral cast-iron staircases, or the glazed facades comprising patented broad sliding windows, or yet still the suspended balconies)[15] make this edifice a milestone in the evolution of industrial architecture and a pinnacle of the art of construction in Geneva at that time.

11

The aesthetics of prefabrication

Following the purist and conventionally built structures of Le Corbusier's houses, the Villa Ruf, built of steel columns and composite straw panels rendered on both faces, shows no fabrication joints and thereby achieves a similar monolithic appearance. That is the key to a future architecture, which was to distinguish itself from the unitary construction style or "construction à rajouts", characteristic of the XIX century. The choice of monolithic construction falls within the context of developing an assuredly sculptural architecture, whose abstract forms are capable of even redefining the essence of a house. It's for this reason that from 1924 onward, Le Corbusier introduced modifying colour into his first purist buildings. He had recourse to a traditional palette of which the effect had undergone the test of time in the fine art of painting. With the help of these tints he succeeded not only in underlining and modifying, but also in correcting the plastic and spatial effects of largely open volumes. He also knew how, by the use of coloured ambience, to restore to a pure dematerialised architecture, the spirit of missing matter. Thus, outside of the physiological, a psychological effect was created by spectrally generated associations; take for example a wall painted in light sienna recalling the colour of brickwork.

While designing the Clarté building, Le Corbusier developed a spiritual legacy of his purist polychromy for the Salubra company. This was a wallpaper collection presenting forty-three plain colours with corresponding colour charts or "claviers de couleurs". These charts took the form of a dozen sample cards, upon which were three broad bands presenting lighter colours intended for the principal walls. Between these, on two parallel narrower bands were located perpendicular arrays of keys of contrasting colours destined for woodwork, for doors, and other similar elements, in a manner whereby the user could, thanks

12
Le Corbusier and Pierre Jeanneret, Swiss pavilion of the City university, Paris, 1929–1939. Nocturnal view of the principal facade showing the symphony of interior colours of the student rooms (version from the polychrome photographs of 1957), postcard.

13
Clarté building, four-room duplex apartment, south side fitted out by Gustave-Adolphe Hufschmid. Furniture in black wood, curtains in white cotton (imposed on the owners), silk fabric, and coral red wool. Movable work surface. Reconstitution from the polychrome photograph by Barbara Thommen/Arthur Rüegg, 1999, photography by Boissonnas, October 1932.

13

to a sliding cardboard cursor, frame a coordinating combination of three to five different colours. Each sample card reflects the colours of a particular ambience: "Space" for example combines light blue walls and light grey, destined to create a sense of greater volume within the room[16].

In the context of "construction à sec" or dry construction – based on the site-assembly of elements – the monolithic impression of a building had been put aside. In the case of the Clarté building, Le Corbusier and Pierre Jeanneret drew for the first time, while yet incomplete, important conclusions regarding aesthetics. The characteristic elements of this new aesthetic are notably: the glass bricks, the dressing of friezes and plinths with finely jointed travertine[17] sheets, the metallic structure of the facades treated with a particularly dark green colouring rhyming with vast panes of glass and the natural wood blades of the shutters; the raw finish remaining visible for the majority of these construction materials. Nonetheless, the visitor who expects to see an expressive and structured architecture can only be disappointed. Le Corbusier had not renounced forms devoid of all joints without a fight. On the contrary, he affirmed: "Industrialisation has never prevented architectural creation"[18]. For example the technique of arc welding allows the production of square section structural steel elements that show practically no trace of the means of fabrication, such as rivets or bolts. For the interior, Salubra wallpapers mask both joints and changes of material. However, as a consequence the tenants were obliged to choose from the Le Corbusier wallpaper collection. And while they were able to determine their own ambient colour scheme, they had in return to accept the hanging of uniform coloured curtains. By this means, Le Corbusier succeeded not only in creating a purist interior space, but also in applying the concept of colour charts on a grand scale. It's easy to imagine the striking effect of the building at night when, like a giant ocean liner, it dominated a neighbourhood comprising smaller houses. With its long glowing transparent facades, the "houses" behind, each with its own range of colours, contributed to the creation of a vast polychromic symphony. The rhythm of the colours thus expressed the individuality of the inhabitants, while the framework of the facade embodied the collective structure [19].

From the house to the urban building, from moulded form to prefabricated element, from abstract sculpture to expressive structure, the Clarté building foreshadows new themes in the work of Le Corbusier and Pierre Jeanneret and, in addition, constitutes an extraordinary experiment to bring together the most important elements of their research within a large building and in exemplary harmony.

1 All the citations are drawn from Le Corbusier and Pierre Jeanneret, "L'immeuble Clarté à Genève, 1930/32", *Œuvre complète de 1929–1934;* Le Corbusier, Pierre Jeanneret and Pierre Scheidegger, "La Maison de verre: l'Immeuble Clarté", *L'Art en Suisse,* special edition without pagination, Geneva, April–May 1933. – The first monograph was only published fifty years later: Catherine Courtiau, *L'immeuble Clarté,* SHAS, Berne, 1982. – See also the analyses of Christian Sumi, *Immeuble Clarté Genf 1932 von Le Corbusier & Pierre Jeanneret,* gta/Ammann, Zurich, 1989, as well as the complete presentation in Luca Bellinelli (ed.), *La construction de l'immeuble Clarté,* Accademia di architettura, Mendrisio, 1999.

2 Audience with Georgette Wanner 22.8.1978, in the presence of Jacqueline Jeanneret, Arthur Rüegg, Christian Sumi. See also Christian Sumi, "Il progetto Wanner", *Rassegna 3rd*, July 1980, pp. 39–46.

3 "Firstly the 'Immeubles-villas' were born of a memory after a dinner, an Italian Chartreuse (happiness by serenity) and sketches on the back of a restaurant menu": Le Corbusier and Pierre Jeanneret, *Œuvre complète de 1910–1929,* published by W. Boesiger and O. Stonorov, new edition, Girsberger, Zurich, 1937, pp. 40–41. In his buildings of dwellings, Le Corbusier drew some of his fundamental ideas from origins far from architecture.

4 *Œuvre complète de 1910–1929, op. cit.,* pp. 180–185. The scheme of habitable cells juxtaposed along "corridor roads" – first tried during the "projet Wanner" – is at the origin of the habitation units from the post-war years. For that which concerns the projet Wanner, see also Armand Brulhart, "Villereuse et Rive droite. Le Corbusier urbaniste", in Isabelle Charollais, André Ducret (ed.), *Le Corbusier à Genève 1922–1932,* Payot, Lausanne, 1987, pp. 79–92.

5 Le Corbusier, "La Ville radieuse", *L'Architecture d'Aujourd'hui,* Boulogne-sur-Seine, 1935, pp. 143–146 (facsimile Paris: Vincent et Fréal, 1964).

6 For that which concerns the evolution of dwelling types, see Christian Sumi, *Immeuble Clarté Genf 1932, op. cit.,* pp. 87–119.

7 *Ibid.* note 1.

8 The citation's author is Alfred Roth, cf. Arthur Rüegg, *Die Doldertalhäuser. Ein Hauptwerk des Neuen Bauens in Zürich,* gta, Zurich, 1996, p. 46.

9 For an exhaustive analysis, see Arthur Rüegg, "Couleur, meubles et photographie: 'J'ai deux amours'...", in Luca Bellinelli (éd.), *La construction de l'immeuble Clarté, op. cit.,* pp. 50–71.

10 Cf. The five points of a new architecture are illustrated in an exemplary manner in the Villa Savoye (Poissy, 1929–1931).

11 Otherwise known as shotcrete – https://en.wikipedia.org/wiki/Shotcrete

12 Société anonyme des produits "Le Solomite"/Matériau pour la construction et l'isolation/Bureau: Terrassière 27/Usine: Sécheron/Genève (according to the firm's visiting card). In the case of the Villa Ruf, the firm Wanner had also made available the architect Francis Quétant.

13 *Œuvre complète de 1910–1929, op. cit.,* p. 180. See also Christian Sumi, *Immeuble Clarté, op. cit.,* pp. 44–70.

14 See also Arthur Rüegg, *Le Corbusier, Edmond Wanner, Francis Quétant und die Villa Ruf,* EPFZ, Zurich, 1987; French version in *Faces* No. 17, 1990, pp. 46–54.

15 On this subject see: "Technische Angaben" in the annexes of *L'Art en Suisse* 4/5 1933 (op. cit.).

16 Concerning polychromy in general and more particularly the 1931 colour charts, see: Arthur Rüegg, *Polychromie architecturale. Les claviers de couleurs de Le Corbusier de 1931 et de 1959,* Birkhäuser Verlag, Basel–Boston–Berlin, 1997; 2nd revision, 2006.

17 Travertine is a form of limestone deposited by mineral springs, especially hot springs, and resembles marble.

18 Le Corbusier, "Un nouvel ordre de grandeur des éléments urbains, une nouvelle unité d'habitation", *L'Ossature métallique,* mai 1934, p. 235.

19 Since then, Le Corbusier only used the Salubra collection on a large scale on one occasion in 1931. In the Swiss pavilion (Paris, 1929–1933), he nonetheless personally chose the colour variation for the student bedrooms. See also Jan de Heer, *The Architectonic Colour,* 010 Publishers, Rotterdam, 2009, pp.157–161.

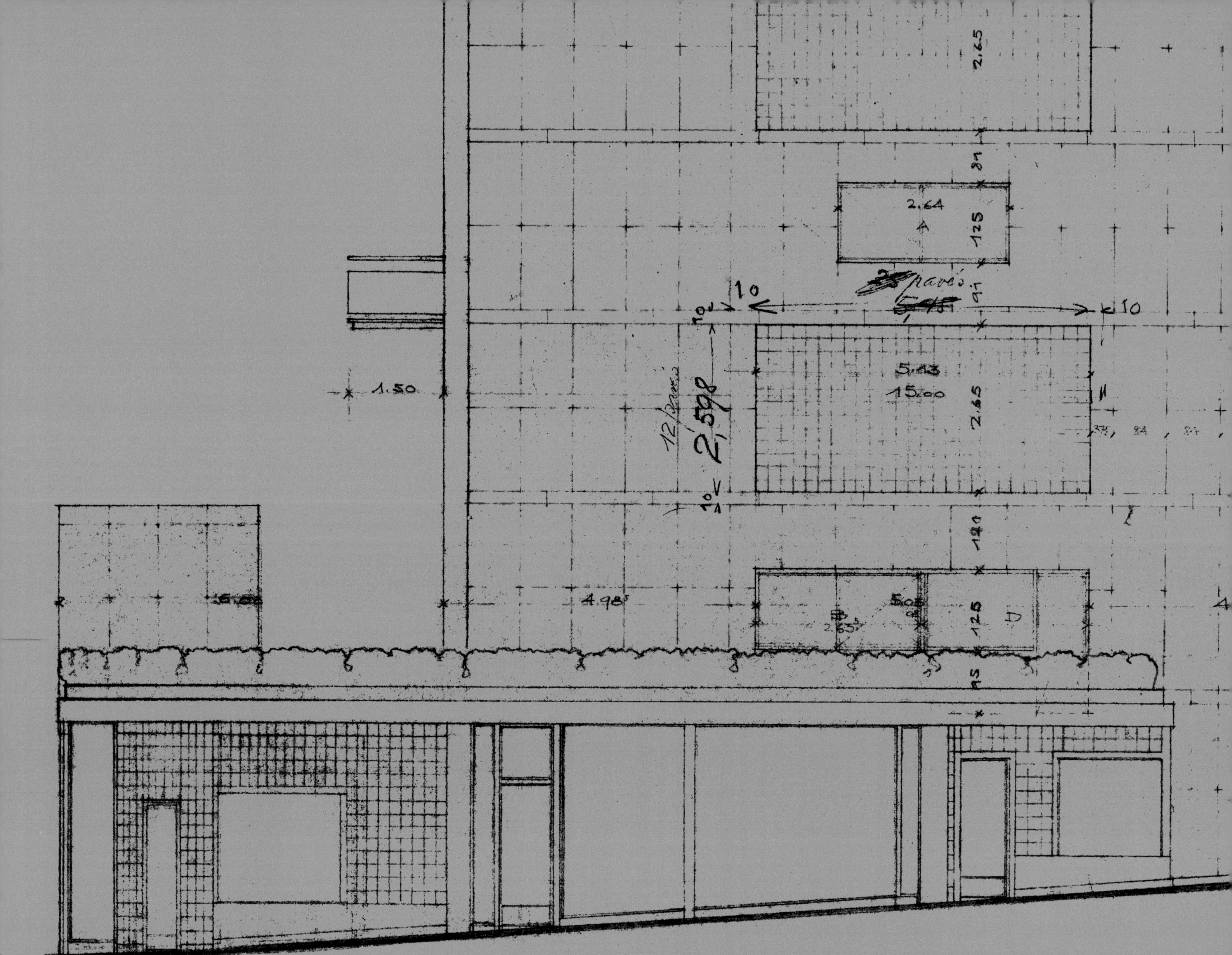

1.50
4.98
5.13
15.00
2.65
2.64
125
10

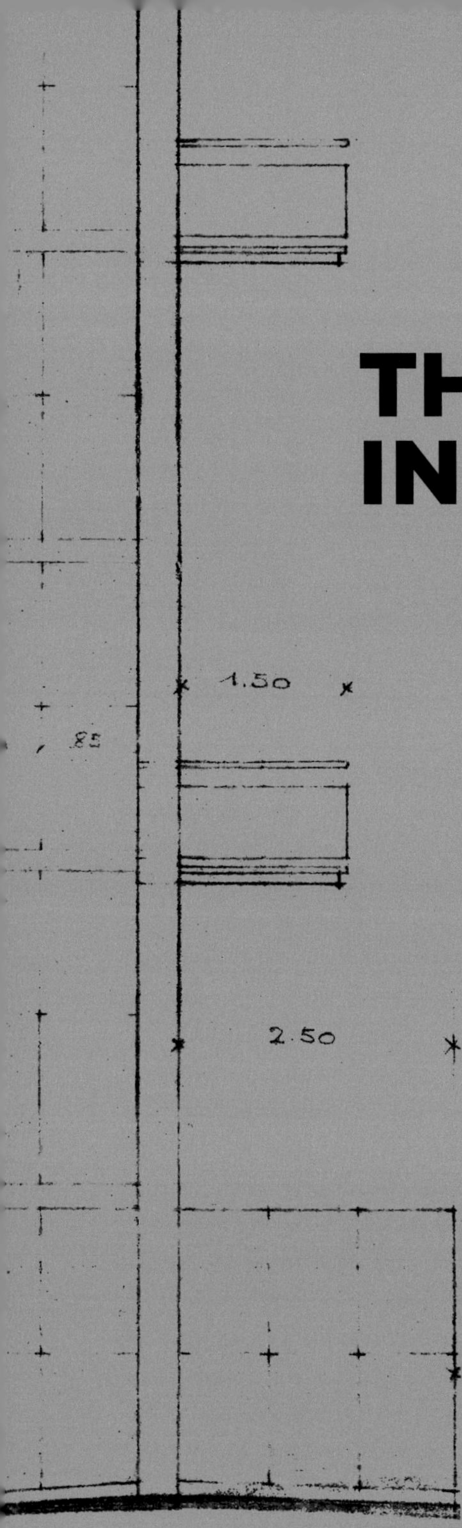

THE RESTORATION IN QUESTION

Lessons of a rehabilitation

Bernard Zumthor

"Architecture is to be regarded by us with the most serious thought. We may live without her. And worship without her, but we cannot remember without her."[1]

Today, according to Ruskin, the architecture born from the rubble of World War II fully assumes this memorial function so essential to our awareness of history. The witnesses to this founding period of our contemporary age are, in the public's opinion, no longer works of "folly". They now deserve to be considered seriously, as any object of our familiar environment for which the passage of time has conferred the attributes necessary for recognition, cataloguing, and public awareness[2], or, in short, their heritage credentials.

However, the preservation of this architecture, in terms of both the relevant values and required procedures, is still largely unknown territory, a bundle of ethical and technical problems whose complexity is a measure of the heterogeneity of their subject.

The XX century has in practice required the coexistence of more expertise and traditions than any other period. Characterised by the non-monumental and standardisation, Le Corbusier's architectural production revolutionised construction methods and materials. Faced with these changes, the concepts of conservation and restoration developed by Camillo Boito and Alois Riegl, the first theorists of the discipline at the turn of the last century, only remained truly valid as long as the legacy of the Modernist Movement was not recognised as heritage. Since then, the gap has widened and today, while the general principles for conservation enshrined in the Charter of Venice (1964) remain valid precisely because of their generality, their practical implementation amidst the hard reality of the worksite often appears unsuited to the construction characteristics of buildings of this modernist era.

Such was the case for the rehabilitation of the Clarté building between 2007 and 2011. The paradox was that this object, whose heritage value was once unquestioned, to the point where it was proposed for inclusion on the UNESCO World Heritage List, only had at its disposition an anachronistic methodology of restoration, imprecise and generating more questions than answers regarding the necessary decisions.

From then on, the project offered an opportunity for reflection and experimentation, and even, depending on the complexity of the problems, the reformulation of theoretical and empirical frameworks for the conservation and enhancement of this extraordinary architectural heritage, designed by an inventor of modernity. The following notes outline some theoretical issues.

The first conclusion to be drawn is that if the construction of the Clarté building had indeed been placed historically at the crossroads of two urban housing philosophies, broadly speaking the individual and the communal, its rehabilitation three generations later would logically be a point of division between two conservation practices, different depending on whether they applied to architectural types resulting from the constructive singularity of the one or from the standardisation of the other.

This statement, which despite the unique character of the Clarté[3] building perfectly summarises the issue of the treatment of post-1920 heritage, led to the project leaders' need to qualify their approach from the perspective of ruptures in the historical significance for this type of architecture, on the sociological level (between the individual and the collective), the philosophical level (between the ornamental and the utilitarian), in terms of methodology (between the artisanal and the industrial), and, finally, in terms of materials, between masonry (stone and mortar) and technologies involving the assembly of prefabricated components (especially glass and steel).

The protagonists of this adventure were therefore obliged to confront, with a "new spirit" as Le Corbusier would have said, a perilous balancing act common to all heritage preservation, between these three competing exigencies:
— conservation, that is to say, the preservation of the work's "authenticity" [4] in both formal and material terms, as found in its archaeological state, with the aim of maintaining the heritage object in a condition as close as possible to the original;
— restoration, the repair or recovery of fragile or hidden authentic components to render them more visible and/or intelligible, so as to preserve them while meeting the requirements for their presentation or reuse;
— renovation, the rehabilitation or adaptation of the building with the aim of returning it to a "new" condition so as to reproduce as far as possible its original state while adapting it to today's demands in terms of performance and quality of life.

Given the specific architecture of the Clarté building and the distinctive nature of its construction history, the translation of these three principles into an integrated strategy of architectural intervention required all the knowledge, creativity, judgement, and imagination of the architect in charge of the project.

It was initially necessary to acquire, with the help of experts, historians, curators, conservationists, and engineers, a detailed knowledge of the substance of the building. That is to say, to identify the meaning and the matter of its authenticity, that which establishes its heritage value, defines its intrinsic qualities, and constitutes its characteristics with respect to the built environment of the time. These are, namely: the architectural history, the socio-cultural context of the design and its implementation, the construction techniques, and the details of the whole process.

This empathic understanding of the building then allowed the development of a methodology and plan for a staged rehabilitation programme of all identified original elements, while drawing upon, depending on the particular condition of their various components, the techniques either of restoration or of renovation, without ever losing sight of the overall concept of the building. Thus it was a question of finding means of intervention reusing construction methods as implemented in 1930, for example, the welding of the metal frame.

Finally it was necessary to find and incorporate solutions to improve the technical performance of the structure, particularly in terms of sustainable development, insulation, heating, waterproofing, safety, durability, etc., without stripping away the building's identity or origins, rendering it preserved and yet fully renovated.

The convergence of these dimensions made this exceptional project a sort of experimental laboratory, giving rise to inexhaustible questions and surprises.

One of the many observations, particularly interesting because of its methodological implications, was that of the difference in the on-site modus operandi between an older building and one of the Modern Movement. Beyond the basic theoretical rules set by the Venice Charter, which apply to all situations, whatever the object or historical period, the difference in approach between "traditional" and "modern" architecture remains absolute in terms of their particular building techniques. On the part of the architect, this necessitates the use of analytical and empirical instrumentation that often needs to be invented for the purpose.

Confronted with this duality, one is not simply faced with the dichotomy of different approaches but, more fundamentally, that of two moments in time. On the one hand, an architecture built for the long term; on the other, an architecture obeying a functional logic of production and use, the famous "machine for living", as Le Corbusier defined it. That is to say, a conception that, in the creative will of its author, is a tool, a mechanism to be replaced without regret when it no longer fulfils its function, an object whose very design embraces obsolescence.

Therefore, the differences between the specific and firm intentions of conservation, taken according to whether we are dealing with a traditional or a modern structure, are strictly dependent on the interpretation given to the aging of materials.

In the classical masonry monument, a patina, a degree of wear, or indeed, if one refers to Ruskin, a state of normal deterioration, are external signs of the passage of time to conserve, or even to highlight as an attestation of a proud heritage. In contrast, in buildings of the Modern Movement, of concrete, glass, or steel, what counts is the "good working order" of the structure. That which must be explicit in the beauty of its functionality. For the conservationist-restorer, this entails an approach diametrically opposed to traditional practice: the restitution of an as-new condition, of seeking a result that abolishes wrinkles, dents, and scars, that removes the years' injuries, rendering time invisible, in a sense dematerialising it.

One is thus faced with the apparent contradiction that a correct restoration, that is to say one that betrays neither the spirit nor the letter of this Modern Movement edifice's heritage value, can only take the form of a renovation leading to the reproduction of the original.

A perverse effect of this aesthetic of timeless youth is frequently discernible in the high degree of obsolescence attained far more quickly by modern architecture from the 1920–1940 period than by traditional construction, exactly because of the mechanical principle of a precise match between form and function. For well-known ideological reasons, the functionalist conception was significantly more rigid during the avant-garde interwar period than in previous architecture, which was more attentive to formal expression. This greatly reduced, in principle, the potential for modern architecture's adaptation to new uses and the comfort and safety standards of the time.

In fact, the "modernisations" to accommodate a change of function more often caused irreversible disfigurement with this type of building than was the case with buildings made before World War I. Numerous valuable XX century works, like the Clarté building, suffered severe alterations in a relatively short time; there is virtually no building of that time fully preserved in its initial state (but when by chance it does happen, in what state of conservation!). Conversely it is not unusual to find older structures, still in their original condition having simply aged, and offering substantial potential for reuse without loss of heritage value.

For the Clarté building, the problem of a change of function had fortunately not arisen. However, the authorities had to grant unusual exceptions to normal regulatory requirements, in order to preserve the formal integrity of the building.

There is a singular connection between the durability of this architecture and the experimental nature of its original construction. This issue, fascinating in terms of the orthodox principles governing restoration, was particularly evident in the case of the Clarté building. Its original construction, using new materials and assembly techniques without the benefit of experience, was in time to prove downright faulty.

The history of XX century architecture is riddled with countless stories of leaky windows, windows that do not close properly, corrosion, appalling heating and ventilation, and building owners furious after the handover of the building.

Just such a situation was encountered at this restoration site. The rule of "identical reconstruction" – the requirement that the structure be restored to its initial state – is questionable, to say the least. Should we go as far as to restore the "factory defects" simply because they were in the original building? The descriptions in the following pages give details of corrections made to the original structure, notably with regard to waterproofing, insulation, the treatment of metalwork, and, more generally, the durability of the materials.

These reflections could be elaborated ad infinitum. Here I only touch upon some paradoxical aspects encountered in the course of this project because of the historical links with an architecture that sought to be timeless, insofar as the horizon of its purpose was the present, that famous end of history announced by the ideologies of the twentieth century.

However, the awareness that emerges through these observations is that of a more complex and fundamental question. When on the scaffolding we are confronted with seemingly simple questions such as "What really is the substance of this building?" or "What are the invariable characteristics that will ensure without betraying authenticity?", we realize that what we're actually asking the building is, "What is the real significance of this architectural heritage you exemplify?"

Clearly, the architecture of the Modern Movement is not measured by the yardstick of its own historical, technological, or aesthetic dimension, nor by its legal status as a protected monument. Economy, sustainable development, social continuity of use, and urban symbolism are as important as the structure's age, elegance, the prestige of the architect, etc.

In other words, the patrimonial quality of this particular architectural heritage, its meaning and thus the value that the community gives it, resides less in its substance – that should of course be saved and rehabilitated at all costs – than in the symbolic force of its existence, in what the building represents in terms of social history, and for the crucial exercise of our power of memory, as pointed out by Ruskin in the preamble[5].

Thus, we might ask, have the careful development of the project and the pragmatic management of the rehabilitation allowed us to put our finger on, through the confrontation with many technical and theoretical uncertainties, something of the apparently contradictory nature of the architecture of the Modern Movement? Similarly to what was happening at the same time in abstract art, which represented a revolution in painting and sculpture[6], modernist architecture drew its conceptual definition more from the philosophical categories of essence rather than substance, which, therefore, brings it back, somewhat unexpectedly, to ... the classical tradition[7].

The Geneva building therefore provides a practical and elegant demonstration of Le Corbusier's paradoxical false ruptures: an object whose modernity itself is foreign to the traditions of its substance but that nonetheless proclaims its loyalty to them in its idealistic relationship to history.

How to manage this ambivalence, where to place the cursor of the selection criteria, which methodologies to approve when deciding what action to take to transmit this heritage to future generations? One of the lessons from the regeneration of the Clarté building has been the urgent need, for the future of XX century architectural heritage, to place at the service of conservation an ethic of preservation, an obligation of intervention, and a renewal of how we conceive restoration[8].

1 John Ruskin, *The Seven Lamps of Architecture; The Lamp of Memory,* London: George Allen, 1880.

2 We must remember the important role played in this area by international agencies such as ICOMOS, DOCOMOMO, or, in this case, the Le Corbusier Foundation, the History of Art Society in Switzerland and its Inventory of Swiss Architecture INSA; the conservation associations, notably the Swiss Heritage Geneva and the relevant government departments, such as the Cantonal Office of Heritage Buildings and Sites in Geneva that conducted a systematic inventory of the canton's twentieth-century heritage and regularly publishes examples in its heritage and architecture magazine. One can observe, however, that if the architecture of the first half of the twentieth century is no longer in question, recognition by the community and the political and cultural authorities of the heritage value of buildings subsequent to World War II, which owed much to the work of the pioneer generation of the years 1920–1930, is still far from certain.

3 It should be remembered that the Clarté building was originally conceived as the first piece of an ensemble that would redefine the entire Villereuse neighbourhood. Unfortunately there was insufficient financing for this.

4 In this regard, the ambivalent nature of the notion of authenticity should be emphasised. It is often confused with seeking the original, the initial state at the time of construction. However, it is extremely rare that a building survives its history intact. When classifying a historical monument, it is the evolved state that one preserves, that is to say, usually the original state as altered by time. See the Nara Conference on authenticity of 1994, notably Françoise Choay's "Seven proposals on the concept of authenticity". See also the Nara Document on Authenticity, ICOMOS, 1999.

5 The long agony of the Frederick Metzger building at Vieusseux, a contemporary of Clarté, is exemplary in this respect. What conservation advocates have sought to preserve is more the concept of "Existenzminimum", which was instrumental in the process of social progress in Europe between world wars, than these modest structures deliberately vandalized by the stupidity of their owners.

6 Just think of the close intellectual and formal collaboration between artists and architects of the Russian Constructivists or the De Stijl movement or, in another way, the close relationship between Le Corbusier's pictorial practice and architectural design.

7 John Allan, "Points of Balance", *Architectural Review* 1321, March 2007, p. 84. See also John Summerson, *The Classical Language of Architecture,* London: Thames and Hudson, 1963, ed. rev. 1980; Susan Macdonald, Kyle Normandin, Bob Kindred (eds)., *Conservation of Modern Architecture,* Shaftesbury: Donhead, 2007; Susan Macdonald (ed.), *Modern Matters, English Heritage,* Shaftesbury: Donhead, 2013.

8 The proliferation of recent experiences similar to Clarté begins to draw a new theoretical and technical operating framework, essential for the preservation of the architectural heritage of the twentieth century. Take, for example, the Nestlé administrative centre in Vevey, the Van Nelle factory and Bergpolder building in Rotterdam, the Pirelli skyscraper in Milan, and the remarkable conception of the Lignon complex in Geneva, directed by Franz Graf and Giulia Marino should also be mentioned, in order to introduce a body of procedures to support all future interventions with operations respectful of the building's heritage substance.

The restoration of the Clarté building, an introduction

Jacques-Louis de Chambrier

The project really began the day the Geneva Cantonal Bank's[1] Asset Valuation Foundation gave us the mandate to study the restoration of the building envelope in autumn 2003. The Valuation Foundation, which was at that time the majority owner (more than fifty per cent), was ready to advance the funds needed to start drawing up the vital plan for the restoration of the Clarté building.

The building was fairly run down in general appearance, having been irregularly maintained, despite a general renovation of the exterior and interior dating back to 1976. In addition, the establishment of a restaurant on the ground floor of 5, rue Adrien-Lachenal had radically altered this part of the building by removing several garages and important common premises, which posed a functional and aesthetic problem with the facades in particular.

A first inventory of damage had highlighted many leaks in the roof and facade; facade elements deformed, numerous windows broken or opaque; widespread rust on all external metal parts of the facades, balconies, and shutter boxes; broken shutters and tattered canvas awnings; deteriorated balcony floors no longer up to security standards; travertine stone facade cladding split and ready to fall; and glass brick panels completely shattered. In short, the building envelope showed advanced deterioration of almost all its elements.

Following the preliminary study, which was based on the assumption of a simple restoration of the envelope, the residents' association unanimously handed back responsibility for the final project to the Valuation Foundation. The work had now to include, in addition to the outer envelope, restoration of common interior areas and technical services. The start of the project also received a decisive boost from the State of Geneva. They ordered that essential works be done in the event that the residents' association would be unable to carry out the necessary remedial repairs, and promised subsidies from the Confederation and the canton of Geneva in proportion to the recognized architectural importance of the building.

The restoration project therefore developed simultaneously along several principal paths, notably including the following:

— an inventory of documents and plans, and a cultural and historical inventory (publications and documentation of studies of existing conditions),

— a condition survey of the building structure, on-site and laboratory investigation and detailed report, an evaluation of the structure by specialist companies and consultants;

— design of the general restoration project, including upgrading the service installations, to be drawn up in agreement with the building administrator and the residents' association, and detailed with respect to the diverse financial and technical aspects as well as those related to the future construction site;

— preparation of the project, including application for the building permit, taking into account the various legal provisions and the need for the approval of the restoration concept itself in consultation with the Swiss Confederation's expert and the Geneva State Heritage Directorate;

— preparation of the project documents, to include: all general and detailed plans, the procedures and specifications, the authorisation documents for site work, the tenders, the bills of quantities, and the site work schedule.

These different aspects of our work merit the following remarks.

Inventory and research of documents, records, and plans[2]

The first source of documentation on the building was found in the Torcapel archive kept at the Federal Institute of Technology Zurich (ETHZ). This archive, which takes its name from the construction company responsible for the Clarté building site 1931/32, contains plans and construction details of which only part – obtainable as a copy – corresponds with what was actually built.

In addition to the above, the general section showing the building's construction at a scale 1:20, prepared by Devanthéry & Lamunière in 1990 based on a comprehensive review of the Torcapel archive, summarises the details and shows the probable original state of the building[3]. This remarkable document has notably served as a constructive and formal hypothesis with which we could compare the results of surveys and examinations of the facade and the building interior throughout the project's development, continuing well into the site work programme.

The second source of documentation was the Clarté archive at the Le Corbusier Foundation in Paris. This archive collection consists of scans, sketches, and plans tracing the evolution of the project from the outset, including construction details, correspondence, and other documents.

In third place, the archive that was the most immediately useful to us, though incomplete, was that of the surveyor, Buffet, who had served in the establishment of property in 1986, and whose minutes include original copies of plans of some storeys, to a scale 1:50.

Finally, a document giving a complete inventory of all apartments from the first to the ninth floor, drawn up by the architect Laurent Chenu on behalf of the State of Geneva Heritage Directorate, turned out to be essential. This study, completed in 2007, includes all the interior plans of the different storeys (excluding the ground floor), a list of the various fittings, an inventory of the characteristic interior elements, and a typological analysis tracing the interior modifications since handover of the building. These files have been able to be reused, with some updates (some apartments had been inaccessible during the inventory), and integrated into the overall plans.

Published literature, specific studies

The fundamental works enabling one to position the project in its historical and cultural context are the study by Christian Sumi[4] (1989), the historical brochure written by Catherine Courtiau[5] (1982), and the two catalogues accompanying the exhibitions on Clarté in Geneva[6] (1987) and Mendrisio[7] (1999).

Concerning the detailed and technical study of the project, useful information for the restoration of materials and colours and better understanding of the building's original construction methods came from detailed analysis of the archives in Paris, Geneva, and Zurich. This painstaking and lengthy process was directed by Catherine Courtiau, mandated by the State of Geneva to do additional specific research (balconies, coloured canvas awnings, glass bricks, bills of quantities). Moreover, she drew up a very comprehensive summary document, including a significant body of old photographs, essential references for the preparation and carrying out of the restoration project from start to finish.

Hence we see the fundamental importance of the documentation and the huge amount of work that went into research, the interpretation of documents, sorting through what remained at the design stage and what was actually built, and linking that with the realities discovered during the restoration. Often, these two sources of information (the available documentation and the building itself) complemented each other, which was indispensable for better understanding an assembly detail or a construction element.

Records

In early studies, we were surprised to discover that, for a building so well known and documented, no systematic survey had ever been undertaken and no complete set of plans existed. While the original floor plans were reliable and easy to verify and compare with Chenu's records, all the 1:50-scale cross-sections and elevations were wrong.

Our efforts in this sphere began with the overall ground floor plan (basements, garages, technical rooms, restaurant), in reality the most modified part of the building. In the original terminology, this level was called "street level" and "ground floor" to designate what today we call the first floor. Then came the inspection of the facades, a task of considerable duration, which was completed during construction with the survey of the west gable, composed of multiple travertine elements. This phase was completed by a survey of the ground floor facades and details of the eight and ninth floor superstructures, in plan and section.

Note that the survey work (measurement and drawing), which can also involve soundings, trial pits, and laboratory analysis, is of paramount importance for any archaeologist, architect-restorer, or builder. This investigative tool necessitates approaching the material, and the constructions, in all its complex and composite reality.

1 The owner of the majority of the building at the turn of this century had taken out a loan from the Geneva Cantonal Bank in 1988 and gave his part of the Clarté building as security. In 2004 this loan could no longer be serviced, the interest on the debt having doubled as a result of the extraordinary rise of interest rates in the 1990s. The Geneva Cantonal Bank's Asset Valuation Foundation, a division of the bank created to manage such loans, therefore became the major owner of the Clarté building and had auctioned the lot comprising this property. Initially it was the Foundation that mandated Jacques-Louis de Chambrier's architectural practice to manage the building restoration but subsequently the residents' association, of which the Foundation was a member, took overall responsibility for the mandate. See *La Tribune de Genève*, 27 February 2004.

2 Here we cite only the principal documents.

3 This document is the result of a mandate given to Devanthéry & Lamunière by the Geneva State Heritage Directorate.

4 Christian Sumi, *Immeuble Clarté Genève 1932, von Le Corbusier* & *Pierre Jeanneret*, gta/Ammann, Zurich 1989.

5 Catherine Courtiau, *L'Immeuble Clarté Genève. Le Corbusier – 1931/1932, Guides de Monuments suisses SHAS*, series 32, no. 319, Berne: 1982.

6 *Le Corbusier à Genève, 1922–1932, projets et réalisations*, catalogue for the exhibition held in the Clarté building, Lausanne: Payot, 1987.

7 Catherine Courtiau, Inès Lamunière, Arthur Rüegg, *La costruzione dell'Immeuble Clarté/La construction de l'immeuble Clarté*, Luca Bellinelli (ed.), Mendrisio: Cataloghi dell'Accademia di architettura, 1999.

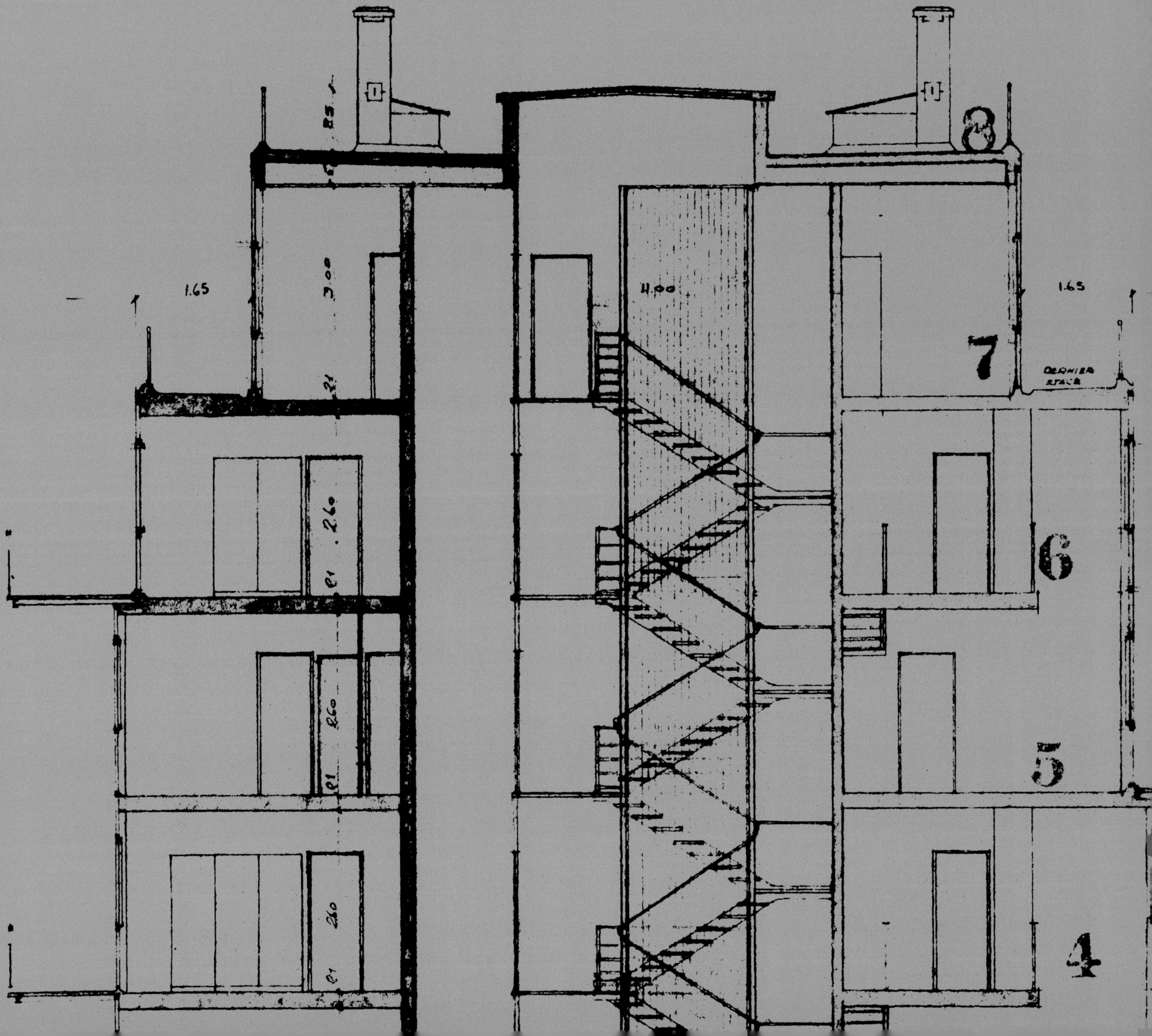
1.65
3.00
1.65
4.00
8
7
DERNIER ETAGE
2.60
6
2.60
5
2.60
4

BUILDING PLANS
HISTORICAL PLANS
RESTORATION PLANS

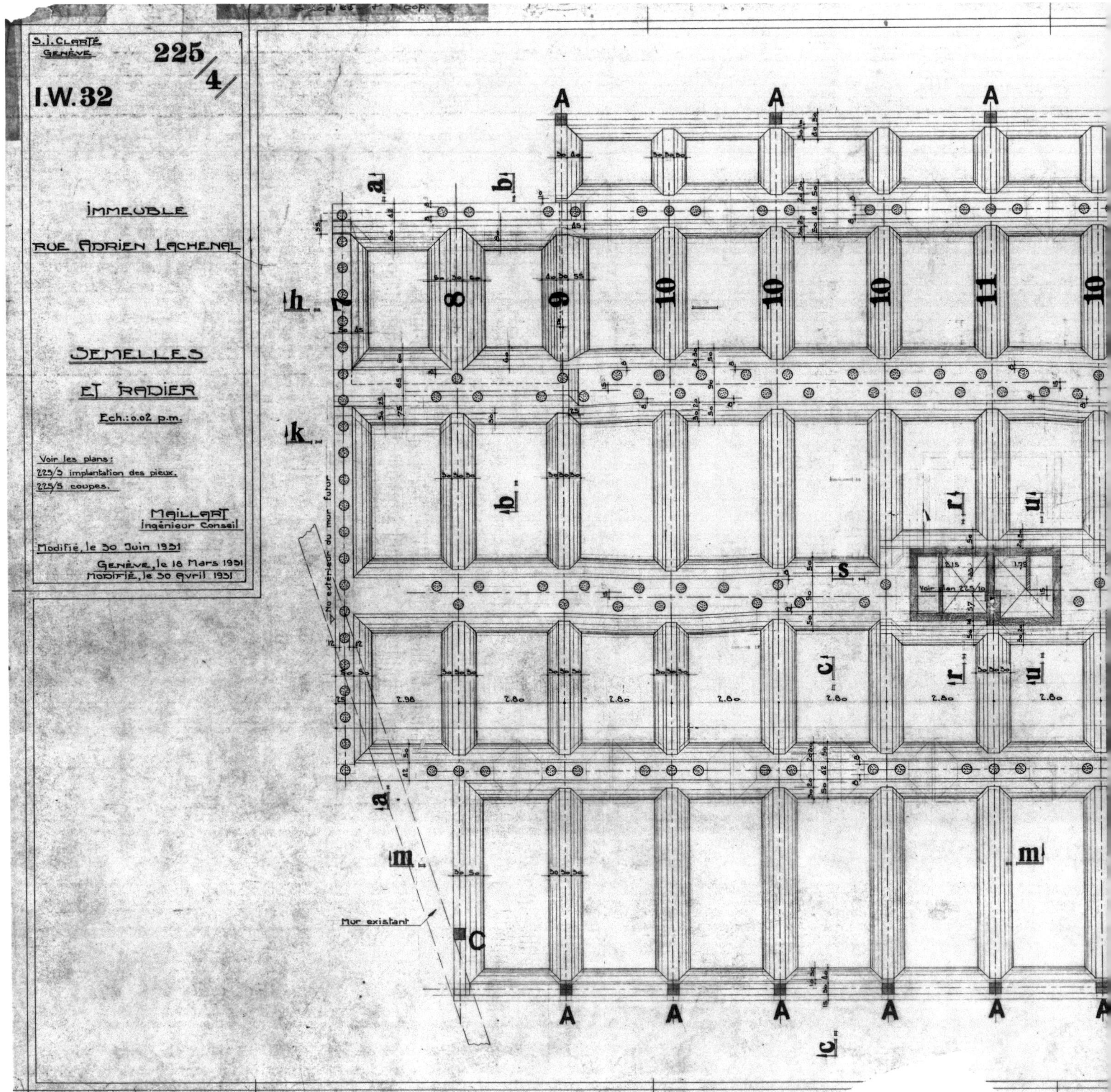

Plan of the footings and of the ground slab, by the engineer Robert Maillart, 18 March 1931, modified on 30 April, and again on 30 June 1931.

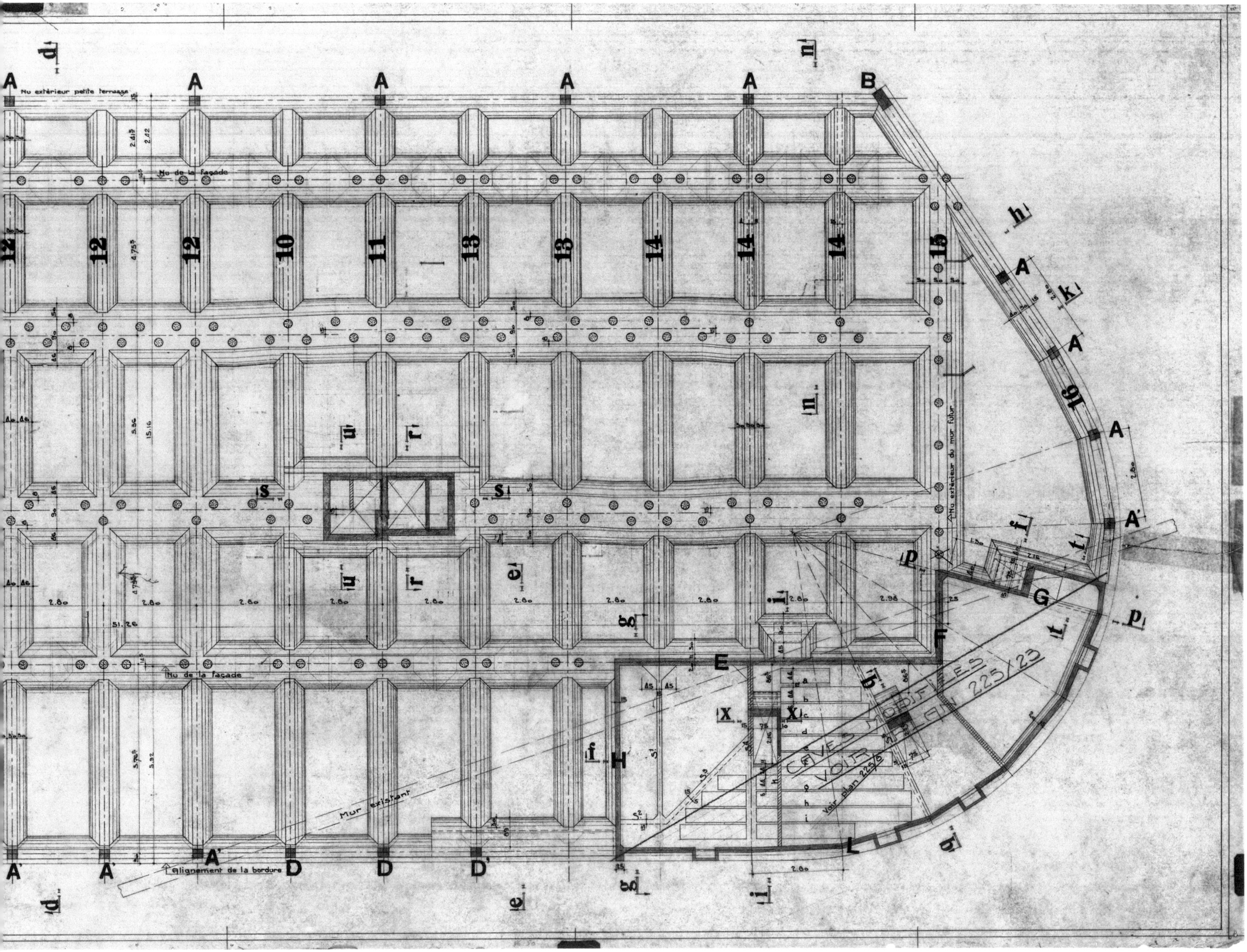
Nu extérieur petite terrasse
Nu de la façade
Nu extérieur du mur futur
Mur existant
Alignement de la bordure
CAVES MODIFIÉES
VOIR PLAN 225/23
Voir plan 225/5

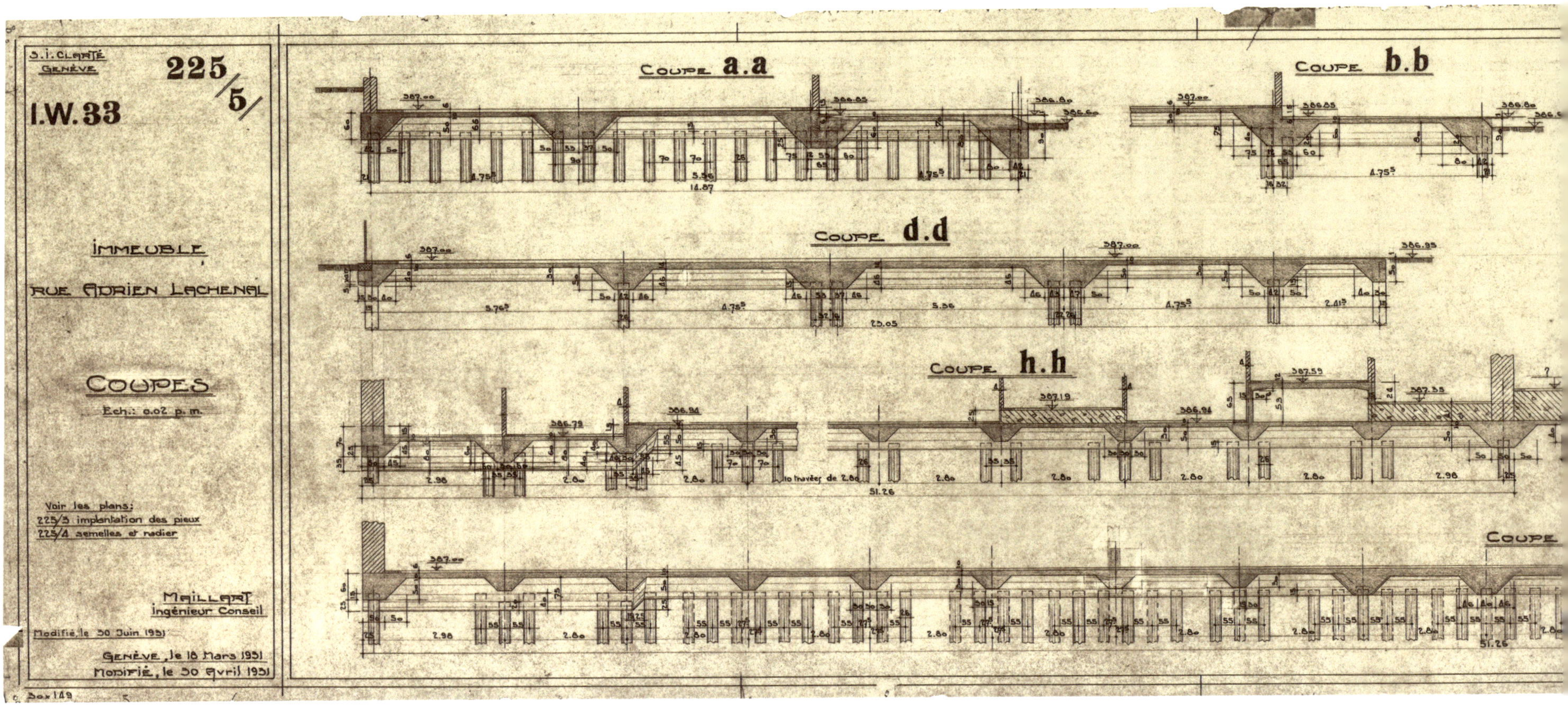

Foundation cross-sections, by the engineer Robert Maillart, 18 March 1931, modified on 30 April, and again on 30 June 1931.

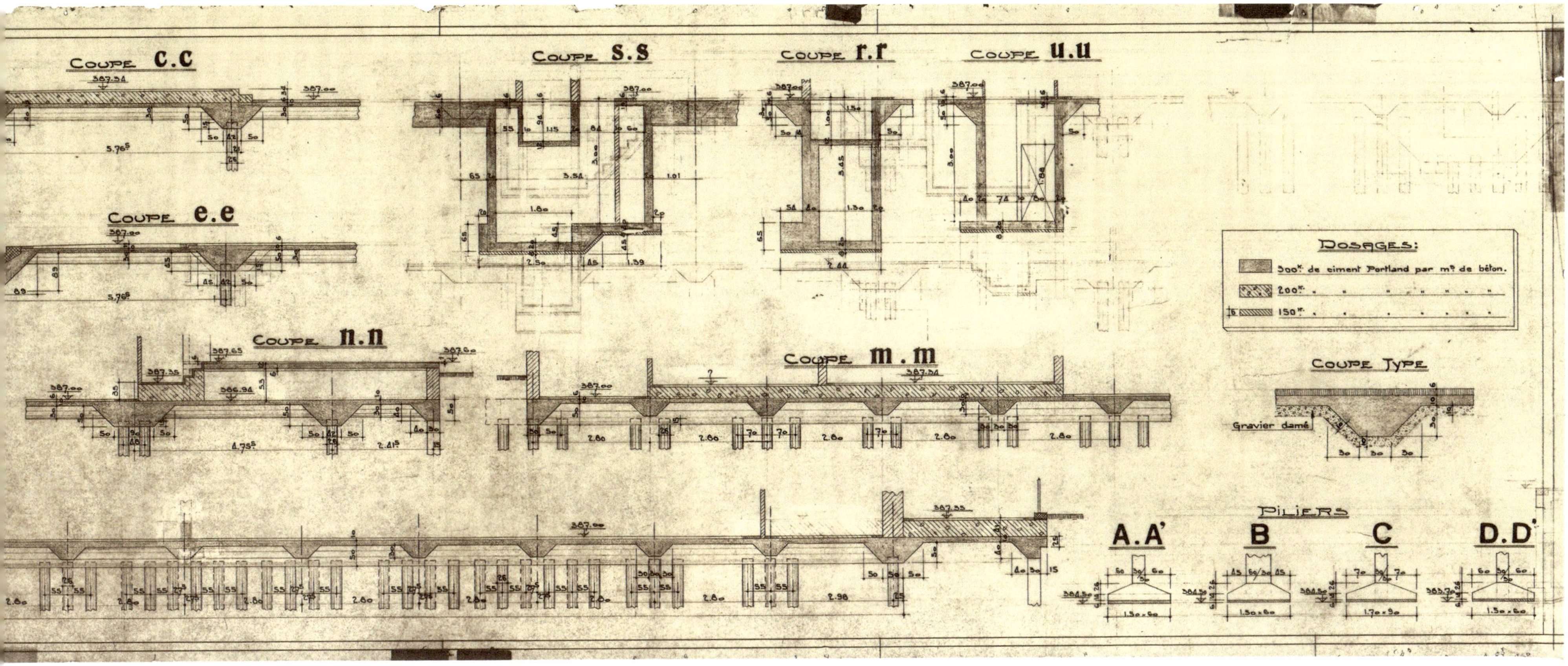
Coupe c.c
Coupe s.s
Coupe r.r
Coupe u.u
Coupe e.e
Coupe n.n
Coupe m.m
Dosages:
300K. de ciment Portland par m³ de béton.
200K. " " " " " "
150K. " " " " " "
Coupe Type
Gravier damé
Piliers
A.A'
B
C
D.D'

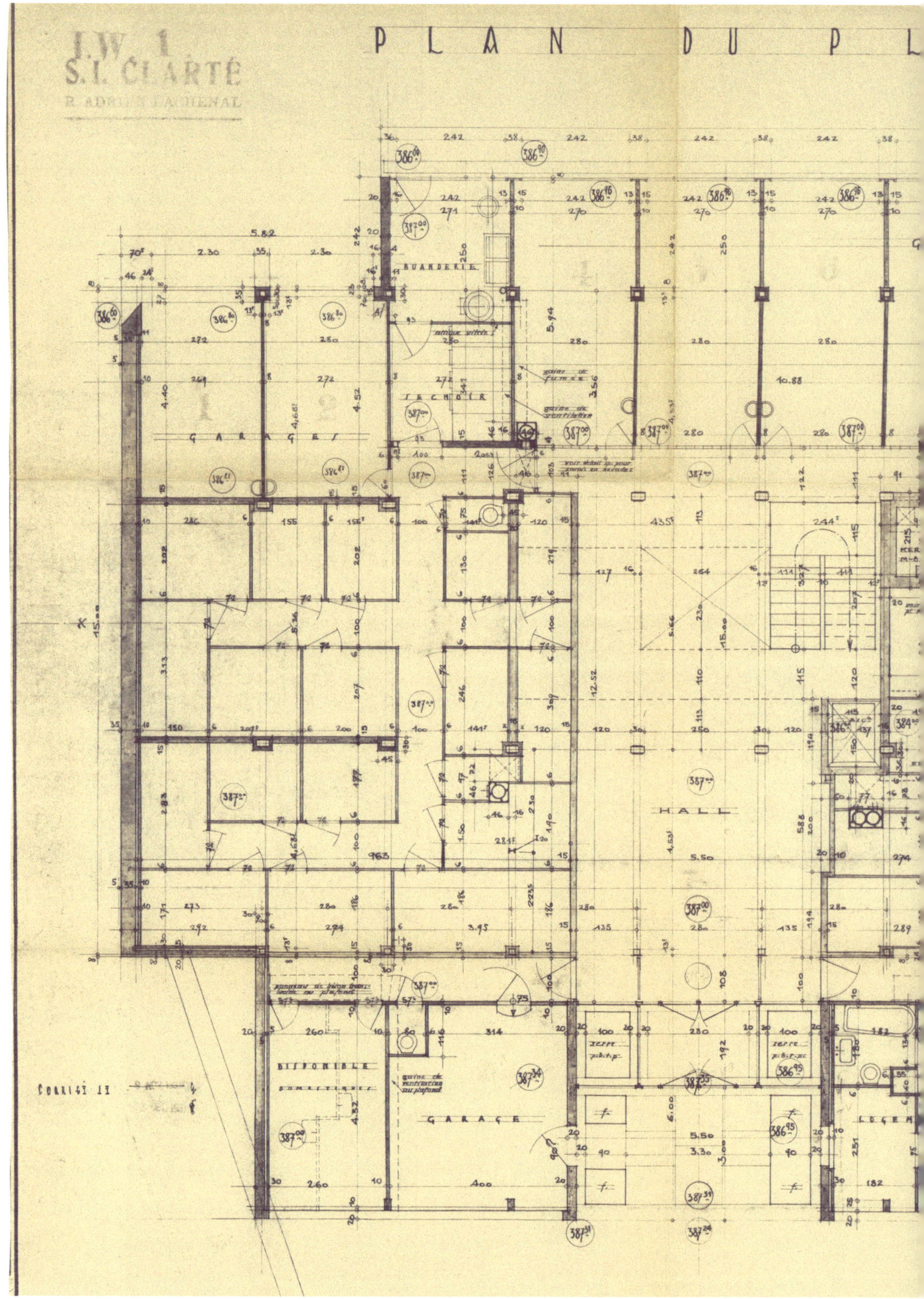

Plan of the first and third storeys (actual second and fourth storeys), dated 22 October 1931, plan kept at the gta of EPFZ.

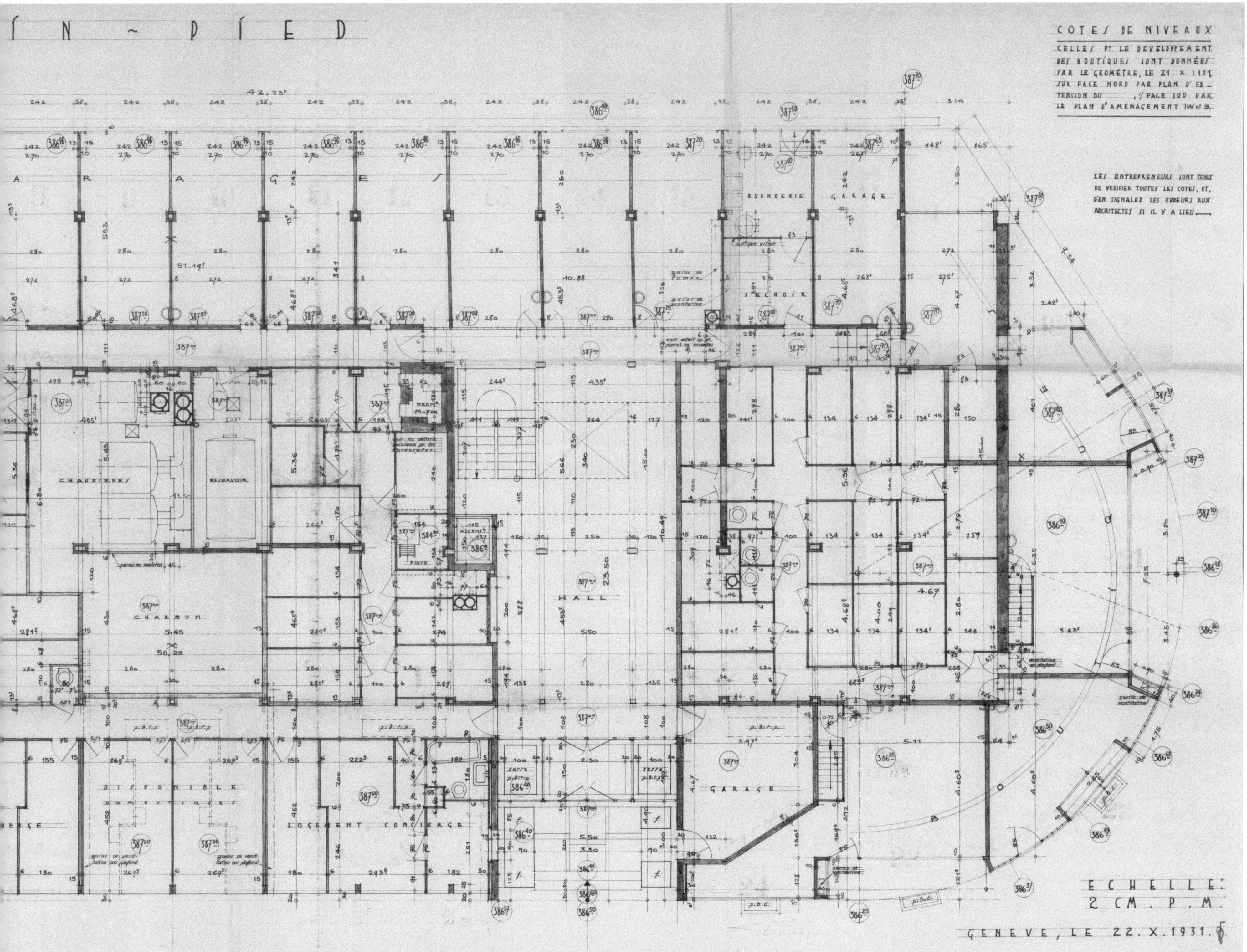
COTES DE NIVEAUX
CELLES P. LE DEVELOPPEMENT DES BOUTIQUES SONT DONNÉES PAR LE GEOMÈTRE, LE 21. X. 1931, SUR FACE NORD PAR PLAN D'EXTENSION DU ....., S/ FACE SUD PAR LE PLAN D'AMÉNAGEMENT
LES ENTREPRENEURS SONT TENUS DE VERIFIER TOUTES LES COTES, ET, D'EN SIGNALER LES ERREURS AUX ARCHITECTES SI IL Y A LIEU
GARAGES
BUANDERIE
GARAGE
SECHOIR
CHAUDIERES
RESERVOIR
CHARBON
HALL
GARAGE
DISPONIBLE
LOGEMENT CONCIERGE
BOUTIQUE
ECHELLE: 2 CM. P. M.
GENEVE, LE 22. X. 1931.

59

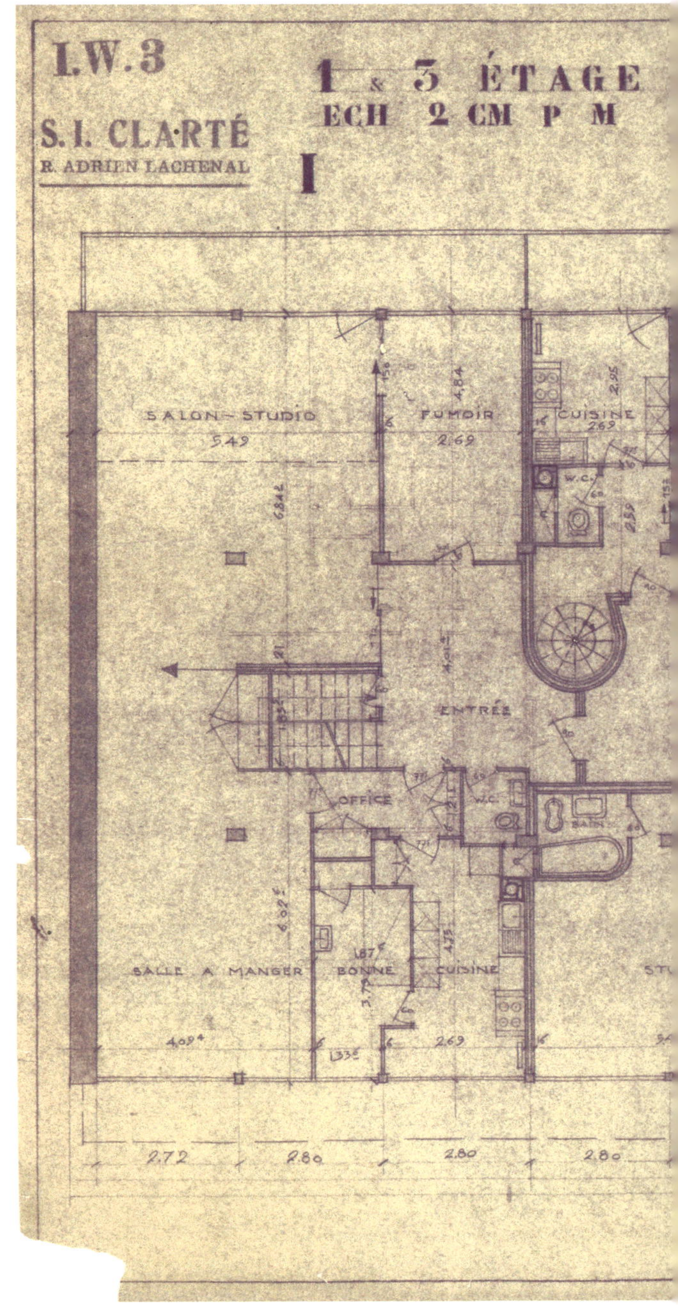

Plan of the first and third storeys (actual second and fourth storeys), modified 18 December 1931, plan kept at the gta of EPFZ.

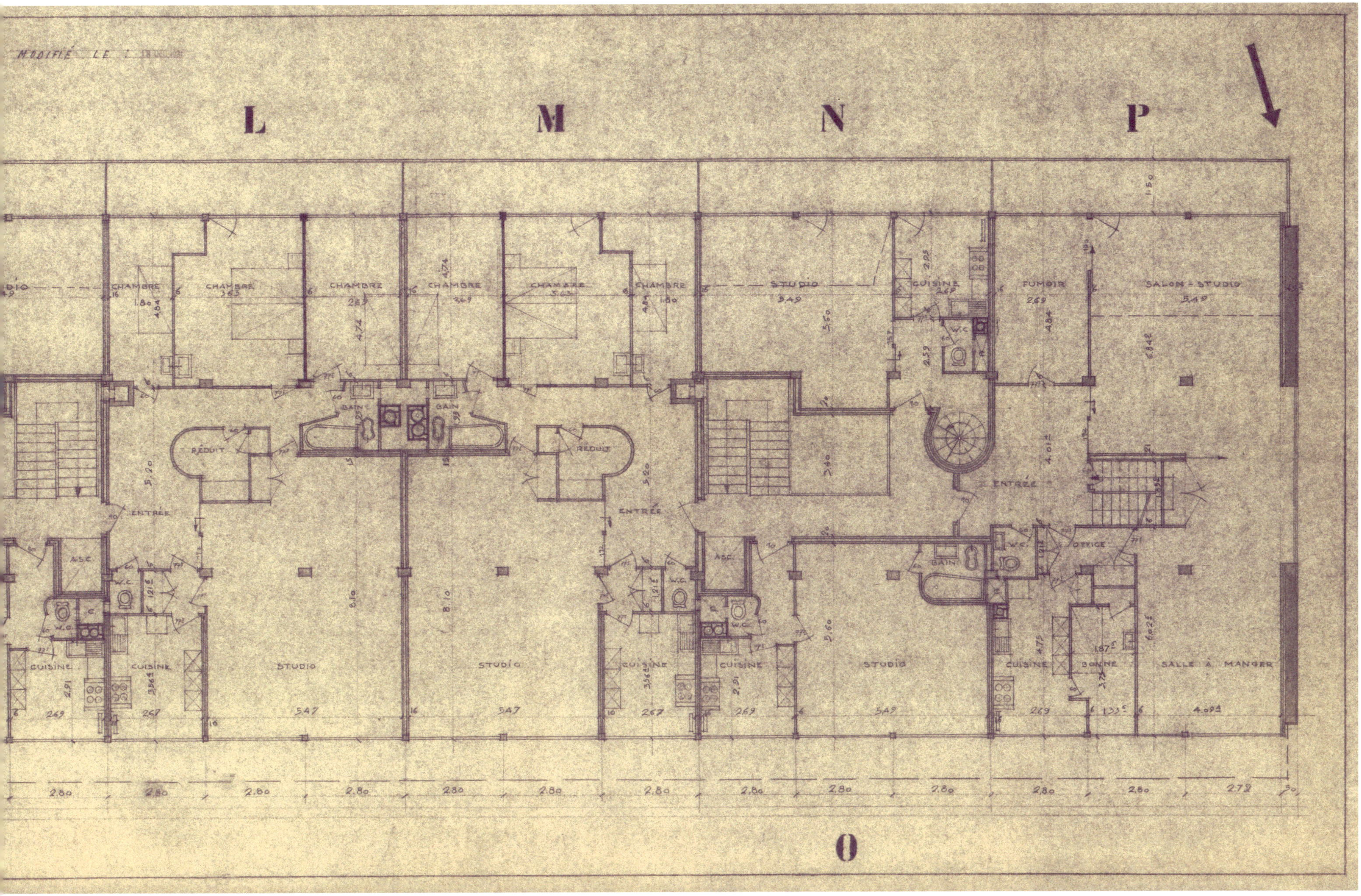
L
M
N
P
CHAMBRE
STUDIO
CUISINE
FUMOIR
SALON - STUDIO
RÉDUIT
BAIN
ENTRÉE
A.S.C.
W.C.
OFFICE
BONNE
SALLE À MANGER
0

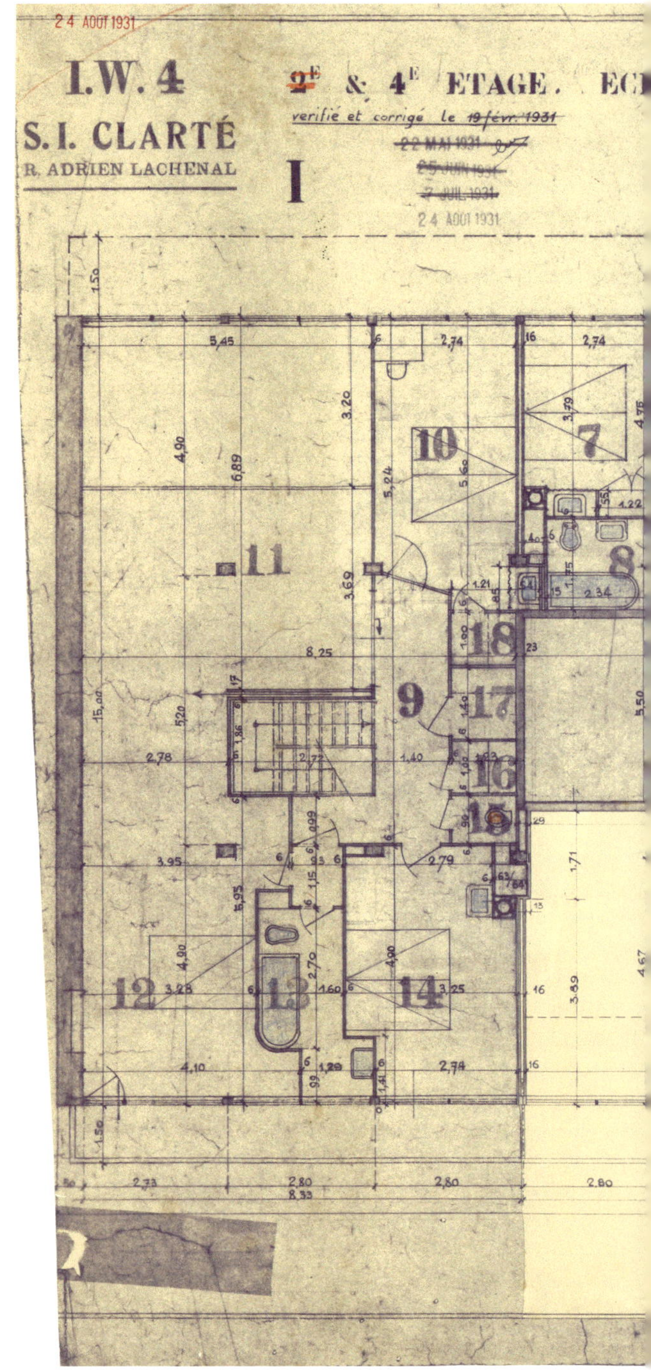

Plan of the second and fourth storeys (actual third and fifth storeys), final revision of 24 August 1931, plan kept at the gta of EPFZ.

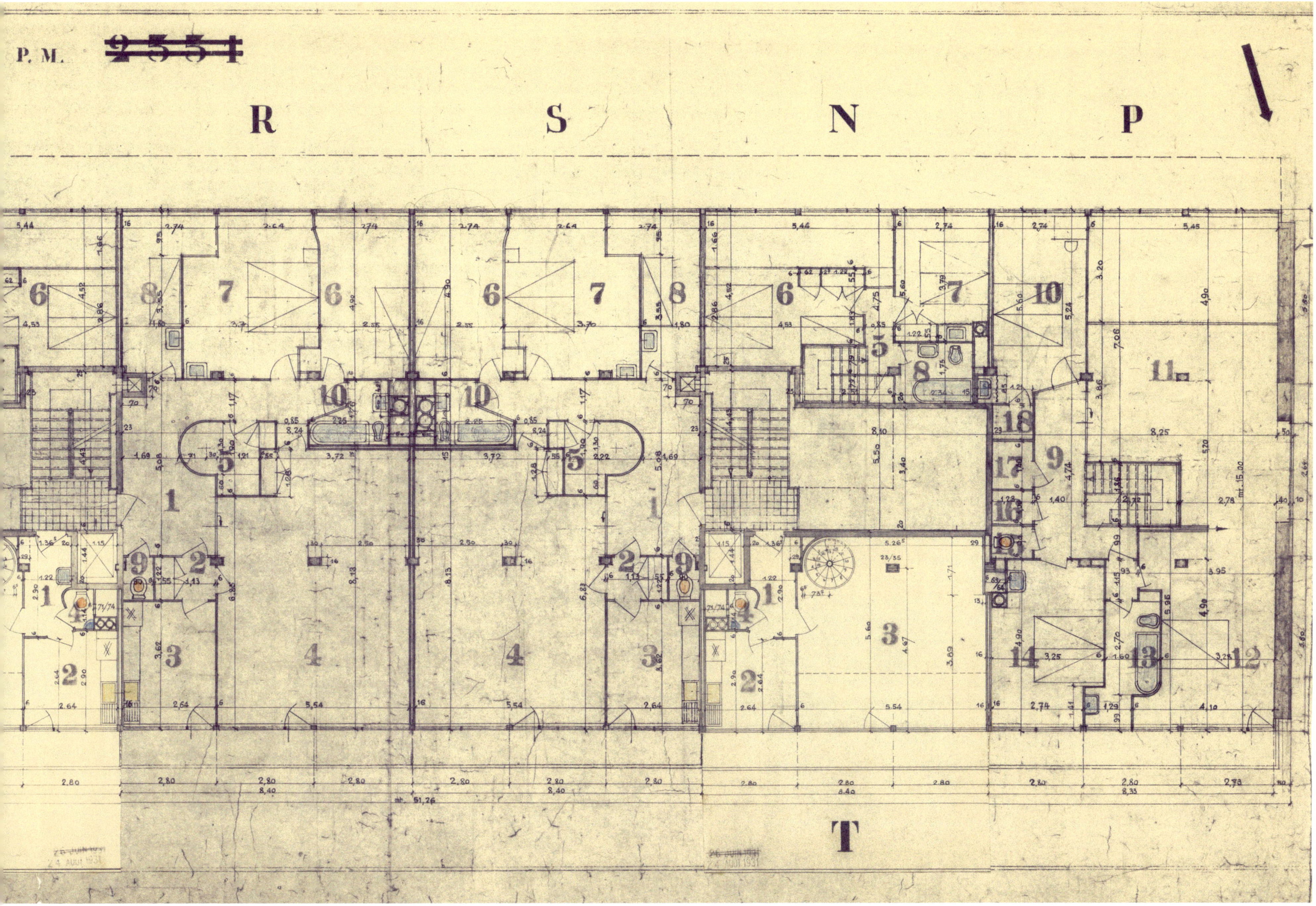
P. M.
R
S
N
P
T

Plan – 1932 detail
ground floor and basement
scale 1:300

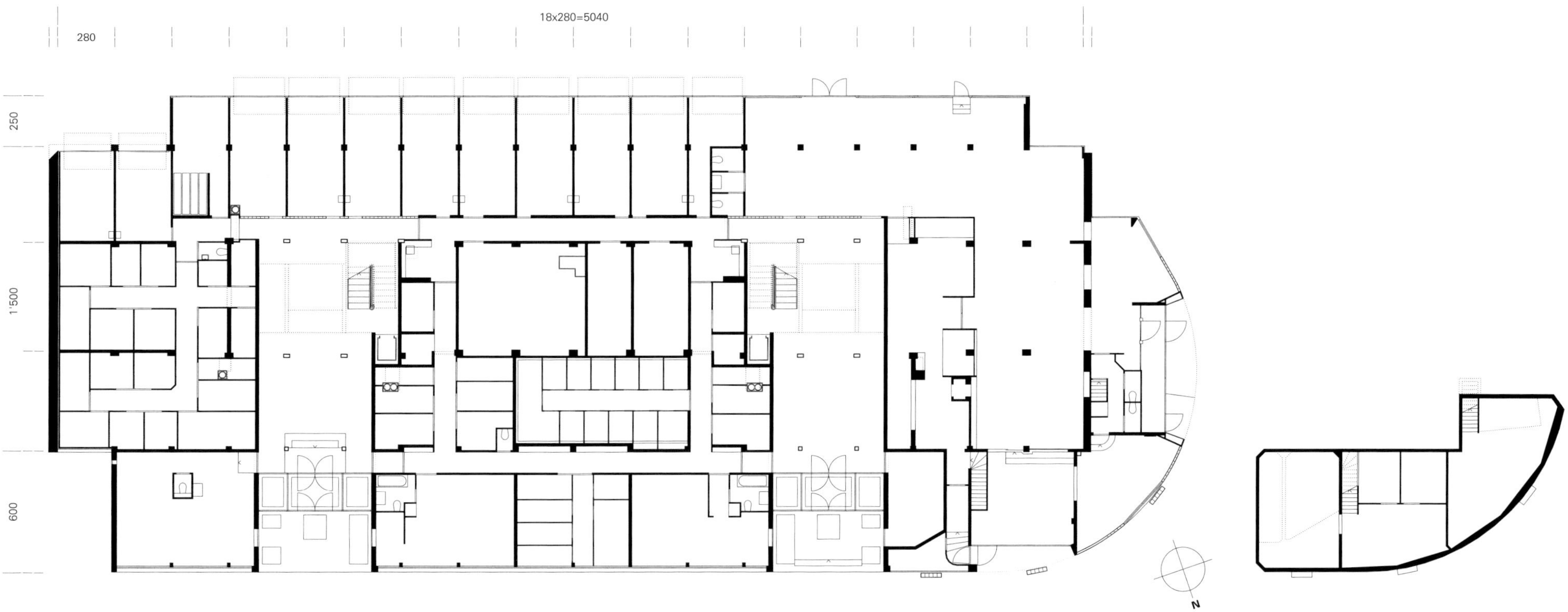

Plan – state 2014
ground floor and basement
scale 1:300

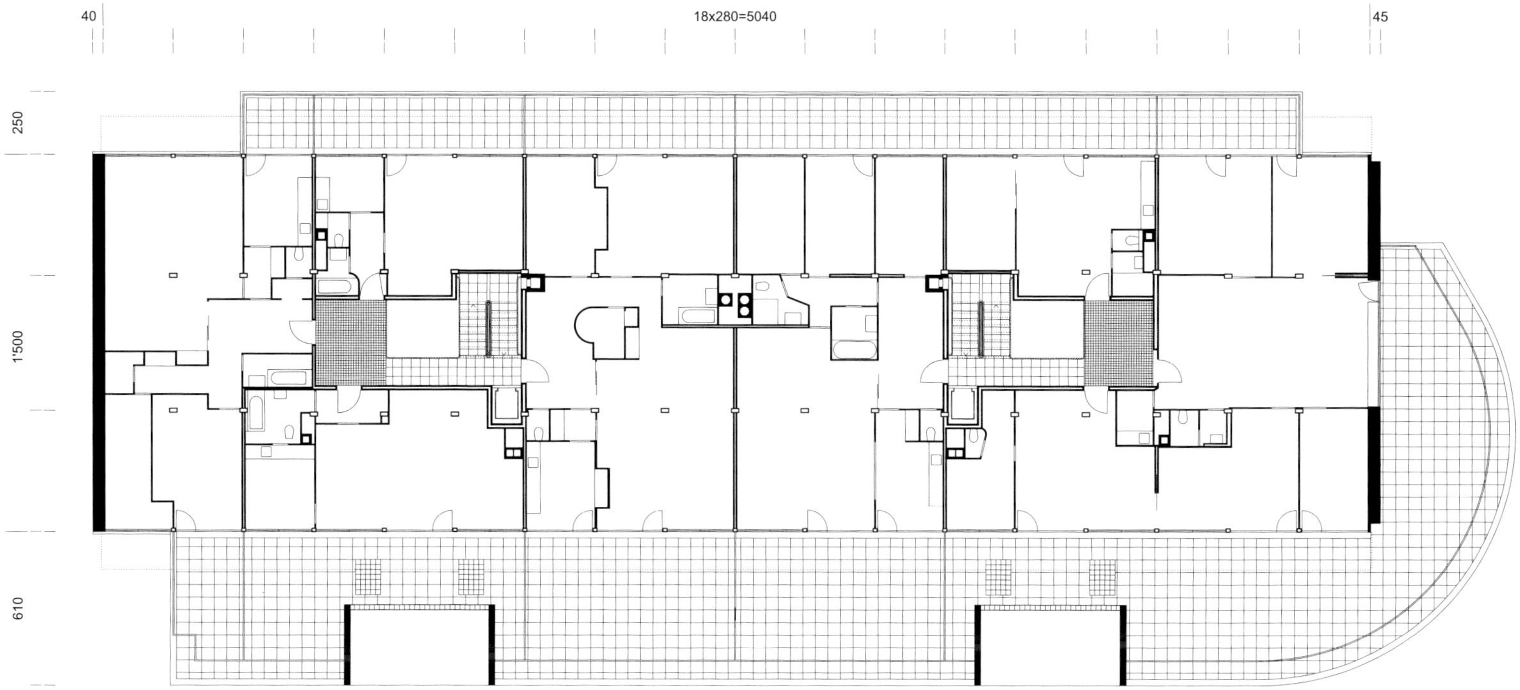

1st storey
scale 1:300

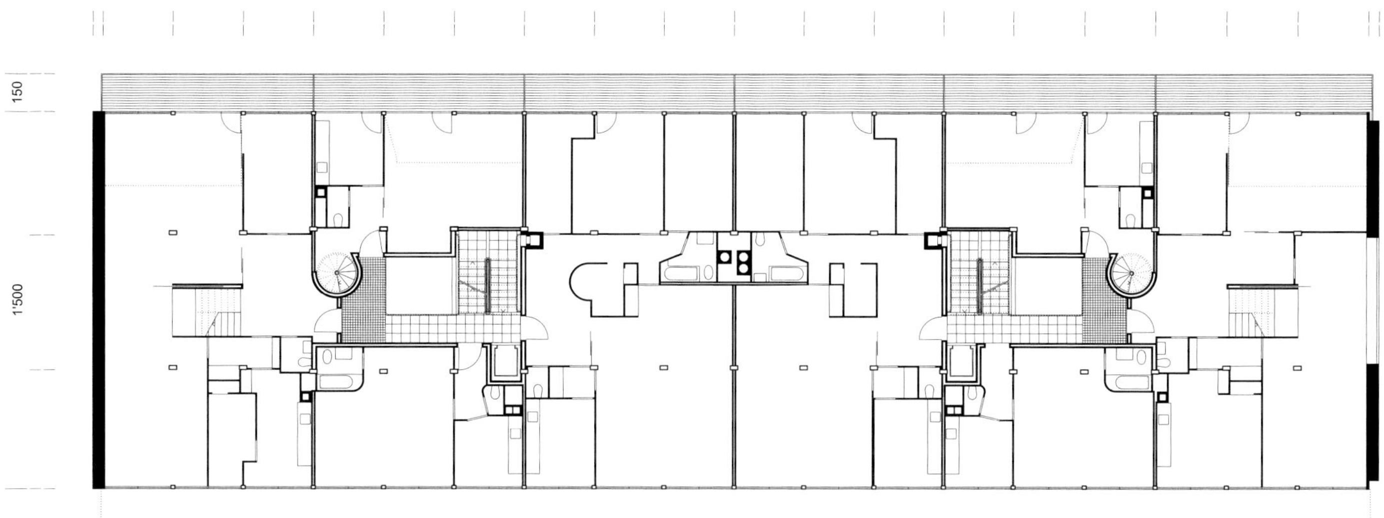

2nd storey
scale 1:300

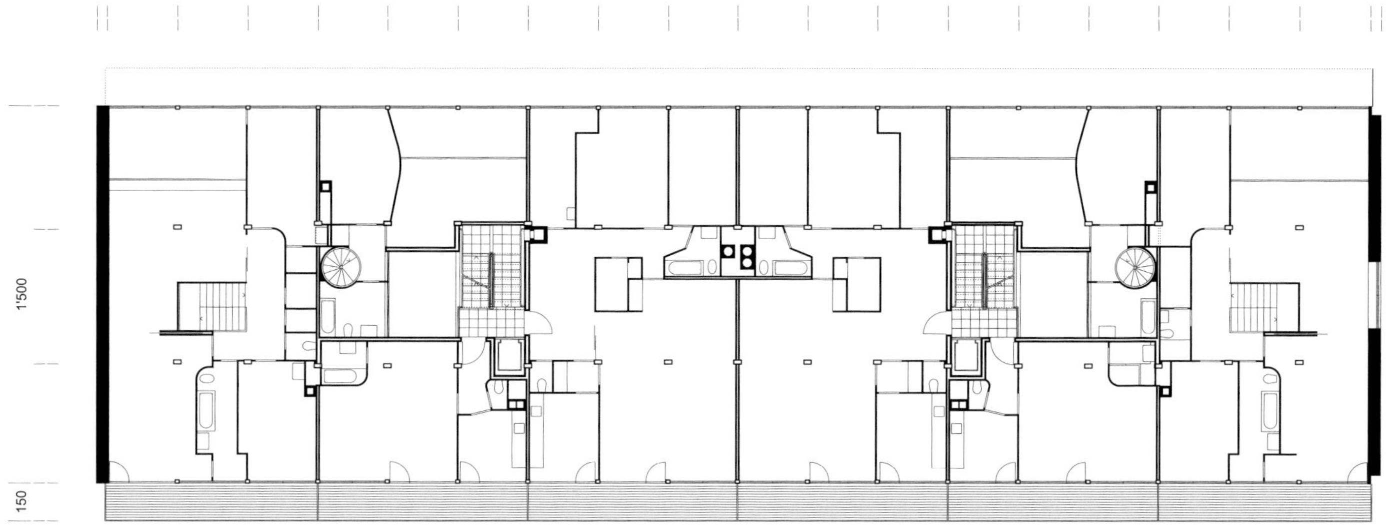

3rd storey
scale 1:300

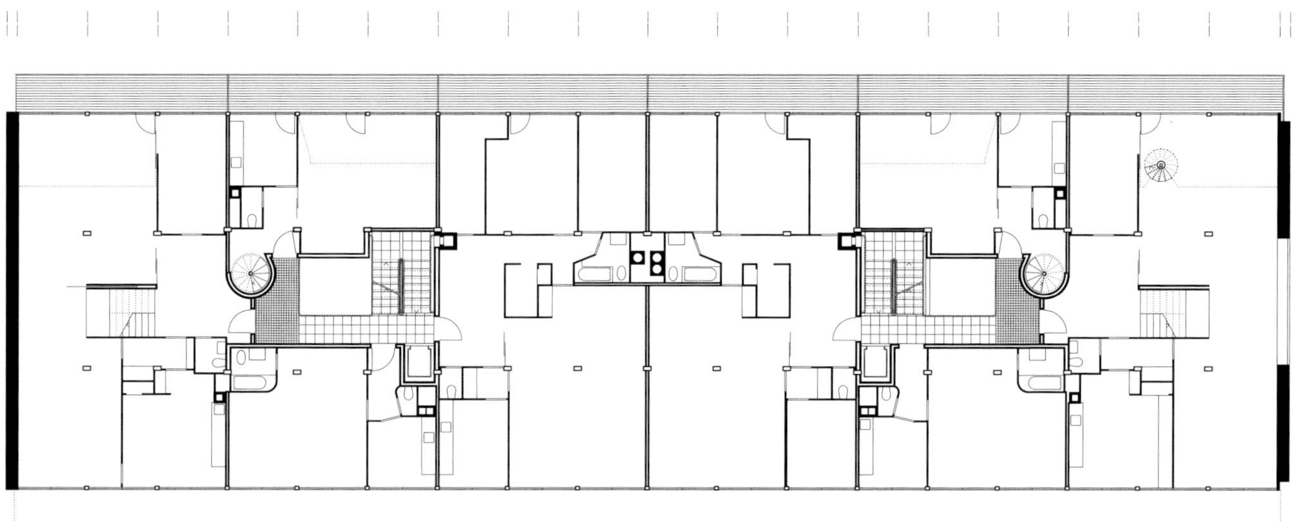

4th storey
scale 1:300

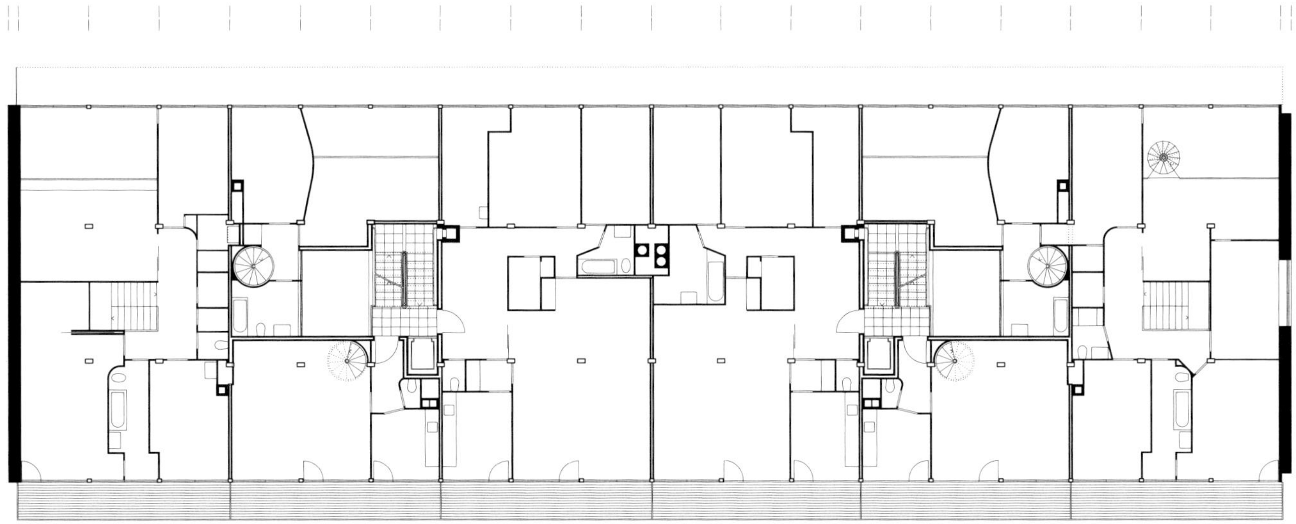

5th storey
scale 1:300

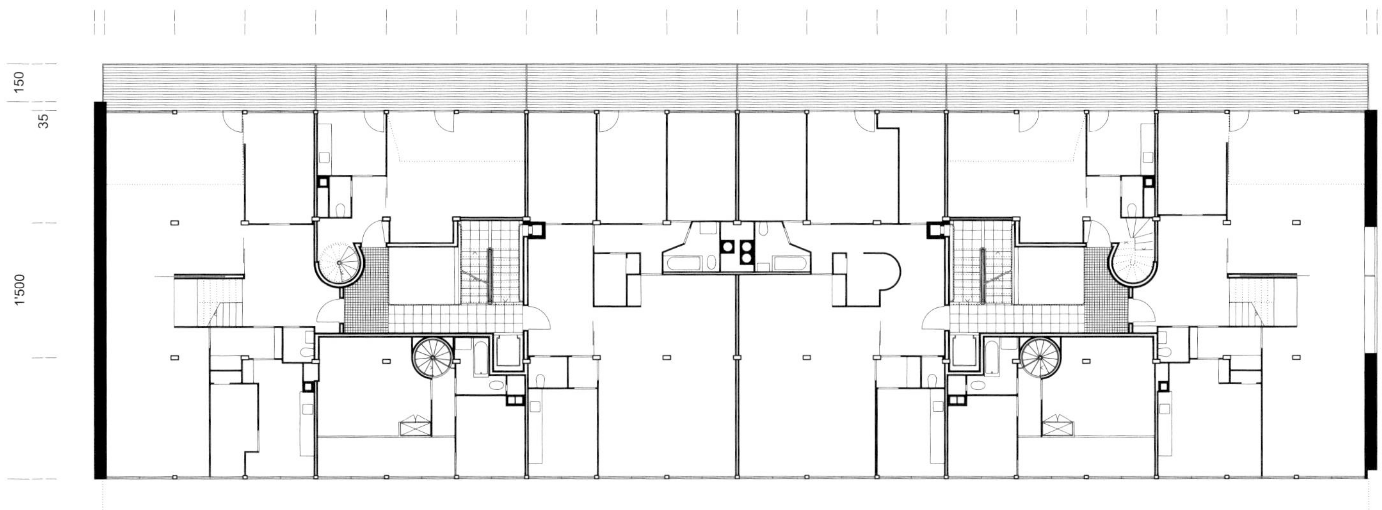

6th storey
scale 1:300

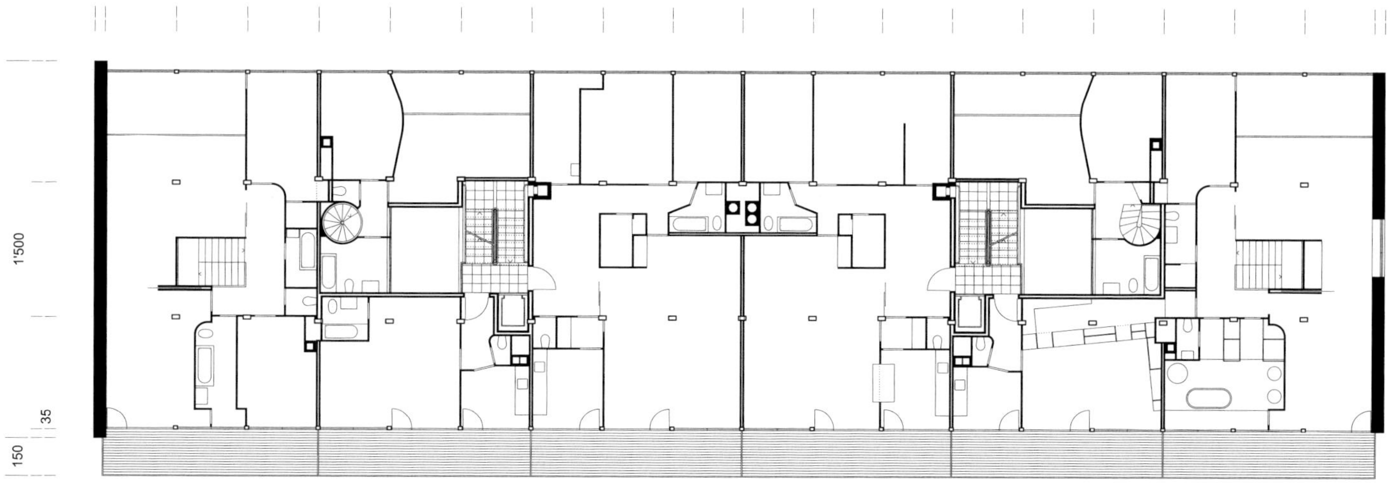

7th storey
scale 1:300

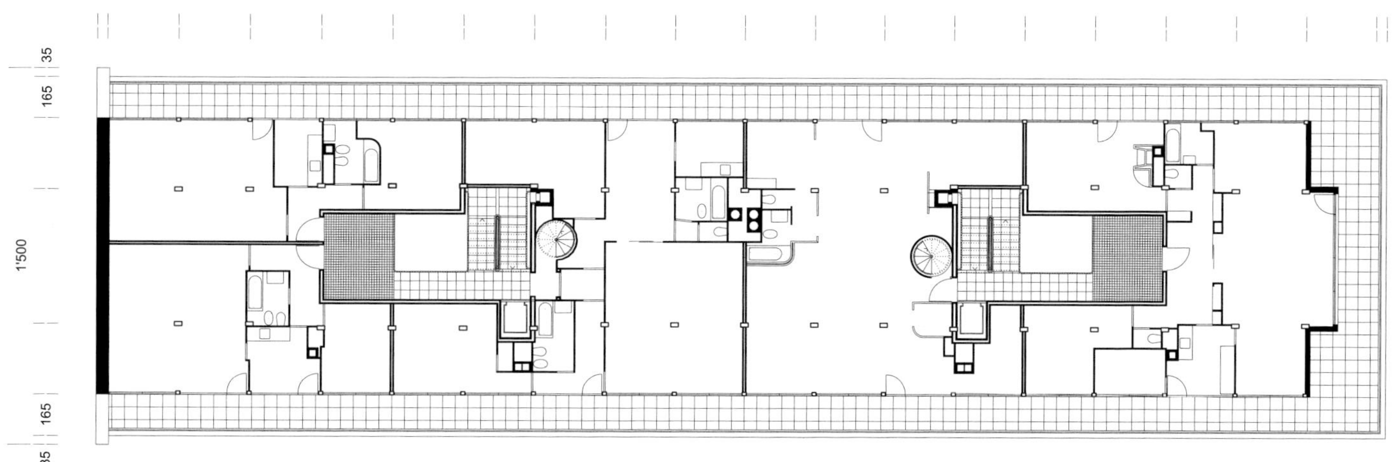

8th storey attic
scale 1:300

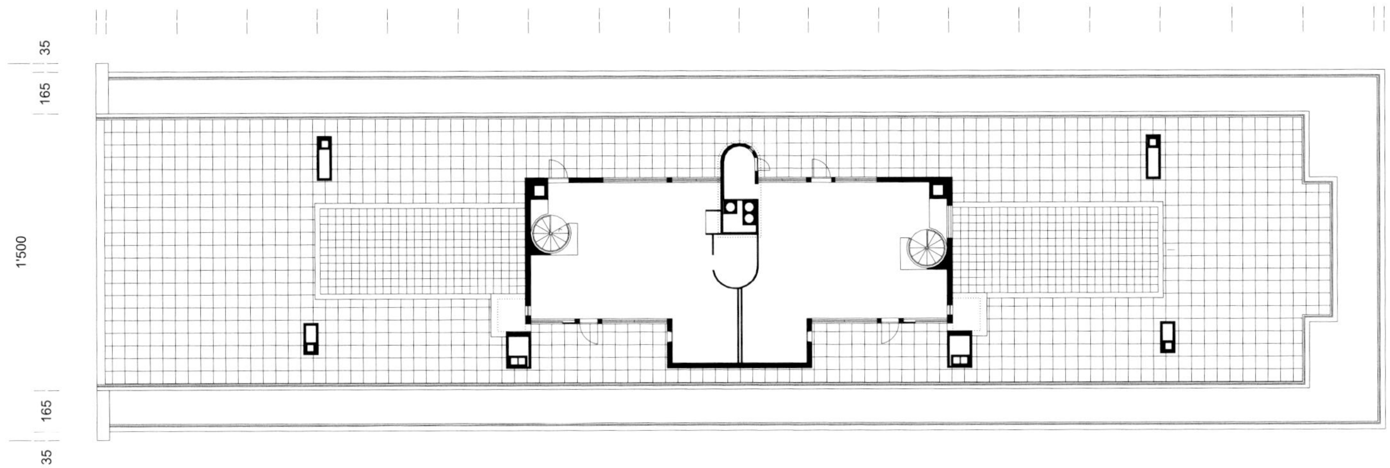

9th storey
scale 1:300

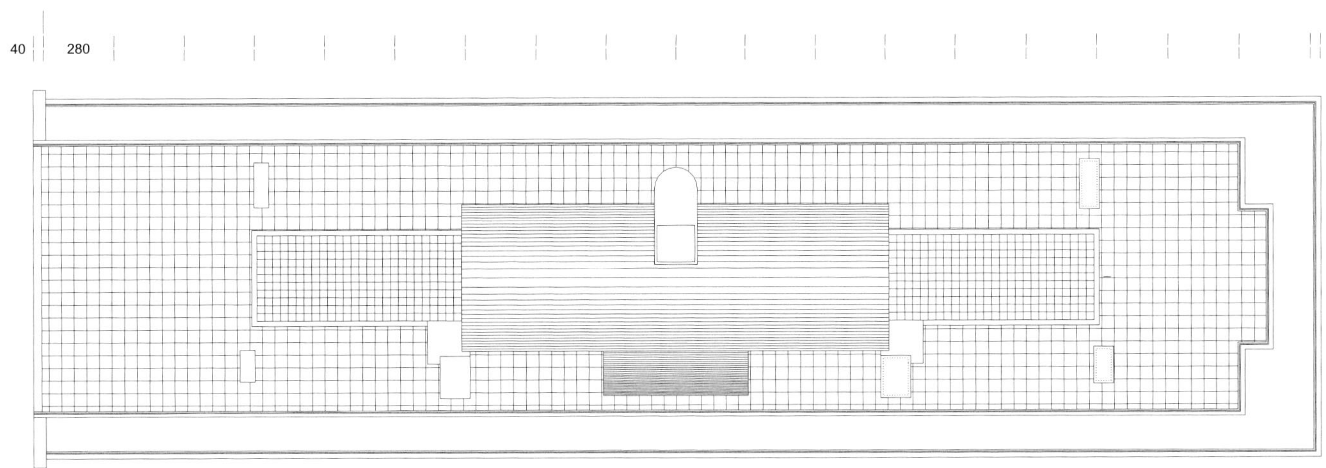

Roof terrace
scale 1:300

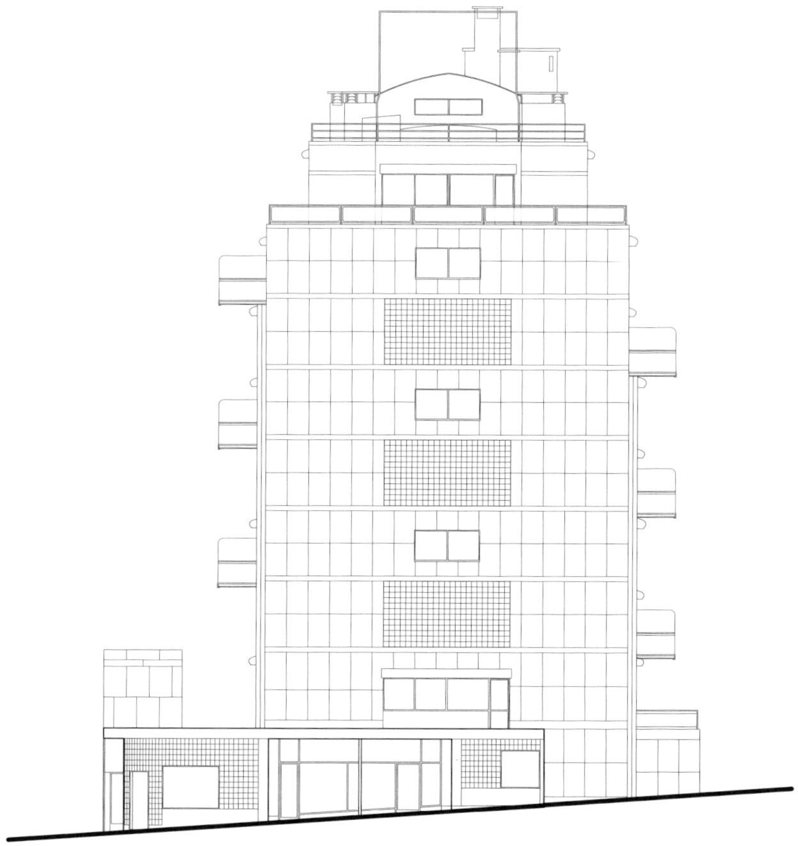

West facade
scale 1:300

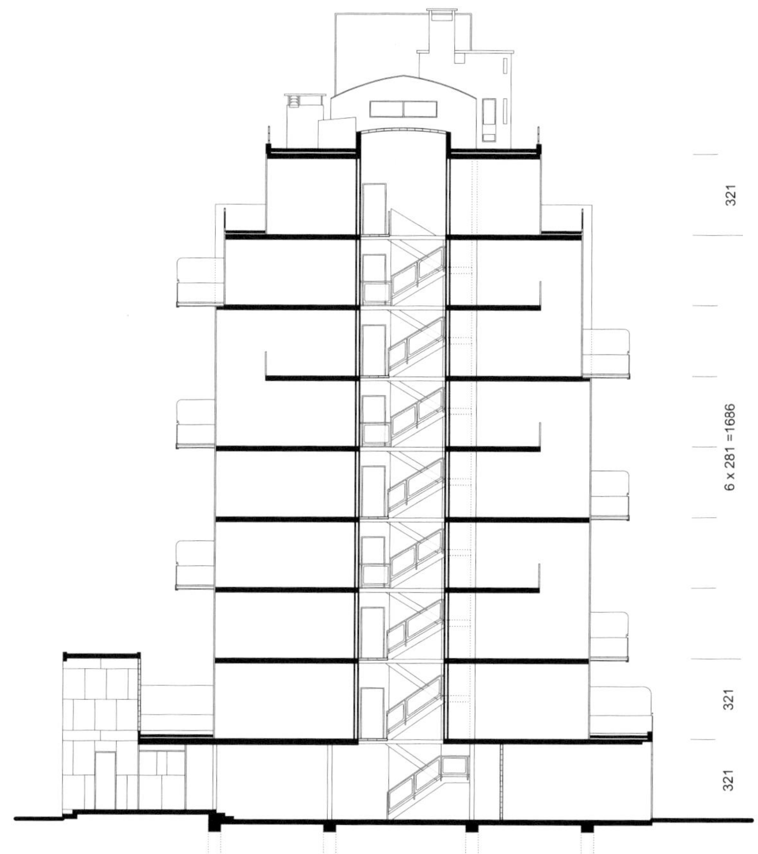

Transverse section
scale 1:300

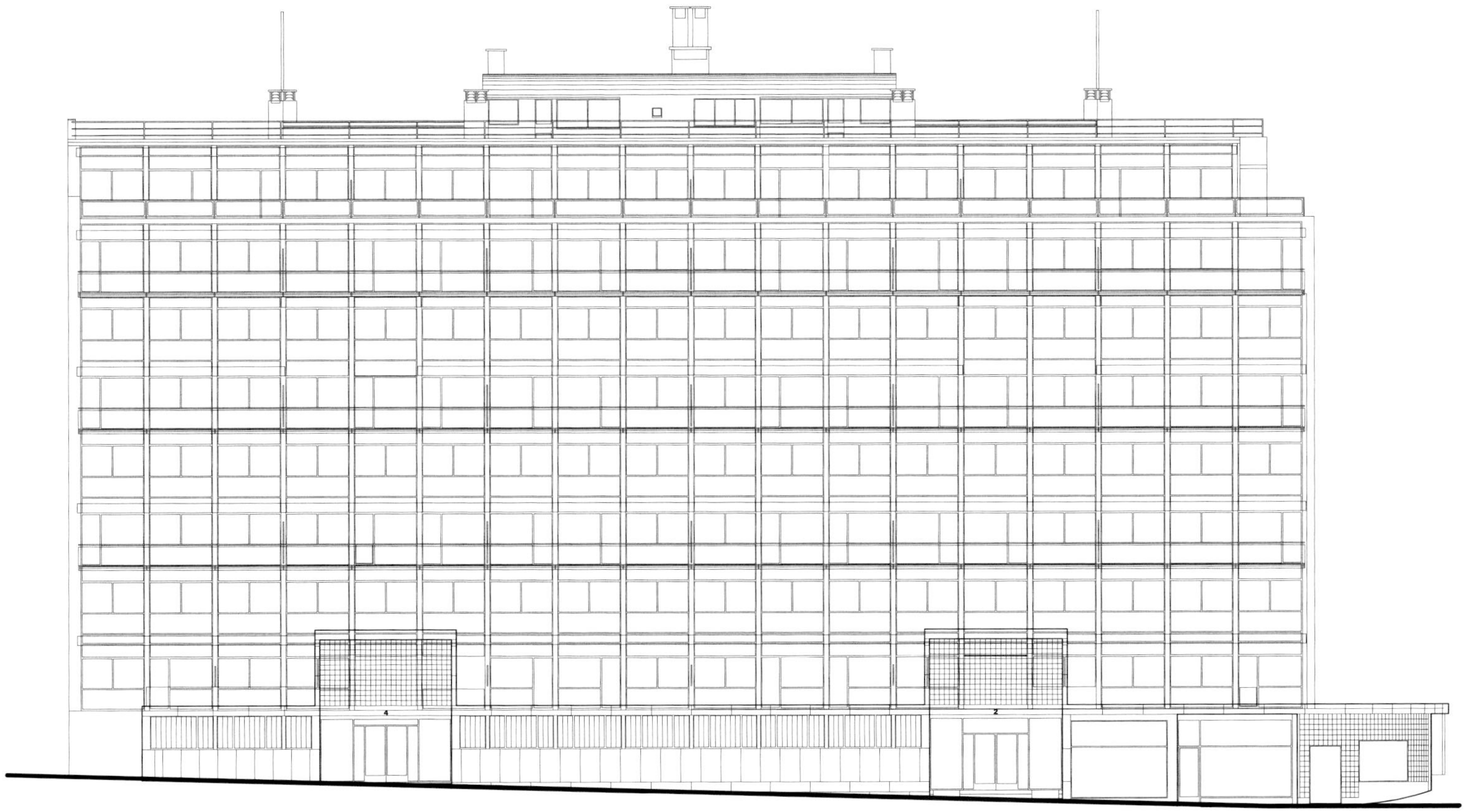

North facade
scale 1:300

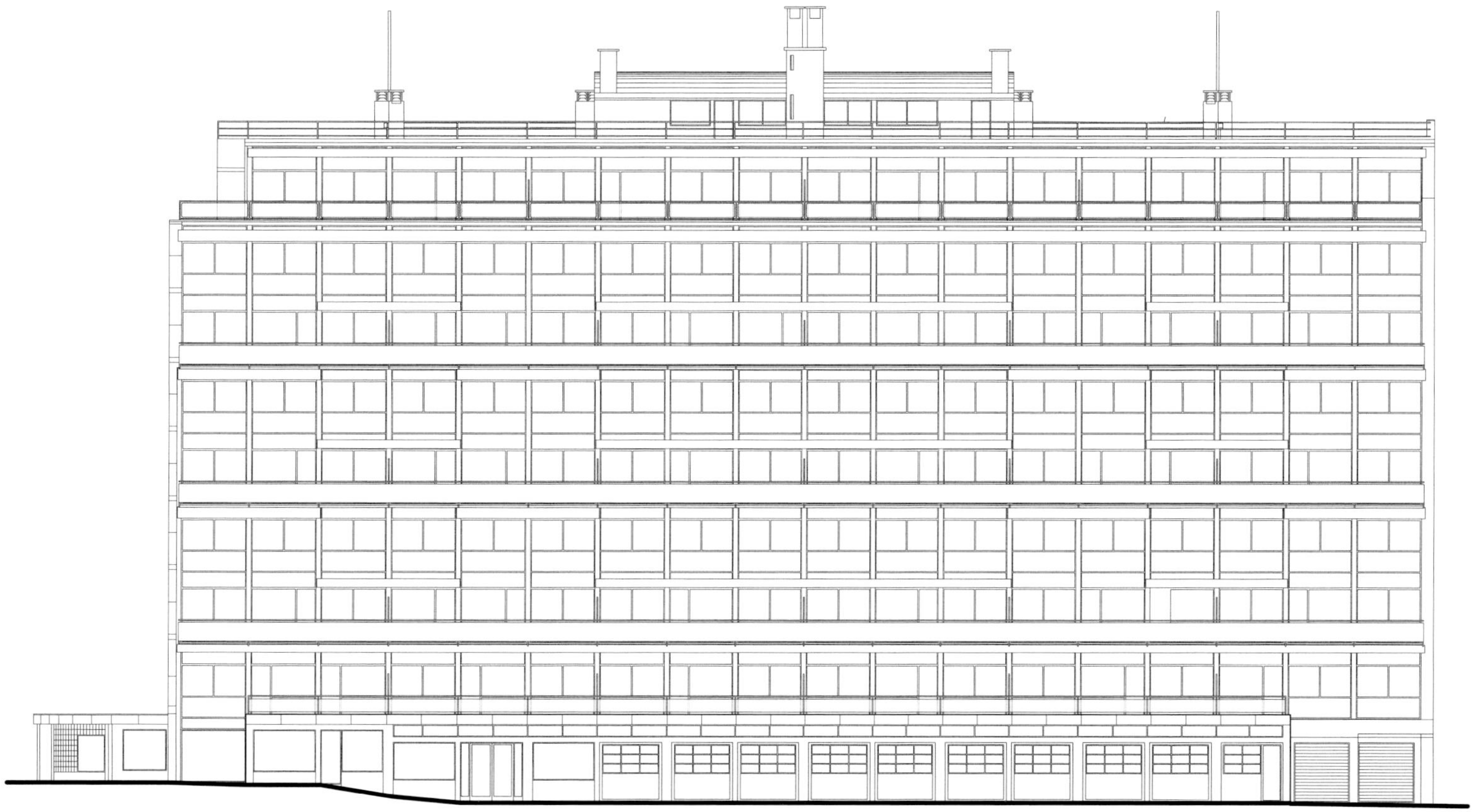

South facade
scale 1:300

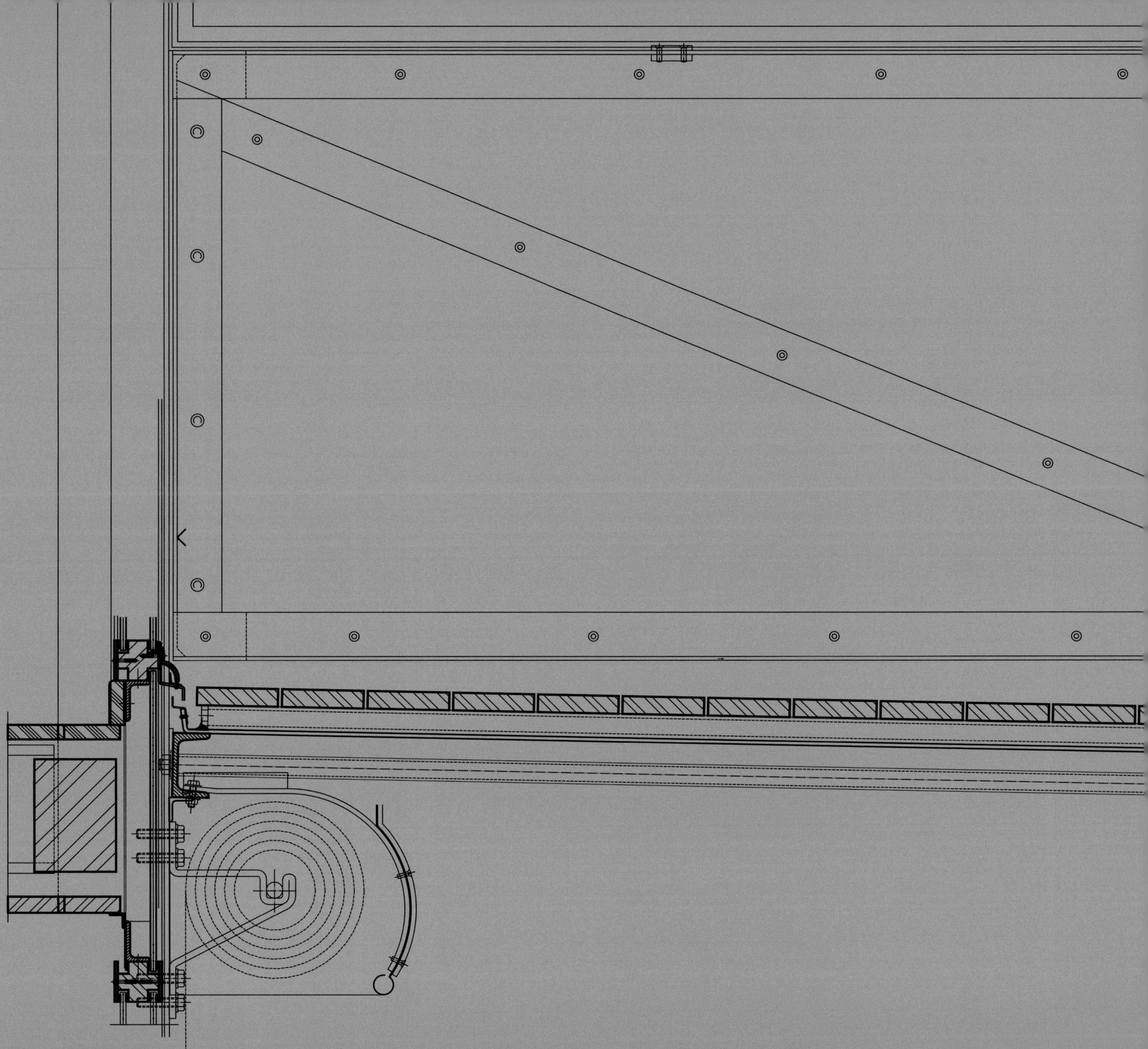

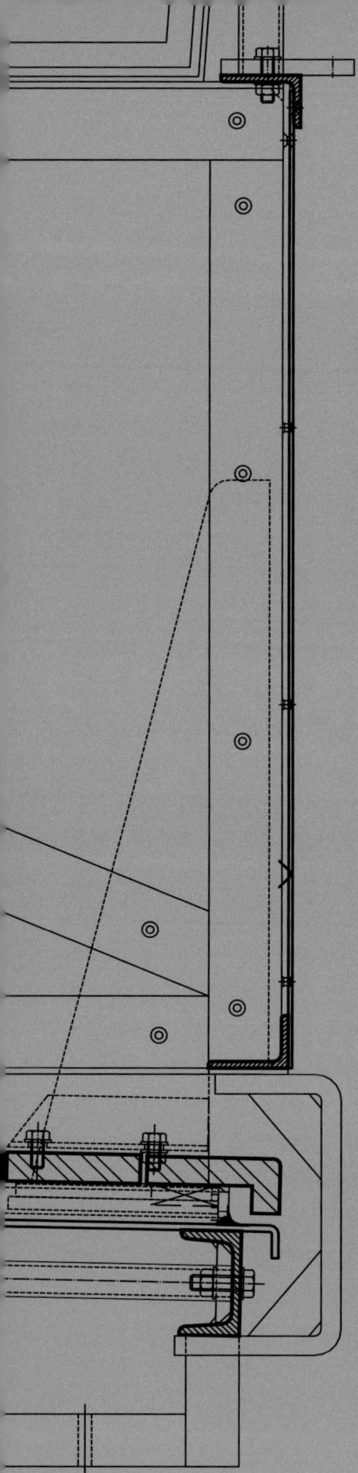

THE RESTORATION OF 2007–2011 AT THE HEART OF THE WORKS

Introduction

Sabine Nemec-Piguet, Marielle Savoyat

Beginnings

The Clarté building, realised in 1931/1932 by the architects Le Corbusier and Pierre Jeanneret, promoted by the entrepreneur Edmond Wanner, is located in the Villereuse district. This architecture of steel and glass is among the most representative of the modern movement in Europe. It summarises an epoch of purism, of engineering aesthetics, and of the machine. The concepts of standardisation and of mass production are shown as never before, making this building a model of experimental rationalism.

In 1953/54, the architect Marc Joseph Saugey undertook some restoration works, notably to the balcony decks, which he directed be covered with asphalt. According to the art restorer Eric-James Favre-Bulle, at around this time Saugey commissioned some large (2.20×8.45 metre) murals in multi-coloured oils to decorate the entrance halls. These were painted on the wall facing the letter boxes and were to a design by Georges Aubert (1881–1961), a friend of Le Corbusier. These works have been obscured by subsequent layers of paint.

In the 1960s the Clarté building, being in a very dilapidated state and threatened with demolition, owed its preservation to an initiative of the Federation of Swiss Architects (FAS) leading to its acquisition in 1968 by a consortium of Swiss architects/shareholders. Soon after, between 1975 and 1977, the architects Pascal Häusermann and Bruno Camoletti bought the building, sold some of the apartments, and undertook maintenance works. They proceeded with general repairs to the roof, waterproofing and flashing, and with reconstruction of the skylights illuminating the stairwells. The repairs included painting exterior metal parts brown, the replacement of some windows, wooden blinds, and textile awnings, and the repair of glass brick panels to the fourth and sixth floors of the west gable-end facade. A general freshening-up of all apartments (essentially the hanging of woodchip wallpaper) and the partial renovation of sanitary installations (replacement of ceramic kitchen sinks with stainless steel units), earth stacks, and pipework was also carried out. The central heating was changed, entrances and stairwells were repainted, and the original letter boxes replaced. Finally, a restaurant was installed at 2, rue Saint-Laurent. “But Häusermann and Camoletti were experiencing grave financial difficulties; in consequence maintenance of the building was no longer assured and in the 1980s it was once again threatened with demolition”.[1]

When classified as a historical monument in 1986, the Clarté building was again in poor condition. In 1993 the Office of Heritage Buildings and Sites engaged the firm of Devanthéry & Lamunière to prepare a specification for restoration of the facades. This work included establishing a 1:20 scale drawing of the building’s outer envelope consigning all changes made to the facades since their construction. However, with no work planned, the state of the building continued to deteriorate, to the point where, ten years later, the Office of Heritage Buildings and Sites had to intervene to oblige the owners to undertake an urgent and immediate restoration. In autumn 2003, the Geneva Cantonal Bank’s Asset Valuation Foundation, at that time the majority owner with more than fifty per cent of the property, engaged the architects Jacques-Louis de Chambrier and Alain Dutheil to undertake a preliminary study. With that, the Foundation was now ready to advance the funds needed to begin the Clarté building’s essential restoration.

This initial study also prompted the support of the residents’ association, who engaged these two architects to conduct the restoration work. The building permit (DD 99’620) was issued on 24 June 2005 and the site work began in June 2007.

While the building’s envelope and communal areas (external areas) are the responsibility of the residents’ association, maintenance of apartments (interior areas) is the responsibility of each individual owner. Alongside the restoration of external areas, specific rules were formulated regarding an apartment’s use and maintenance and incorporated into the residents’ association regulations. These rules ensure conservation of the heritage quality of interior areas[2]. To facilitate their development, a complete inventory was drawn up in 2003 by the architectural firm Laurent Chenu, on behalf of the Office of Heritage Buildings and Sites.

1 Catherine Courtiau, *Le Corbusier – Construction, projects and training in Switzerland*, Swiss Art History Society, Berne, 2012, p. 73.

2 See extract of the residents’ rules for administration and use dating from 2008 (clauses concerning maintenance and conservation), given as an appendix.

The condition before the 2007–2011 restoration

On the upper floors, roof and facade leaks were a recurring problem, as they were at the undersides of balconies. Most of the large wooden roller blinds, of over five meters in height, were broken and their mechanisms not working; in addition the textile awnings were torn. On the southern facade, about thirty per cent of the fixed windows, notably the lower reinforced glass areas, had broken. Corrosion was attacking all facades causing deformations. The rotten balcony decks were threatening to give way. Although seemingly in good condition, the travertine cladding of the western facade and the entrance porches was in danger of falling, due to carbonation attacking the underlying reinforced concrete; all masonry superstructures showed much cracking, notably the skylights illuminating stairwells, which were no longer waterproof. On the ground floor, the outer panels of "Nevada" glass brick were also leaking. In summary, the building envelope was in an advanced state of degradation, while inside, the communal technical service installations had reached a high degree of obsolescence.

The 2007–2011 restoration

This major restoration has focused on the building's envelope and communal areas. It became urgent to resume and continue the work undertaken thirty years earlier during the 1975–1977 restoration, such as that concerning waterproofing, corrosion, and the facade glazing; the structure, decks, and paintwork of all balconies; the superstructure and arched roofs of the "roof apartments"; the travertine facade and carbonation of the reinforced concrete elements; the glass brick panels of the entrance porches and the arcades.

Attention was also focused on issues of energy consumption and insulation (insulating glass, roof insulation, motorised sun screens) as well as on safety, of the user in general and on fire safety (structural steel intumescent coatings, fire-resistant partitions and ceilings on the ground floor).

The owners and tenants continued to occupy the premises throughout the duration of the works, which had to take account of their presence.

The restoration in question

Given the exceptional value of the Clarté building, restoration sought to conserve as much of the building material as possible and to preserve it in its original state, to repair damaged elements or to identically rebuild them. The aim was to preserve the functional and physical integrity of the building while restoring its overall coherence.

A restoration procedure was established, taking account of many, sometimes contradictory, constraints arising from demanding conservation requirements. The work was subject to financial, technical, and regulatory obligations (safety and energy standards) and complicated by the presence of the inhabitants.

The debate between conservation of the original materials or their renewal was the central theme of the work, particularly regarding adaptation to current standards and change of function. The restoration included identical reconstruction work where original elements were too degraded to be saved, so as to preserve the structure and its initial appearance.

There was much discussion about repair of the balconies. The proposal to lay the wooden slats on the balcony deck, orientated parallel to the facade, was, at first, much criticised by the Paris-based Le Corbusier Foundation. This reaction highlighted the controversy involved in the concepts of conservation, of restoration, and of identical reconstruction. However, the historical study revealed that the original perpendicular orientation of the balcony slats had been dictated by economics, not by architectural considerations. Furthermore, Le Corbusier himself had outlined plans showing the orientation of the wooden slats parallel to the building's facade. Thus the latter approach was finally validated by the Le Corbusier Foundation.

 The work was originally planned in two stages, over a total period of two years. Finally this complex project took longer than expected, a total of four and a half years.

The scaffolding was first erected at the north facade, the west gable-end, and the south facade of No. 2. After the restoration of No. 2 it was extended to No. 4 where it was kept at the facade of No. 2 and the west gable-end for eighteen months, then for eighteen months at the facades of No. 4 and the east gable-end. Experience gained at the start of the site work led to modification of the project planning; the complete scaffolding was retained for a period of six months, to allow access to the building's perimeter.

The scaffolding, designed to withstand heavy loads, was sited back from the building's facades to leave vertical gaps through which the installation of motorised winches parallel to the facade allowed the handling of balcony and facade elements during dismantling and rebuilding operations. To facilitate this, reusable floor modules, directly bolted to the facade's support structure, were made wider than usual. The entire scaffolding was enclosed by netting and tarpaulins to provide protection against inclement weather, and dust, particularly for the very exposed north facade.

A scaffolding tower was erected on the pavement in front of the restaurant, in line with the vertical gap at the north-west corner, thereby allowing the delicate manipulation of elements of almost nine metres' length, during the first stage of works at No. 2. A second tower was erected on the south side, in a central position, for the two stages at No. 2 and No. 4. A third tower, located on the pavement, east of the entrance to No. 4 and connected to the scaffolding via bridging platforms, was later erected for the final stage of work to the north facade.

The slender and lightweight nature of the temporary roof structure over the building allowed the vertical and lateral loads from it to be supported and shared between the building's metal facade structure and the scaffolding.

As for the north, south, and west first floor terraces (lightweight structures of cementitious blocks on steel girders) they couldn't support additional charge, such as that of the scaffolding above them. Temporary load-bearing slabs, supported by the terraces' steel girders, were installed to resolve this issue. These areas were also partially used to hold construction materials.

1
The scaffolding is extended from No. 2 to No. 4, along the southern facade, 9 October 2008.

1

80 Two old garages at the heart of the building were used as site offices. The principal site material store was established to the north, on the hard surface of the rue Saint-Laurent and on the pavement in front of No. 4. Electricity supply boards were placed outside, one for each facade, as well as inside in the communal areas.

Scaffolding was also erected inside the building, at the centre of each stairwell. The works' director installed himself at the heart of the site, in a second storey apartment.

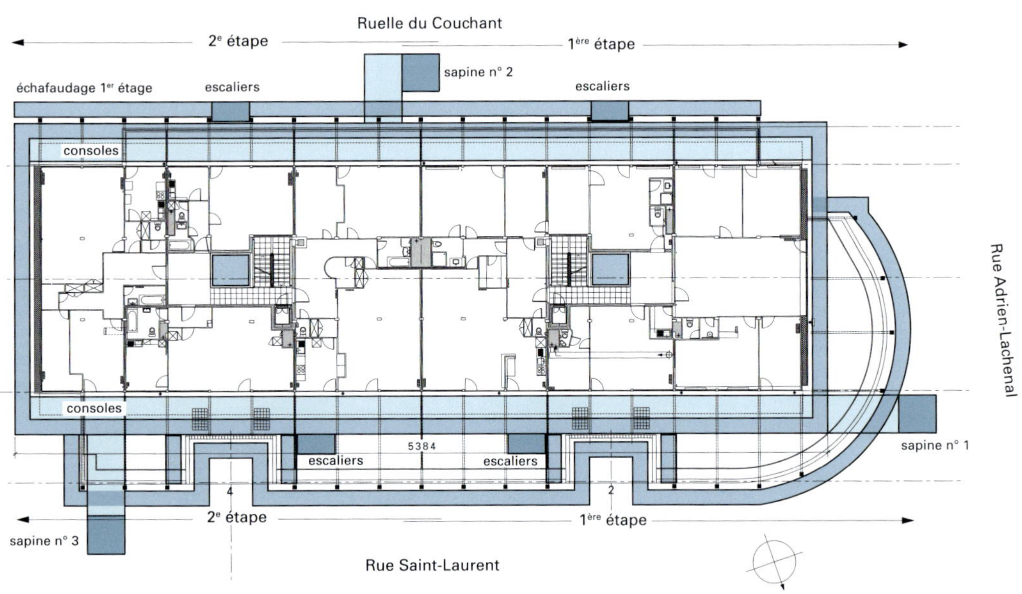

2

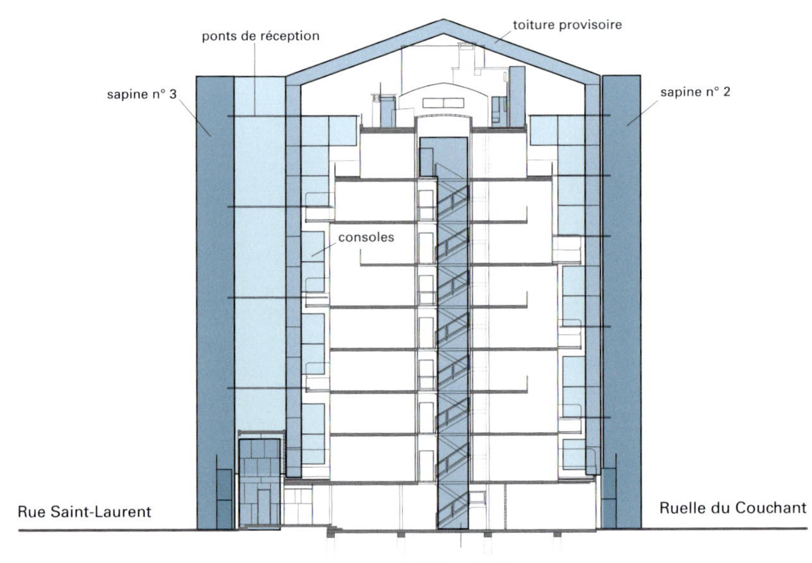

3

5

4

2–3
Plan and section showing the scaffolding installation, scale 1:500.

4
Scaffolding, first stage of works, 8 November 2007.

5
View from the interior of the scaffold, 19 June 2009.

The roof terrace

An outside space with spectacular views of the city of Geneva and its harbour, the roof terrace (ninth floor) was originally destined for use by all residents of the building. It is now privately owned, which is unfortunate because it represented an exceptional communal area for the fostering of social contact between residents. The terrace was originally covered with ninety-centimetre square slabs, spaced about five centimetre apart, with grass growing between them.

Condition

The metal framed structure of the roof terrace, which echoes the construction style of the rest of the building, was originally covered by a shallow screed laid directly on panels of Solomite[3] that spanned between the joists. Over this screed were several bitumen layers covered by fifty-centimetre square cementitious slabs, dating from 1975–1977. They were in poor condition and overgrown by vegetation.

The roof's rainwater drainage system comprised a central channel running along the building's longitudinal axis, either side of the skylights to No. 2 and No. 4, continuing directly around the base of these and, as broad channels, along the facades of the "wagon"[4]; similar broad channels ran along the foot of the facades of the attic on the eighth storey. The rainwater down-pipes were located in the small service courtyards within the building's interior. Thus, aside from the "wagon", there were no rainwater down-pipes on the building's facade.

Rainwater from the first floor terraces was collected by channels located at the foot of the main facades, their down-pipes passing through the rooms beneath before joining the underground drainage network. Ridged metal plates placed over the channels, in front of the glass doors, allowed safe passage onto the terraces.

While the system had been completely repaired during the 1975–1977 restoration, the building was still suffering from waterproofing problems, due to inadequate maintenance.

The works

In order to ensure the waterproofing of the entire structure, the "wagon" and the roof terrace constituted the first stage of the works. The roof terrace was completely renewed; the old waterproofing

1
2, rue Saint-Laurent, roof terrace, before the works, June 2007.

2
2, rue Saint-Laurent, roof terrace, after removal of the concrete slabs, showing the central drainage channel, 2 October 2007.

3
2, rue Saint-Laurent, fixing parapet flashing strips, 10 June 2008.

4
4, rue Saint-Laurent, roof terrace, waterproofing before placing installation and concrete slabs, 9 September 2009.

5
South facade, eighth floor attic, drainage channel with spacer blocks, 9 September 2009.

1

2

membrane was broken up and removed, the screed was repaired, then a new waterproofing membrane together with a four-centimetre thick layer of extruded polystyrene insulation (inverted waterproofing system) was laid across the entire roof terrace area, without modifying the original levels and surface profile to any great degree. Prefabricated concrete slabs, fifty-centimetres square, placed on supporting blocks, replaced those dating from 1975–1977.

The drainage channels serving the roof terrace (ninth floor) and the attic (eighth floor) were conserved and repaired. Their interior surfaces were treated with the same waterproof membrane applied to the rest of the roof. Resin sealed stainless steel protective plinths were installed at the foot of the "wagon" facades. Along the facades, over the channels, a horizontal stainless steel capfacade secures both the concrete slabs and the small spacer blocks placed within the channel.

As part of the renovation, numerous fibre-cement plant pots located on the first floor and attic terraces were removed. On completion of the works, in view of the attic's limited load capacity, the installation of new plant pots was only permitted on the roof terrace and on the first floor terraces.

3 Solomite is an insulating five-centimetre thick composite panel comprising of straw and iron wire bound in cement mortar that was placed between horizontal steel girders or the curved steel rafters of the "wagon" and also used for "dry-lining" the gable-end masonry walls. It's an essential element of the general concept of new lightweight industrial techniques promoted by Le Corbusier.

4 "Wagon" is the name given to the rooftop apartment structures, probably due to their resembling railway wagons.

3

4

5

The balustrades

The balustrades of the terraces on the first and eighth floors consisted of welded steel tubes surrounding a metal grill infill. Those of the roof terrace were made entirely of steel tubes.

Condition

The balustrades showed degradation problems due to corrosion that had resulted in perforations at the most exposed locations.

Intervention

All balustrades were removed for repositioning at their original location, after repair, sanding, and painting. A new detail for connection at the base plate, comprising silicone sealed cups, was adopted for all balustrades.

The chimneys

Condition

The original chimneys had not been maintained. The condition of the chimney stacks, severely cracked in places, was average to poor.

Intervention

The original configuration was restored (covers, stack, and colour), and the old flues were reused. Chimney covers, prefabricated according to the original model, replaced the old ones. Air extraction vents were concealed in the existing chimney stacks. Some modifications were made to these, notably for the two restaurant vents.

1
Balustrades of the roof terrace and of the eighth storey (attic) terrace.
2
Roof terrace, with the preserved former radio antenna, 1 February 2010.

1

2

The "wagon"

At the ninth floor, the superstructure called the "wagon" (a structure originally unauthorised for habitation, then rented as an apartment to Francis Quétant, an architect employed by Edmond Wanner, and responsible for Clarté designs and costings) was divided into two studios.

The original roof, covered in cement render and supported by masonry elements, was a simple structure comprising curved T-shaped steel beams between which were fixed insulating panels of Solomite. Bitumen waterproofing was placed on the upper surface of these panels.

Condition

Steel corrosion and thermal movements between different materials had caused extensive deterioration. There were numerous cracks in the walls, rusted steelwork, broken windows, a leaking roof, and extensively damaged masonry.

Intervention

Damage to the walls of the "wagon" caused by steel corrosion required numerous treatments including blast-cleaning, concrete repair, and filling holes.

The wagon's metal roof structure was conserved, cleaned, and repainted. The works included creating a new roof covering, with insulation (ten centimetres thick) and smooth, reinforced, black bituminous waterproofing. The objective was to recreate the dark tone of the original roof.

1

2

3

1
2, rue Saint-Laurent, roof terrace and "wagon" during renovation, 2 October 2007.
2
4, rue Saint-Laurent, "wagon", south side, condition before works, 5 September 2008.
3
4, rue Saint-Laurent, roof terrace and "wagon" under renovation, 5 November 2008.

4

5

6

7

8

4–5

Damage caused by steel corrosion as well as by differential thermal movement between materials.

6

Metallic structure of the "wagon" cover, 27 October 2008.

7–8

The interior of the "wagon", after renovation of its roof.

The skylights

Condition

The skylights, above the building's two stairwells, adjacent to and on either side of the "wagon", originally comprised a curved reinforced concrete framework of "bottle glass" tiles. In view of the heavily deteriorated state of these structures Marc-Joseph Saugey, in charge of 1953–1954 restoration works, had taken the decision to protect them with shed structures, of which marks were still visible on the gable walls of the wagon in 2006. These glazed protections had been removed by the architects Camoletti and Hausermann during the 1975–1977 restoration work and the original "bottle glass" tiles replaced by new glass tiles installed in a horizontal, slightly curved, metal frame. The original dwarf walls had remained in place.

Intervention

In view of its well-maintained condition, the 1975–1977 structure was conserved. To prevent water leakage, the outer rim was repaired and injected with resin. Elsewhere flexible mastic joints were installed between the glass bricks. To satisfy current fire regulations, two smoke vents with motorised flaps (one at No. 2, the other at No. 4) were placed at the corner of each skylight. The smoke vents also allowed service access to the roof without passing through the apartments.

1

2

3

1
Roof terrace with skylight, west end, before works, June 2007.
2
Roof terrace with skylight, east end, after works, 1 February 2010.
3
Detail of one of the overhead skylights.
4
4, rue Saint-Laurent, landing of the eighth storey attic with overhead skylight, after works.

4

From the initial realisation of the Clarté building, the balconies had proved problematic. Initially projected at the same height on the north and south facades, they were finally constructed at different heights on each facade. They had not been accurately costed in the initial budget, and hence economies were made in their construction, resulting in many technical faults.

During the building's construction, an expert report of 10 February 1932, directed by the engineer Maurice Brémond[6], stated that the structural design of the balconies was "permissible, though not satisfactory" and that the long-term performance was not adequate regarding environmental exposure. Maurice Brémond even indicated that fracture of the welded "C" brackets, used to secure the balcony floor to the parapet, or rupture of the latter, could have serious consequences.

Originally, the balconies were formed from 76 centimetre high load-bearing frames, comprising the balcony parapet and consoles (end-plates), having a width of 1.50 metres at the second, third, fourth, fifth floors and a width of 1.85 metres at the sixth and seventh floors. The consoles were welded to a vertical facade support at every 8.40 meters; all elements being built of strong sheet steel (consoles: 5 mm thick; parapets: 3 mm) reinforced with flat steel bars (section – 60 × 5 mm) and L-shaped steel bars (60 × 40 × 5 mm). The parapet plates were reinforced at two intermediate points (2.8 metres apart) by stiffening gussets[7] fixed to the balcony floor. The wooden floor slats were supported by two UPN 80 channels, one against the facade welded to its vertical supports, the other forming an edge beam, suspended every 2.80 metres from the parapet plate by C-shaped steel hangers, called "swan necks" (approx. 100 × 220 × 40 × 12 mm). The two channels were laced every 1.40 metres by tensioned 16 mm steel rods passing through 25 mm diameter tubes.

The ceilings of the original balconies, covered with smooth panels, had suffered significant water damage. These panels were removed during the intervention by Mark-Joseph Saugey in the 1950s.

Following the 1975–1977 restoration, the floors comprised 40 mm thick slats of larch wood (originally oak), with a grooved and caulked[8] upper surface, oriented perpendicular to the facade.

1
Cross-section showing the balcony offset between north and south facades.
2
West gable-end facade with travertine cladding, after works.
3
South facade, fourth floor, before works, 8 October 2007.

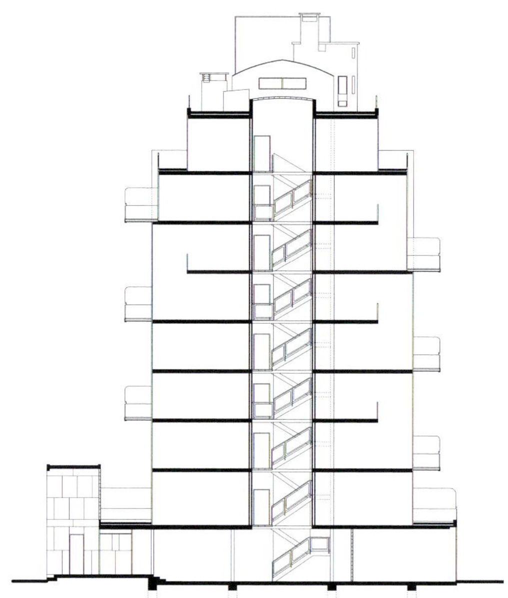

1

2

3

Condition

Given that most of the balconies had little or no weather protection, the metal parts were very corroded, thereby significantly decreasing the section of a large number of steel parapet plates and L-shaped bars. In places their entire thickness had been lost due to corrosion, particularly at the welded and riveted joints of the lower parts of the parapets. There we noted significant deformations resulting from the load of wooden floor slats, and from heavy items stored on the balconies, such as plant troughs. Given the lack of maintenance, these items were extensively damaged.

On the upper floors, the wooden slats of the balcony floors were old and rotten, allowing rainwater to drip onto the lower balconies; there was a significant risk of catastrophic failure.

As noted by the engineer Brémond in his 1932 report, the "C" hanger pieces described above were the most seriously damaged. Furthermore, being undersized, they were notably deformed. Some had not resisted corrosion and had broken, thus jeopardising the balcony floor load capacity with in consequence the danger of collapse. Corrosion damage varied according to the degree of exposure, and was extensive at the upper floors of the south and north sides.

The consoles separating the balcony areas, welded to the facade pillars, had undergone no major damage, with the exception of those located at the ends of the building that were anchored to the reinforced concrete edges of the gable walls. Here, the metal anchors of the balcony consoles had suffered extensive damage due to corrosion and the reinforced concrete edges were weakened by carbonation.

4

5

6

4
Balcony condition before works.
5–6
Corrosion damage of the "C" suspension pieces.

7

8

9

7–8
Balconies, south facade, before removal of the consoles and parapet, 21 January 2008.

9
Anchorage of the hand rail and upper corner of the balcony within reinforced concrete of the east gable-end wall.

Intervention

Before starting work, a balcony restoration prototype was undertaken in January 2007. Indeed, restoring the balconies, given the lightness of their very unusual support structure, proved to be one of the more sensitive operations in the restoration of the outer shell.

It was not possible to disassemble the consoles because they'd been welded to the facade pillars. They were removed by cutting the angle brackets at approximately ten centimetres from the facade. All the dismantled console and parapet plates were transported to the workshop. The parapet handrails and the UPN 80 steel channel floor supports, including their transverse tie-bars, were the only items to be preserved and restored in the workshop. All other structural metal components were identically rebuilt, a decision that was imposed to ensure architectural and aesthetic coherence. This work was dictated by the following conditions and considerations:

— The structure of the balconies met the construction standards of 1932, and although outdated, may still be regarded as sufficient in the context of a restoration.

— A new construction complying with current standards (allowing less restrictive balcony use) would imply a different configuration of the consoles and the upper sections; difficult to connect to the pillars of the existing construction without diminishing the original aesthetic.

— The issue of corrosion of a steel assembly exposed to the elements – a serious problem from the outset – has not been resolved, but the risks have been mitigated, on the one hand by application of a high-performance paint system to protect the steel, and on the other, introducing a new regime of frequent and rigorous maintenance works by the owners.

The C-shaped suspension pieces had to be replaced to ensure adequate long-term security. After several prototypes, a simple solution was chosen that remains as close as possible to the original concept, stiffening the new C pieces by adding two reinforcing corner gussets, thereby increasing rigidity.

The first three layers of protective paint were applied to all metal elements of the balconies in the workshop, before reassembly on site. Reassembly was done after cleaning and restoration of the facades. The console's L-shaped bars were welded

10
Balcony removal, 26 November 2007.
11
Balconies, south facade, before removal of the consoles and parapet, 21 January 2008.
12
Removal of the consoles, after cutting through the L-shaped bars, 24 January 2008.

10

11

12

13

14

15

16

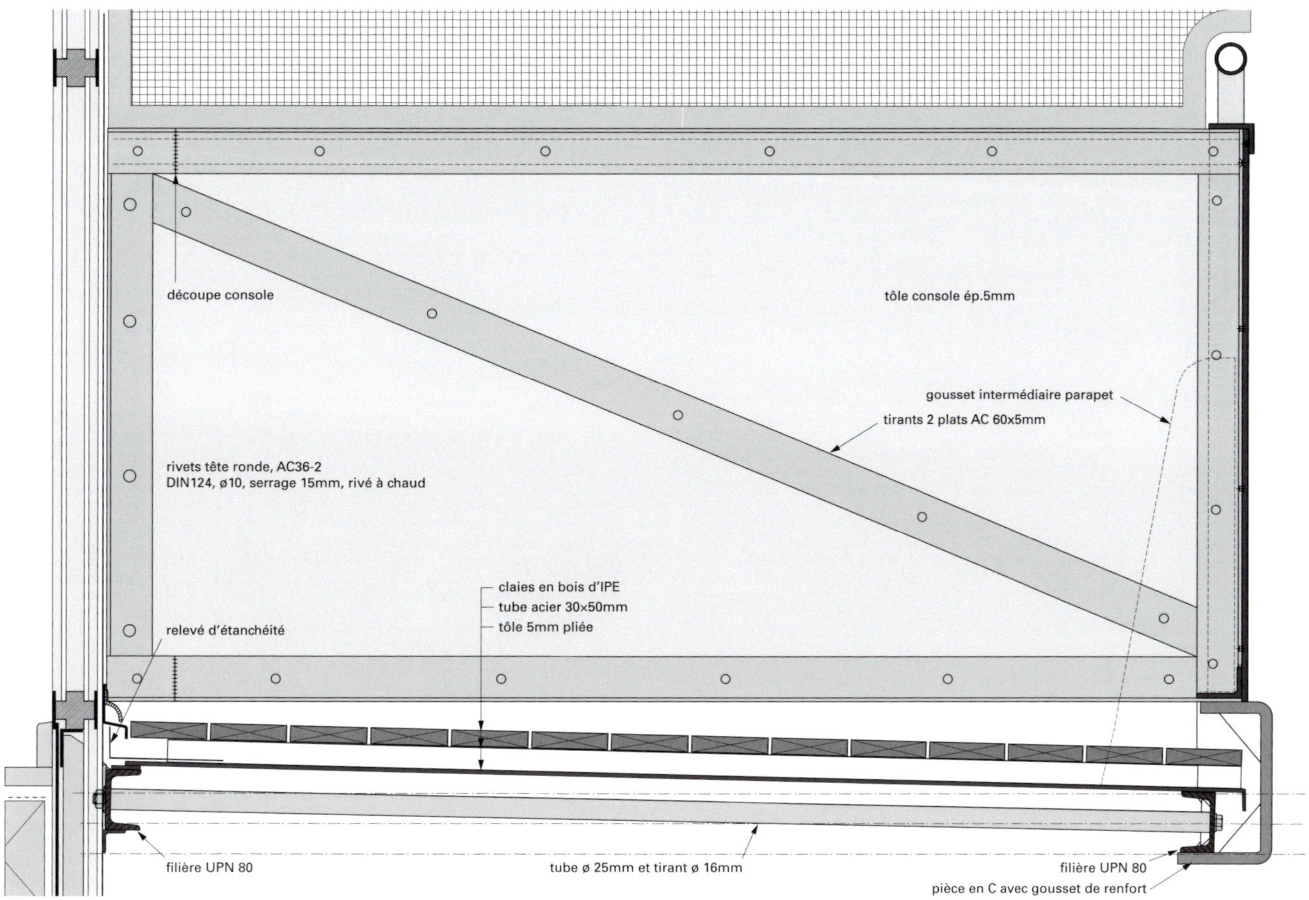

17

13
2, rue Saint-Laurent, south facade, second floor, placing the balcony rivets, 16 July 2008.
14–15
The console's L-shaped bars were welded to the stubs that had remained fixed to the facade pillars, then the steel plates were positioned and riveted.
16
Stiffening the C pieces by the addition of two reinforcing corner gussets.
17
Balcony section, scale 1:10.

to the stubs that had remained fixed to the facade pillars. Then the console and parapet plates were attached to the double frame of L-shaped and flat bars using hot steel rivets in accordance with original construction.

The next step was the installation of the original UPN 80 steel beams, restored with their tie-bars, hung and welded from the new C suspension pieces. The new 5 mm thick steel floor plates were mounted on this assembly, within the supporting framework. This was a delicate operation, given the limited available space for laying sheets weighing almost 200 kilos each, measuring 2.8 × 1.5 metres, and 2.8 × 1.85 metres at the seventh floor. Rigid rectangular steel tubes (30 × 50 mm) were welded to the upper surface of the floor plates, also acting as support for the deck of ipe wood.

During the 1932 structural review by the engineer Brémond, the balcony load capacity was 200 kg/m^2; however the SIA Standard No. 260 recommends a load capacity of 300 kg/m^2 (2010 figures). In order to satisfy the restoration principle for the building envelope, which was to preserve as much as possible the original construction concepts and materials, it was not possible to increase the load capacity in accordance with the current recommendations. Calculations showed nonetheless that the additional load of the new steel plates was permissible.

The new balcony structure, while carefully dimensioned, nevertheless had the effect of raising the finished floor level by 16 mm. This operation further reduced the effective railing height but was considered acceptable.

The introduction of steel plates beneath the wooden floors of the balconies has removed some causes of facade degradation, encountered from the outset due to the use of balcony floors comprising unsealed wooden slats in a very exposed location. With the new elements, a tight fit to the facade proved much easier and long-term protection is thus ensured in a sustainable manner. This vital protective function for all facade levels, including balconies below the sixth (south) and seventh (north) floors, had been largely confirmed by the end of the site work. It will significantly contribute to the facade's overall corrosion protection, and to the sustainable nature of the restoration.

The issue of restoring the original smooth balcony ceilings was debated before being abandoned due to the cost, the additional loads required, and

18
2, rue Saint-Laurent, north facade, after fixing the consoles, 20 June 2008.
19
2, rue Saint-Laurent, south facade, fixing the balcony parapets, fourth floor, 11 July 2008.

18

19

the technical difficulties of achieving the desired appearance. The solution, chosen in consultation with the Confederation's expert and the conservative canton, was to leave visible the fine structure of the dark coloured metal bars against the balcony's smooth sheet steel base, thus allowing an adequate reproduction of the original aesthetic.

Resin seals were placed between the steel plates of the balcony floor, as well as between their edges and the facade structure, thus enabling optimal water discharge during bad weather. Finally, special waterproof and protective seals were placed between the different structural elements. This detailed and essential work, sandwiched between the application of the two finishing coats of polyurethane paint, was aimed at providing the best moisture and corrosion protection to the interstitial spaces between the assembled balcony components.

The slats of ipe wood were installed at the end of renovation work, running parallel to the length of the building, contrary to the original perpendicular orientation. They took the form of pre-assembled racks (two per span) measuring 72 by 279 centimetres, placed on the rectangular steel tubes reinforcing the balcony base plates. The underlying gap allows the flow of rainwater. The ipe wood had been previously rinsed to prevent tannin drips from staining the front textile awnings.

6 Maurice Brémond, *Expert report on the safety of the balconies*, 10 February 1932.

7 Reinforcing element joined, at an approximately 45° angle, between a vertical column and a horizontal beam.

8 Traditional caulking used fibres of cotton and oakum (hemp fibre soaked in pine tar) hammered into joints to render them watertight.

20
Balcony and temporary facade panels, 27 July 2009.
21
The new balcony soffits, after renovation, with metal tie-bars visible.
22
South side balcony after renovation.

20

21

In 1927 Le Corbusier states the five points of a new architecture: stilts, roof terrace, open plan, broad windows, and open facade. The Clarté building includes four of these five points (excluding the stilts).

"These facades are punctuated by three balcony galleries or external walkways whose alignment is staggered by one floor between the north and south facades, unlike the first sketches that aligned them at the same levels. (...) [The latter] also form screens of shadow, serving as sunshades, and are equipped with textile awnings and wooden roller blinds fitted in visible enclosures."[9] The strong horizontal nature of the ensemble is reinforced by the parapets of the balcony galleries, the only "solid" elements in these facades.

The Clarté building's fully glazed north and south facades are drawn on a grid of 2.80 metres; that of the metal frame of rectangular section tubes, comprising a welded assembly of two U profiles, arranged flush with the surface. The facades' glazing comprises transparent and translucent elements composed of two main modules: the base module, of two transparent sliding window units, with translucent reinforced glass panes above the transom and below the sill; another module, comprising a glass door (transparent upper pane and translucent reinforced lower pane), together with a transparent fixed window with translucent reinforced glass above the transom and below the sill. In addition, there are continuous horizontal metal bands, attached to the facades at the floor slab level. These are directly behind the translucent panes above the window transoms. At the location of the duplex rooms, this metal band is omitted across two bays to provide a facade of contiguous transparency.

The 2.60 metre wide glazed facade panels[10] laterally fastened to the vertical facade columns comprise two types of superimposed frames. One type, for the module comprising a fixed window with glass balcony door, is of wood (50×50 mm section pine), with metal strips (50 to 70 by 3 mm section) screwed to the interior and exterior surfaces, serving as beading and protection. The other type, made of steel, is for the module with sliding windows. Their glazing comprised two parallel glass panes separated by spacers, originally made of hard wood (iroko). This was one of the first examples of glazing designed to avoid a cold bridge and hence be thermally insulating.

1

1
Superimposition of metal and wooden frames, after cutting away the L-shaped bars of the consoles, 13 March 2008.
2
Facade modules, after renovation.

2

Condition

The strength of the supporting structure, as confirmed by the structural engineer, meets current safety standards.

With a few exceptions, the facade's wooden frames were generally in good condition, aside from the lower parts, all of which had to be changed due to damage by rot. The metal window frames and glazing beads, some of which were coming loose, were suffering widespread corrosion. The windows' sliding rails were impregnated with dirt, which impeded their functioning. Condensation and dust was penetrating between the double glazing, rendering them partially opaque; their watertightness were clearly defective. A number of the double-glazed windows that had already been installed to replace the original double glazing had escaped this problem, but manifested differences in quality, tint, and reflection.

After many replacements, the different qualities of reinforced glass were a mixed bag. Many of those below the window sills, of which few originals remained, were cracked or broken, particularly on the south facade.

Intervention

At the start of the works, a prototype restoration of a 2.80 metre span over two levels (the kitchen and bedroom of a south side duplex, located on the second floor of No. 4) was completed during the winter of 2005/2006. The architects commissioned several companies in order to evaluate the different methods and times required. This enabled the choice of methods and their associated costs. Because the residents remained in the building throughout the works, the facades were restored in stages of two floors at a time, starting with the north facade of No. 2 and the south facade of No. 2 to No. 4, before finishing with the north side of No. 4. The metal structure did not need reinforcing. All the opening window units, together with all external glazing beads, were dismantled for restoration in the workshop, where they were sanded and repainted.

3

3
4, rue Saint-Laurent, north facade, fifth floor, before works, 3 September 2008.
4
4, rue Saint-Laurent, north facade, seventh and eighth floors, before works, 3 September 2008.

4

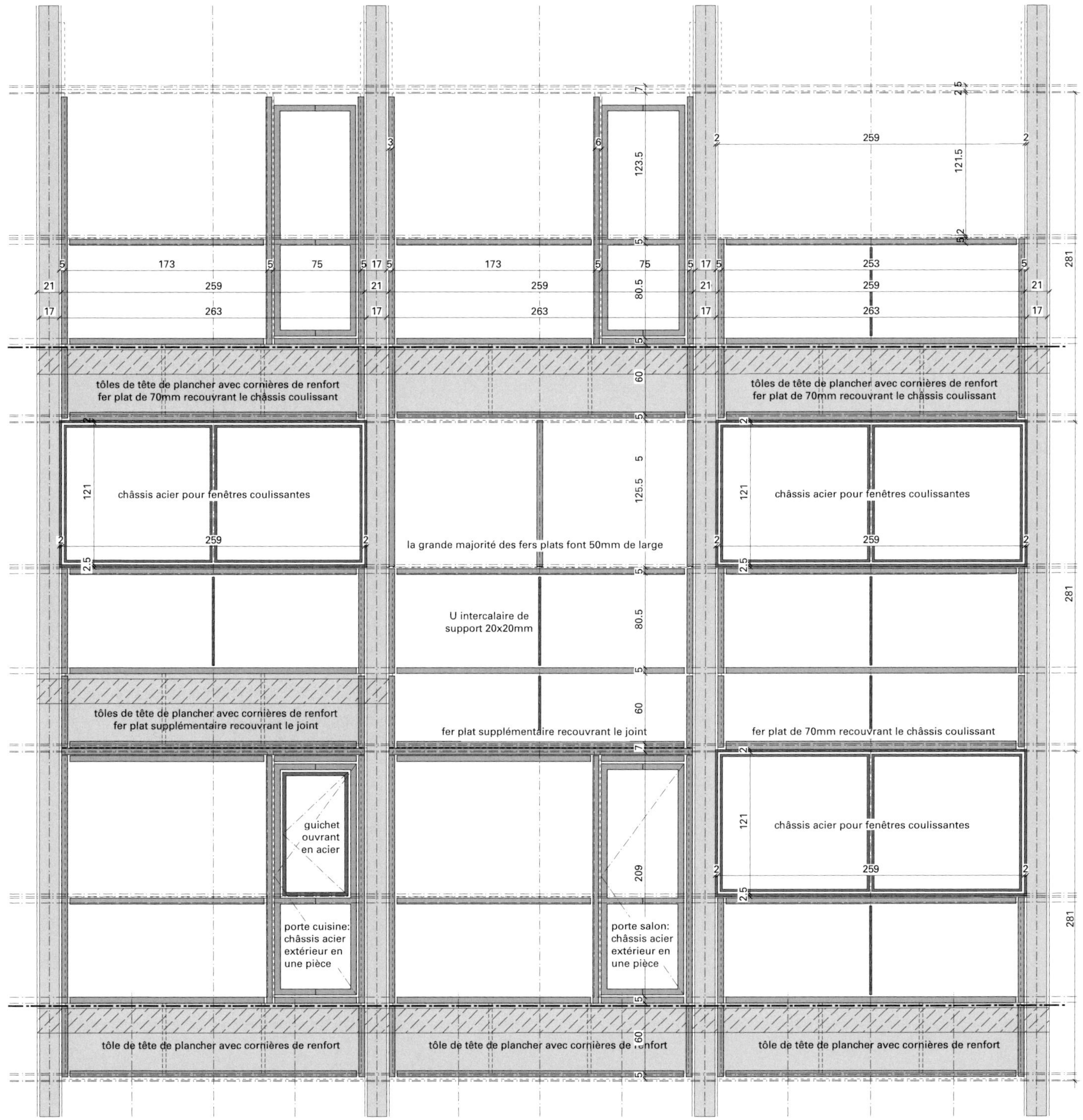

5

5
Exterior glazing detail, triple span small duplex, south facade, scale 1:50, December 2006.

6
South facade, typical detail, scale 1:25, March 2004.

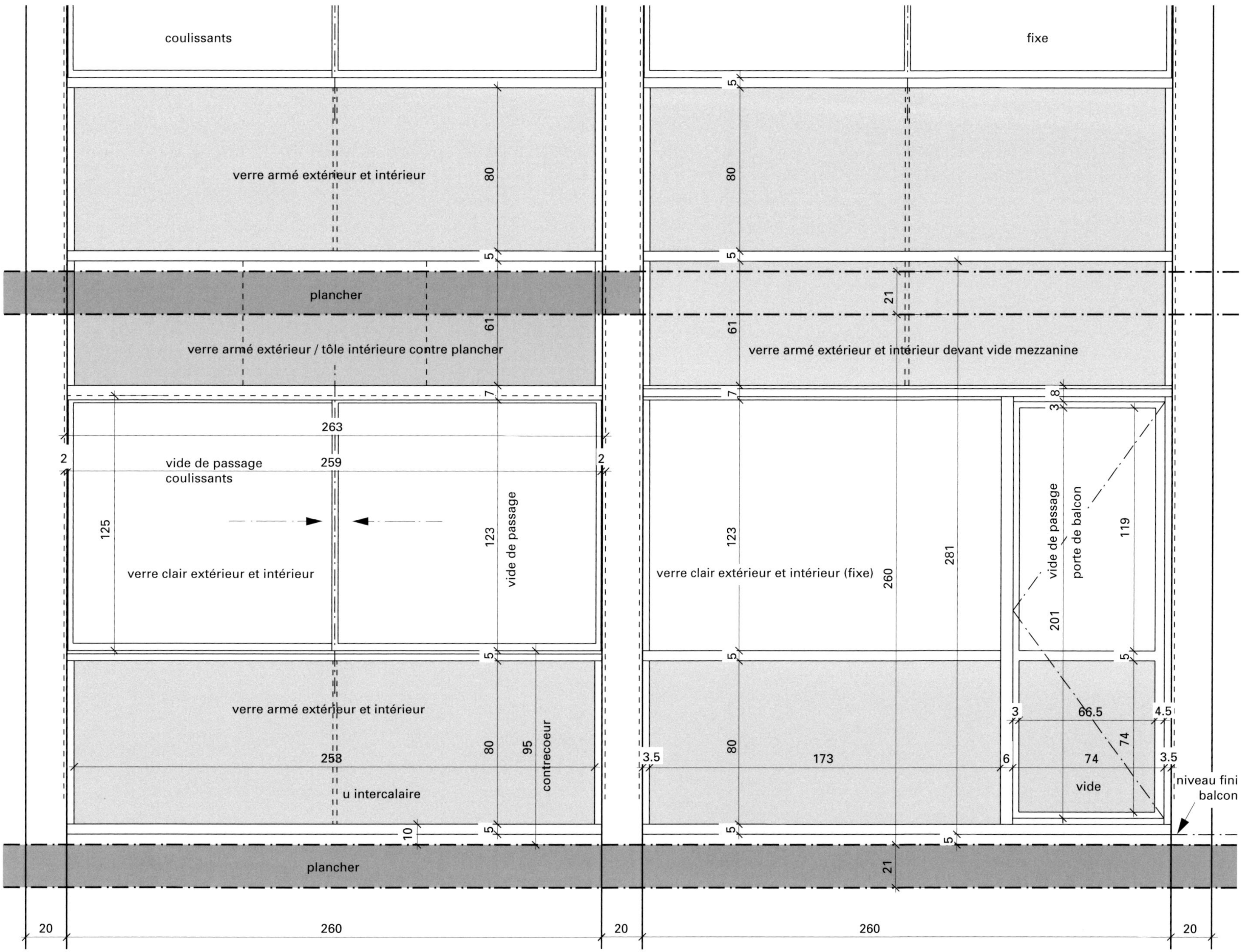

Travée avec vitrage devant plancher

Travée avec vitrage devant mezzanine

6

To replace the dismantled opening elements, temporary wooden panels equipped with small windows were installed. They were fitted from the interior and sealed for protection during blast-cleaning of the exterior facade elements. Interior glazing beads and other fixed elements were treated in-situ (by sanding and painting).

General blasting-cleaning of the structural steel frame allowed the removal of all paint layers and corroded steel (rust). Repeated as required during advancement of the work, the blasting-cleaning required environmental confinement. This was achieved with reinforced PVC screens and ventilation, which included a filtration system installed on the scaffolding, the operator of the blast-cleaning equipment being fitted with a fully enclosed respirator incorporating an independent air supply.

On site the external metal parts of the facade were sealed with a two-component epoxy coating containing anti-corrosion pigments, free of lead and chromate (layers one and two), and then with high performance polyurethane finishing coats (layers three and four). This ensured excellent protection against moisture and the environment.

In the workshop, an initial three layers of coating were spray applied to dismantled elements. Then after re-assembly on site, the fourth and final coating layer was roller applied to large surfaces, and brush applied to smaller surfaces, in order to better match the original appearance. Before the final coat of paint, a suitable compatible acrylic sealant was applied to the spaces between certain metallic elements. During the application process, many coating thickness checks were made.

Steel and wooden pieces were either repaired or replaced with identical elements. That concerned the steel frame and the sliding windows, the corroded lap-joints, the fittings and handles, the wooden frames, especially at the thresholds of the balcony doors, particularly those of the very exposed upper floors.

The double, single pane, windows have been replaced by factory sealed insulating double glazed units. To promote the movement of the sliding windows, they had been mounted on a series of steel balls, themselves located within a U-profile forming the lower part of the fixed frame. To facilitate the sliding, a stainless steel runner was placed in the "rail". Twenty per cent of the original reinforced glass was in an acceptable condition and has been preserved, the remainder having been replaced

7

8

9

10

11

12

13

14

15

16

7
2, rue Saint-Laurent, north facade, 16 November 2007.
8
2, rue Saint-Laurent, application of waterproofing to the eighth floor attic storey, 21 January 2008.
9
4, rue Saint-Laurent, south facade, fourth storey, 5 September 2008.
10
4, rue Saint-Laurent, north facade, 3 November 2008.
11
4, rue Saint-Laurent, south facade, sixth storey, detail after removal of the balcony floors, 9 September 2008.
12
4, rue Saint-Laurent, south facade, sixth storey, after removal of the balconies and the roller blind enclosures, 16 September 2008.
13
4, rue Saint-Laurent, south facade, sixth storey, detail before blast-cleaning, 5 November 2008.
14
4, rue Saint-Laurent, south facade, blast-cleaning, 17 November 2008.
15
4, rue Saint-Laurent, south facade, sixth storey, first layer of paint, 20 November 2008.
16
4, rue Saint-Laurent, north facade, eighth attic storey, view of the balcony from apartment interior, 16 September 2011.

with new reinforced glass, all installed with reinforcing wires running in the same direction (horizontal wires straight, vertical wires woven). The balconies and terrace doors were restored in the workshop. At the eighth and ninth floors, the thresholds and vertical door seals were replaced.

The facade of the south-facing studio on the first floor of No. 4 (three bays) has been conserved as an example of the original construction and was restored without sealed double glazing units, but with the installation of new single glass panes placed in double layers and sealed (sliding windows, glass doors, and fixed parts), as was done when first built.

Regarding the handles of the sliding windows (398 pieces in total) in sintered stainless steel, 174 pieces were conserved and restored (stripped, cleaned, and nickel coated), 189 new brush finished sintered stainless steel handles (copies of the originals) were fitted, and 35 pieces have been preserved as is.

9 Catherine Courtiau, *Le Corbusier, Formation, projets et constructions en Suisse*, Swiss History of Art Society, Berne, 2012, pp. 63–64.

10 The term "facade panel" describes the contiguous surface between the facade's load-bearing columns.

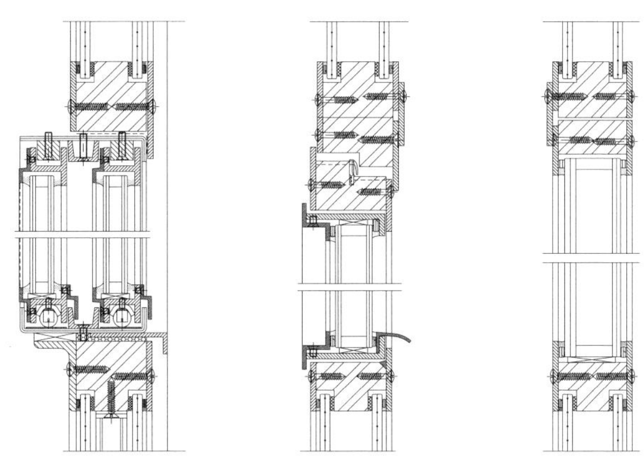

17

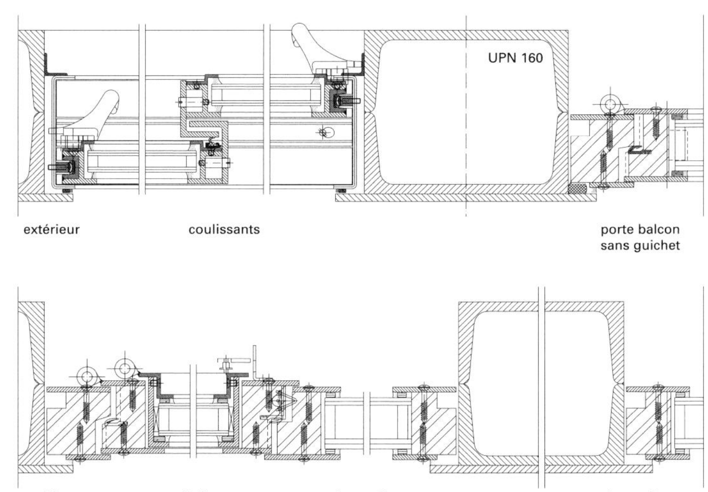

17
Window frame detail.
18
Facade window frame detail, scale 1:10.

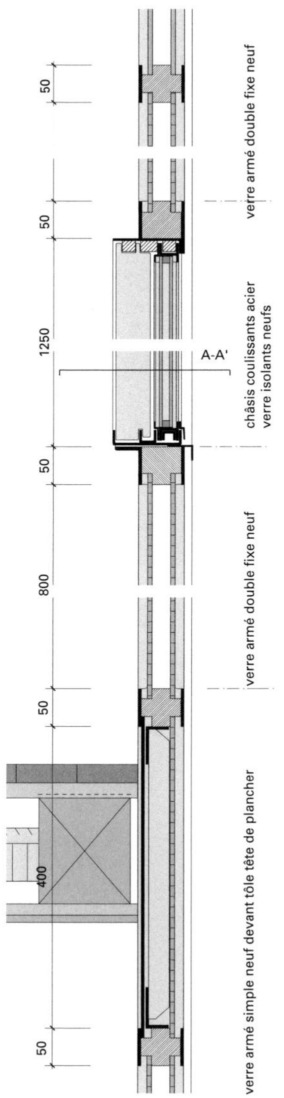

A-A

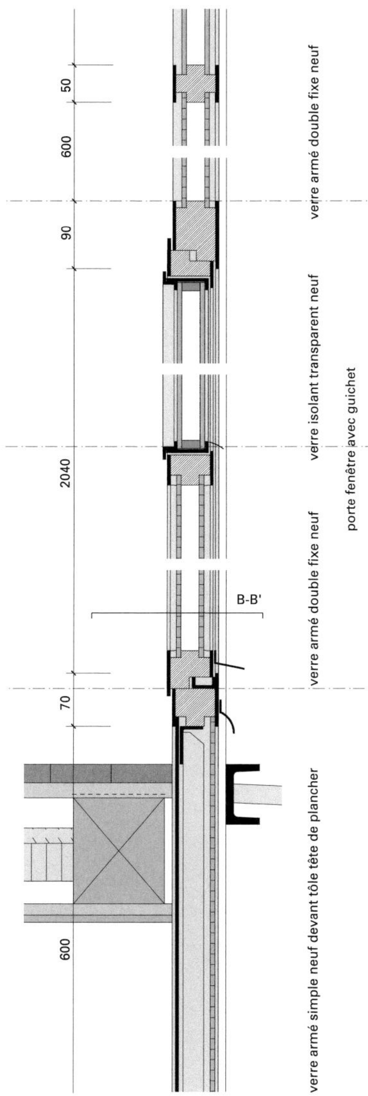

B-B

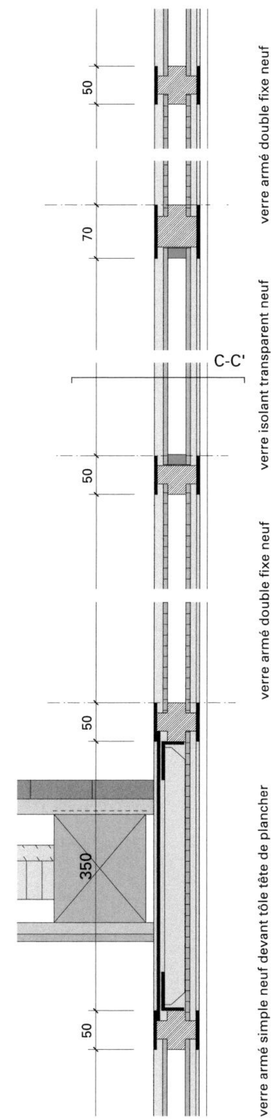

C-C

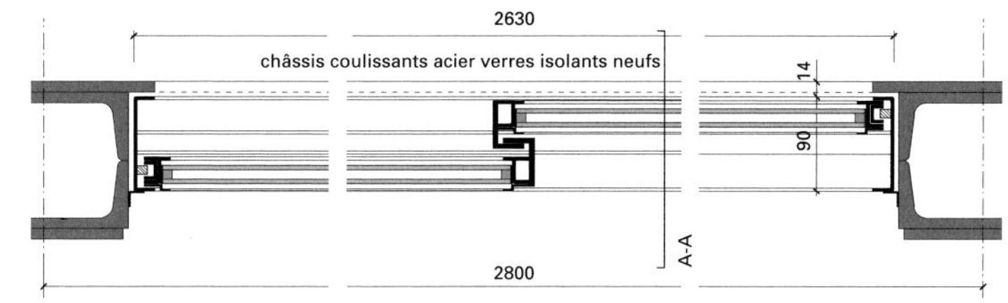

A-A'

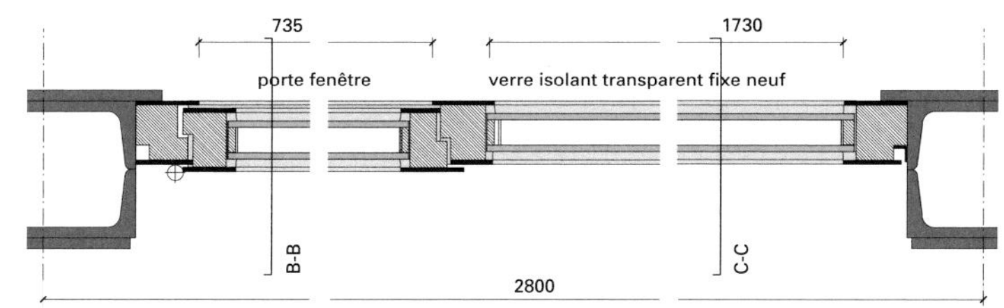

B-B' C-C'

On the north and south facades, cylindrical-shaped steel enclosures, the width of a facade span (2.80 metres), housed the 2.60 metre wide roller blinds, of which the blind comprised multiple pine-wood slats. The enclosures were bolted at each end to steel stirrups, secured to the vertical load-bearing facade columns, and at mid-span, to a lug fixed to the facade. They have a diameter of 30 or 40 cm, depending on the length of the blind, unrolling to either 2.45 metres (94 units), 3.00 metres (70 units), or 5.50 metres (26 units) in the case of the duplex windows. The blinds were guided by open slides to retain them when at the desired height. Original mechanisms included a cast-iron pulley guiding an interior cord for raising and lowering the blind, a steel tube with a screw-fastened metal strip for securing the blind, and a flat section return spring inside, running the entire length of the tube. The textile awnings measured 2.80 or 5.60 metres wide and 2.5 or 2.0 or 4.0 metres high. They were guided by lateral rods, vertical or inclined, or by a pair of pantographs (articulated device) between which a horizontal steel tube (drop bar) placed in a hem at the bottom of the awning gave it horizontal support.

The awning mechanisms were similar to those of the wooden blinds, but with a belt and pulley (original) or a gear mechanism (more recent).

Condition

At the upper floor levels, some roller blind enclosures, dented and rusted (to the point of forming holes in some places), had been found in a very advanced state of decay; at the less exposed lower floor levels, there was less damage. Some roller blinds had broken and the textile awnings were in tatters. The mechanisms were bent and broken, but less so at the lower levels. The small protective screens which extended some roller blind enclosures at the upper floor levels were in a very poor state.

At the eighth floor gable-ends of the building, the only place where the roller blind enclosures were fixed to concrete, corrosion of the stirrup's anchors had caused considerable damage within the concrete.

The axles and mechanisms were of the period. All the wooden blinds had been replaced during the 1975–1977 restoration. A number of pulleys were missing from internal blinds.

1

1
Roller blinds, 21 January 2008.

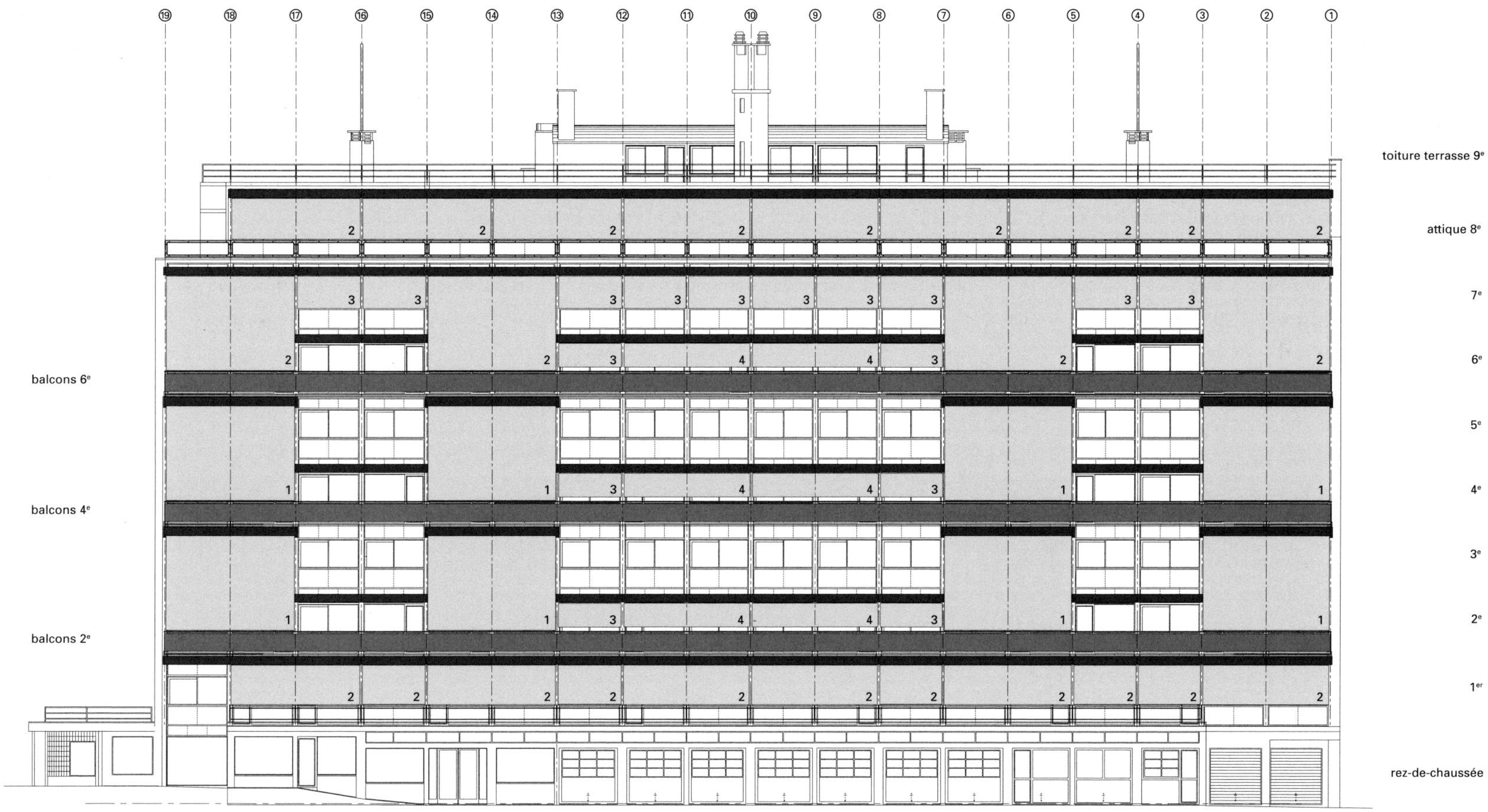

1 Awnings on vertical guides
2 Awnings on inclined guides
3 Awnings on lateral pantographs
4 Awnings on central and lateral pantographs

Position of the textile awnings, south facade, scale 1:300.

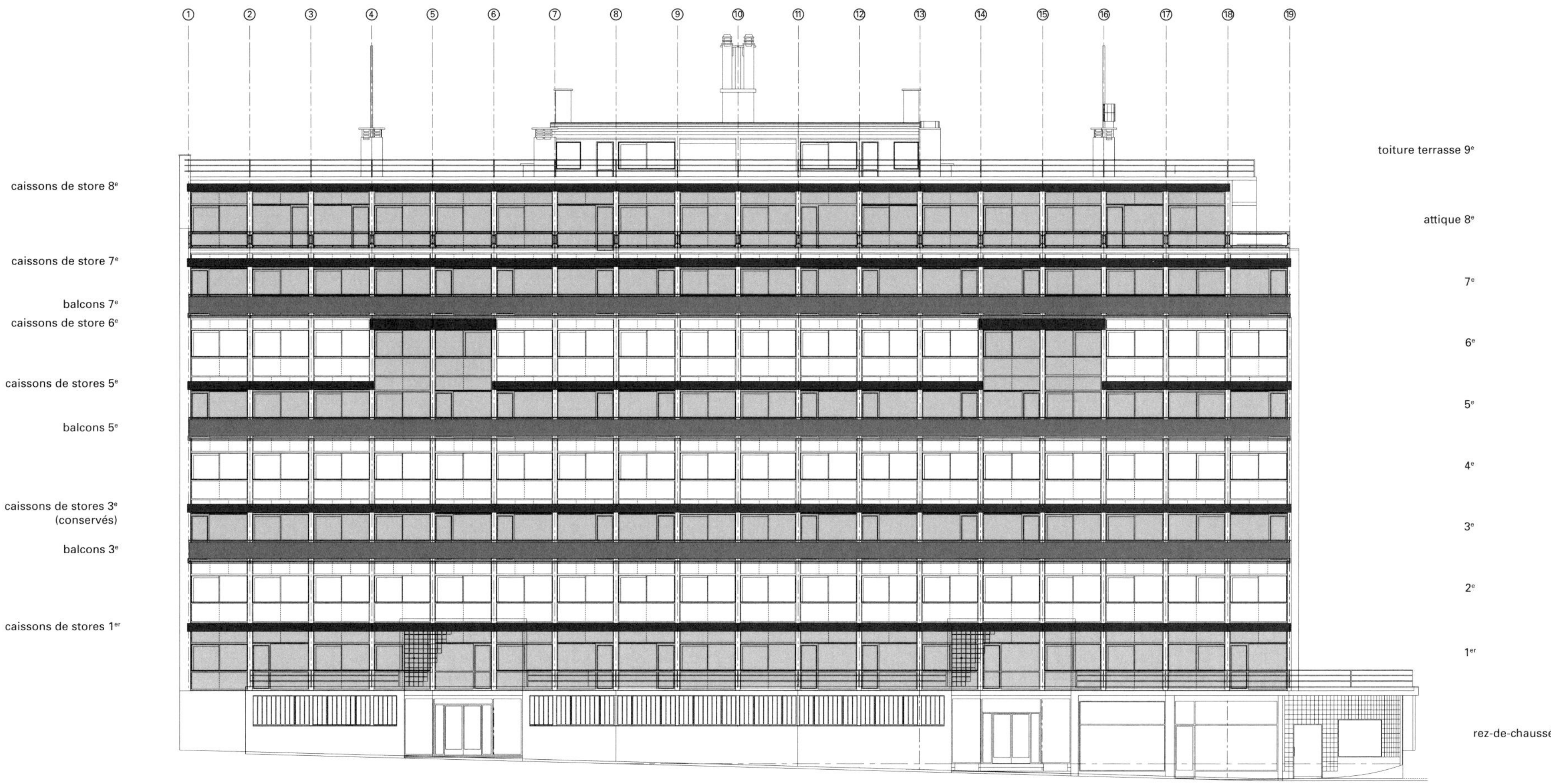

Position of the roller blind enclosures, north facade, scale 1:300.

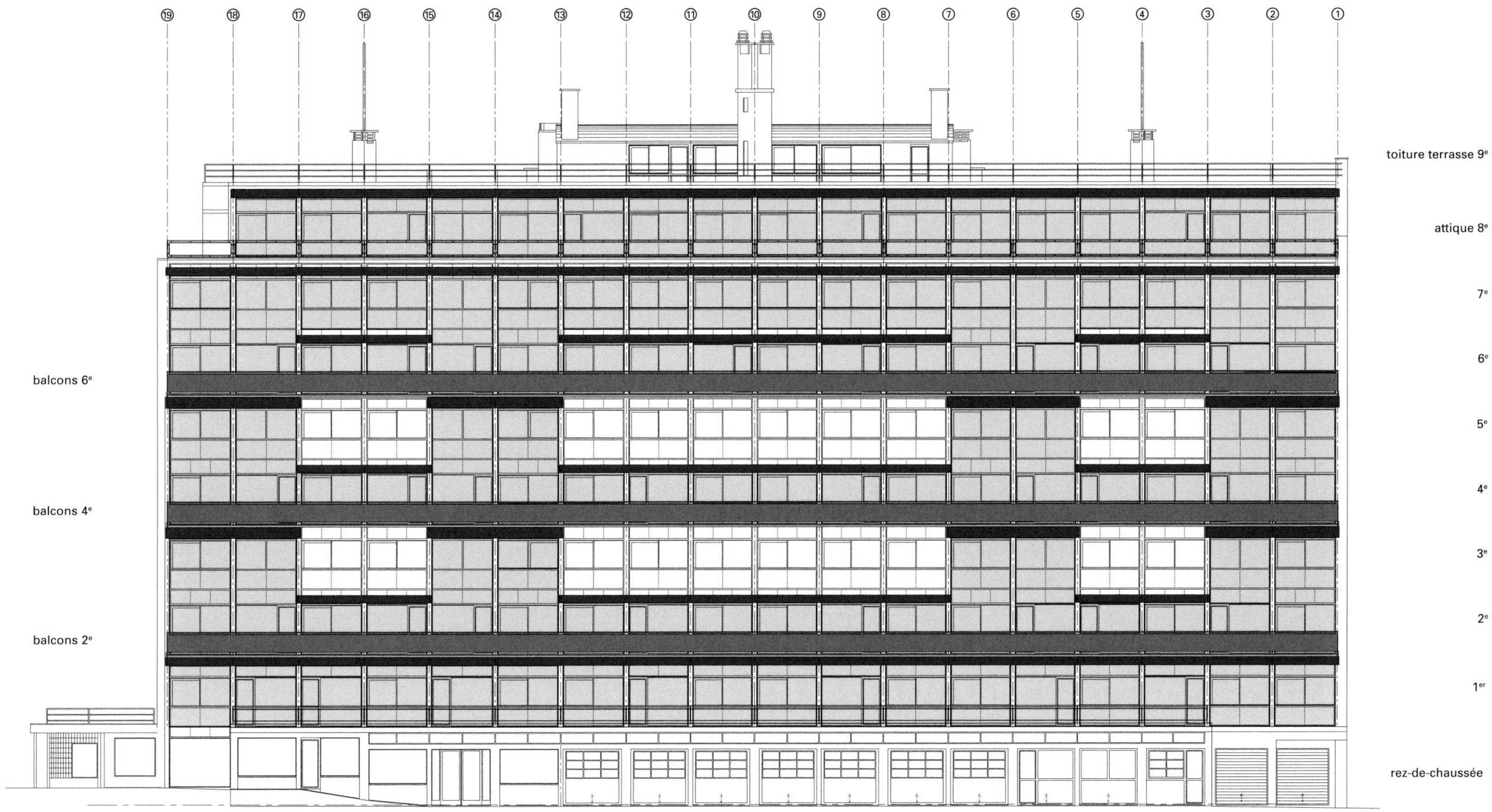

Position of the roller blind enclosures, south facade, scale 1:300.

Intervention

The majority of the roller blind enclosures (173 of 195) had to be replaced (everywhere except the north face of the second floor) by new enclosures made from 0.6 millimetre thick stainless steel sheet. The roller blind mounting stirrups have been preserved; the mechanisms and slides were completely dismantled for repair, sandblasting, and painting (three layers) in the workshop, or for replacement where necessary. New blinds were installed with slats of Oregon pine, a species of wood known for its durability and natural resistance to weathering.

New stainless steel lateral rods were put in place to guide the textile awnings; some have been preserved. The awning fabrics have all been replaced by natural coloured cloth [11].

In addition, the blinds and textile awnings were motorised (modification of axles), while retaining the existing winches and cords. The electrical cables were routed in conduits within the facade's load-bearing columns and then in stainless steel pipes hidden inside the roller blind enclosures. Some of the original slides, while initially preserved and restored, had subsequently to be changed.

11 See the chapter on colours.

2
2, rue Saint-Laurent, original fixings for the roller blind axle and for the cylindrical enclosure, 5 October 2007.

3
4, rue Saint-Laurent, south facade, eighth storey, removal of roller blind enclosures, 3 September 2008.

4
4, rue Saint-Laurent, southern facade, eighth floor, installing the roller blind enclosures, 15 January 2009.

5
2, rue Saint-Laurent, northern facade, eighth floor, roller blind detail adjacent to the western gable-end, 22 January 2009.

6
4, rue Saint-Laurent, southern facade, motorised roller blind axles and stainless steel tubes containing the electric power cables, 9 September 2009.

7
4, rue Saint-Laurent, southern facade, detail showing a roller blind and its enclosure, 7 October 2009.

2

3

4

5

6

7

At each floor the gable-end walls comprise large concrete frames with a filling of hollow concrete bricks and a lining of clay brick on the inner face. The western facade is composed of two distinct areas: the gable-end itself, covered with travertine panels, and the recessed facade of the eighth floor.

The ground floor and the large entrance porches are also of reinforced concrete, as are the superstructures on the roof.

The original foundations, designed by Robert Maillart, are illustrated by a construction plan showing a dense network of large reinforced concrete foundation beams[12] with steel piles beneath them[13]. They were discovered during the restoration works while filling a cavity beneath the electrical services room, a cavity probably formed by the passage of groundwater coming from Malagnou.

Condition

Concrete carbonation is a phenomenon that appears on many structures built during the twentieth century. The Clarté building did not go unscathed, although its superstructure, consisting of a metal frame and wooden floors, contains few concrete elements. In his report on the condition of the structure's envelope, the civil engineer noted that "while the analysis of the gable wall between the ground and the seventh floor was not done in detail, the survey confirms that the load-bearing area of the gable-end wall is in good condition, with no apparent trace of carbonation. As regards the eighth floor facade, we found an advanced state of carbonation and cracking of the load-bearing elements; these are lightly reinforced concrete walls. (...) The other reinforced concrete superstructure elements are more or less in the same state as those of the eighth floor's western facade, that is, in a yet more deteriorated condition."[14] The north-west corner of the building was in general badly damaged by carbonation.

Intervention

Regarding the carbonated concrete, repairs were carried out by removal of the damaged concrete, blasting-cleaning and passivating the reinforcement, then reinstating the concrete. The entire north-west corner of the building was so treated, from top to bottom. The eastern gable-end facade was re-rendered.

1–2
Fixing brackets of the roller blinds of the eighth floor: before/after concrete repair.
3
Concrete carbonation of ground floor concrete columns: repairs in progress.
4
Concrete carbonation of the gable-end wall concrete: repairs in progress.
5–6
Concrete repair at the north-west corner of the gable-end wall, 24 January 2008.

1

2

3

12 Foundation beams serve to support and distribute the large mechanical loads from the supported structure.

13 See chapter III. The building plans.

14 Civil engineering consultants Pierre Moser, Survey report on the condition of the Clarté building's envelope, by the civil engineer, Geneva, February 2004, pp. 9–11.

6

4

5

The west gable-end wall, the two major entrance porches, and part of the north facade of the ground floor are clad with travertine panels. On the gable-end wall, the original two-centimetre thick travertine panels were each fixed at eight points, with steel wire held by cleats. On the ground floor, the panels were secured in place by adhesive. The panels were of variable size, up to 75 by 140 centimetres for the largest.

Condition

On the gable-end facade, the cladding partially comprised the original panels, and partially those dating from replacement in 1976. In appearance it appeared to be in good condition, but was actually in an extremely precarious state regarding structural stability. In effect, the original travertine slabs had been laid with closed joints, and the thickness of the plates and the mounting system were inadequate. The lower panels had undergone compression from the upper panels. The effects of UV rays and freeze-thaw cycles had caused a loss of strength, causing microcracks and distortions in approximately five per cent of the panels; some had even become detached from the facade.

On the ground floor, the original panels were still in place and twenty per cent of them were cracked and delaminated.

Intervention

The carbonation damage to the gable-end wall was locally repaired and the entire surface rendered. Then the new fixings (stainless steel bars and studs) were sealed in place with resin. The original cladding panels were replaced by three-centimetre thick Roman travertine from the Tivoli quarries, leaving open joints of 2 mm, to allow for expansion.

On the two entrance porches and the north facade of the ground floor, the original travertine panels were conserved. Isolated repairs were carried out comprising the removal of some pieces and securely glueing them back in place. Certain panels were replaced by those recovered from the gable-end wall.

1

1
West gable-end wall, installation of travertine cladding panels, 15 May 2008.
2
Entrance porch and ground floor with travertine cladding, after restoration.

2

The glass bricks

Glass is omnipresent in the Clarté building. Le Corbusier held fast to the idea of transparency and of light transmission from one side of the building to the other.

Light passes through the secondary ground floor rooms, such as small storerooms or caretaker lodges located on the north side, and through the garages on the south side, to penetrate to the heart of the building.

A special feature of this building lies in the use of panels of glass bricks. Inside, we find them between garages and entrance halls on the ground floor. Outside, they are found above the entrance doors. They also constitute the curved wall of the former shops at street level and illuminate the duplex apartments from the west gable-end facade. The glass "Nevada" bricks, translucent, 20 cm square (4 cm thick), were originally produced by the Saint-Gobain company, who conceived and developed them at the end of the 1920s.

Condition

Outside, on the west gable-end facade, the three large panels of glass bricks were in fairly good condition. Those of the fourth and sixth floors had been replaced during the 1975–1977 restoration. The second floor panel was original, but in a fragile condition, with some broken bricks.

The two curved walls, originally of shops, but now enclosing the restaurant, were very deteriorated, while thirty per cent of the glass bricks located above the building entrances, also original, were cracked and broken. Much damage was due to corrosion of the panel's metal framework.

Inside, at No. 2, the glass bricks had been replaced during the 1975–1977 restoration; at No. 4, they were original.

Intervention

Outside, the glass bricks were partially replaced by new. On the west facade, the glass brick panels were left untouched. To the left of the restaurant entrance, the walls and their metal framework have been completely remade. The very fine joint thickness made any repair delicate. Indeed, it was not possible to change a broken glass brick without damaging the adjacent bricks. One panel to the right of the restaurant entrance was fully

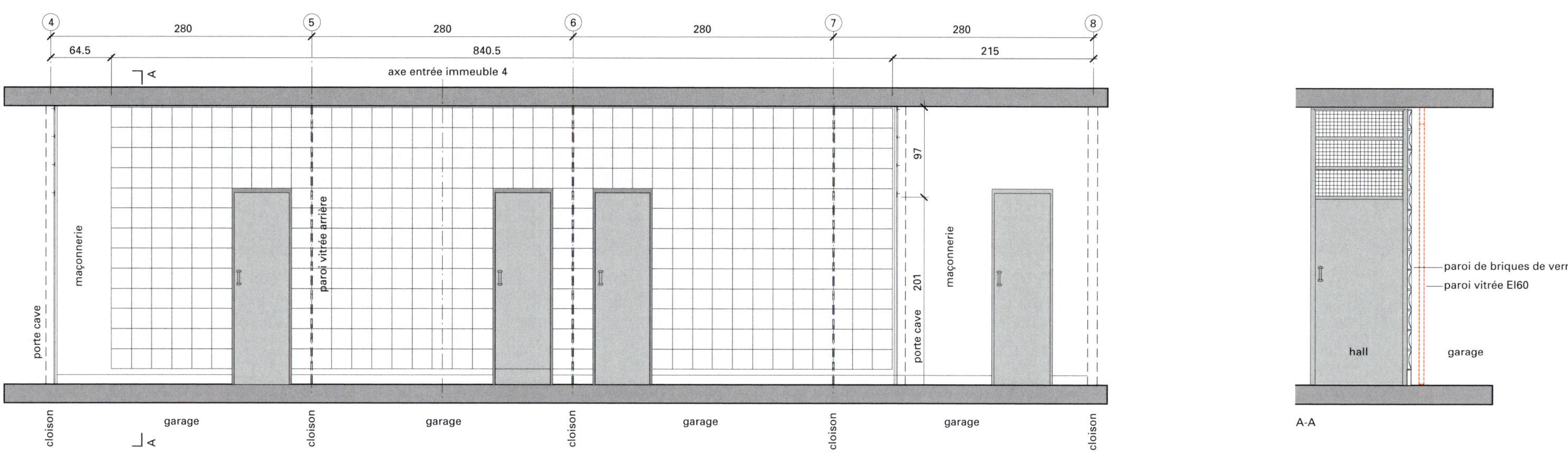

1

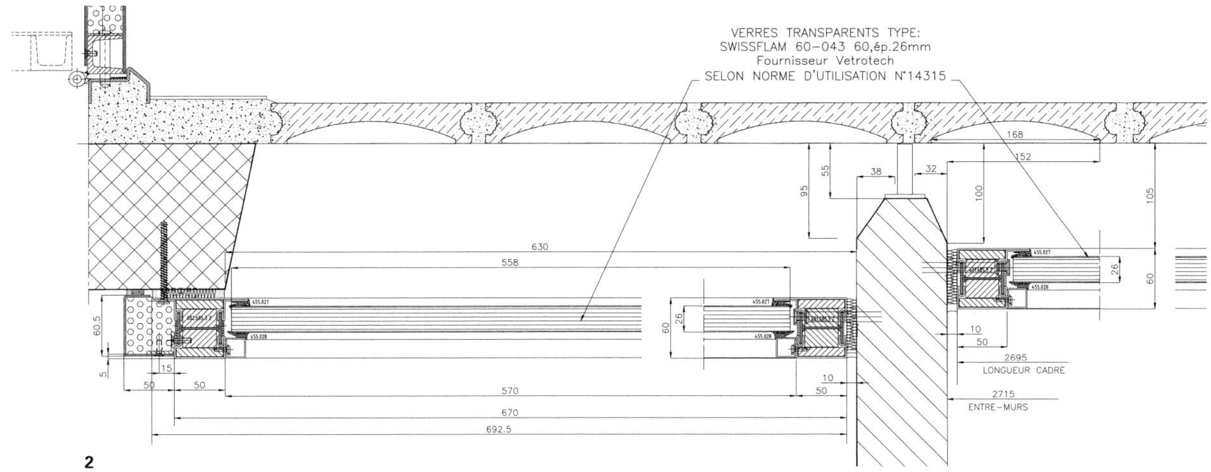

2

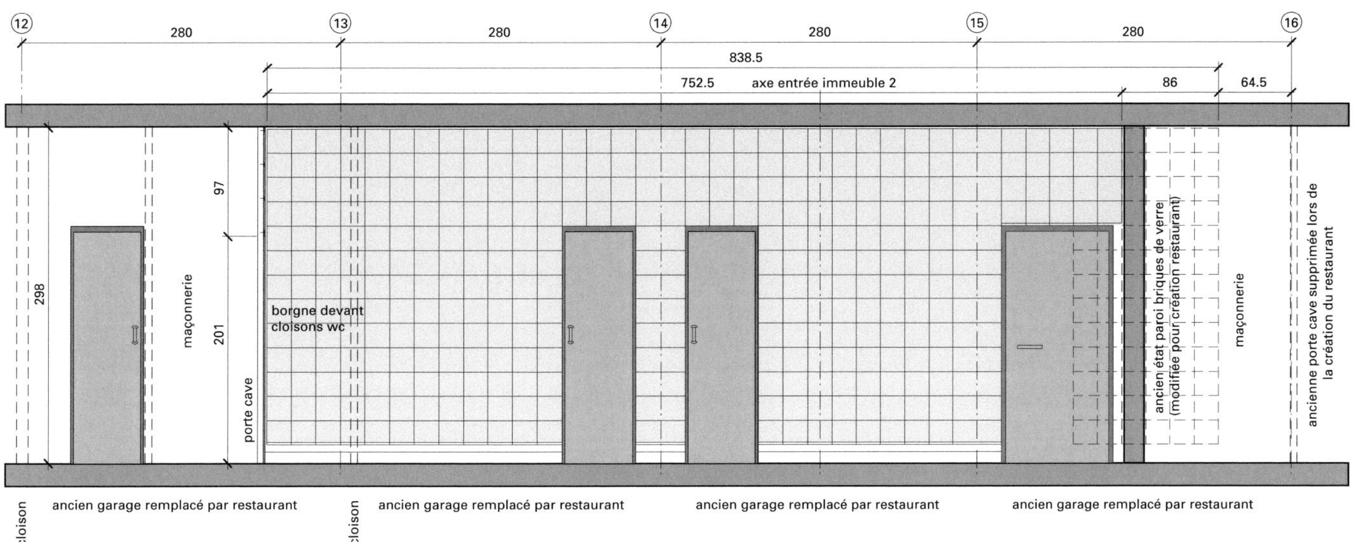

3

1
4, rue Saint-Laurent, elevation showing the glass brick panel between the entrance hall and the garages.

2
Section showing detail of the glass bricks and of the EI60 glazed wall, garage side.

3
2, rue Saint-Laurent, elevation showing the glass brick panel between the entrance hall and the restaurant (former garages).

conserved, together with its metal framework and including its cracked bricks, as an example of the original construction. Some adaptations were necessary: in the complete reconstruction of the curved wall of glass bricks to the left of the restaurant entrance, the restaurant door has been moved to the extension of the glass brick wall. This places it in the position originally occupied by the door to one of the shops. The joints between the glass bricks, originally very slender, have been enlarged.

Inside, at No. 4, the original glass brick panels have been entirely conserved. Fire barriers had to be installed between the garages and the communal areas. This was necessary to ensure optimal fire protection, and was achieved by installing an insulating wall of EI60 glass against the glass bricks at the far end of each garage unit. All of the internal metal doors connecting each garage to the entrance hall were kept in place, but they are no longer in use. This solution, fully reversible, preserves the transparency effect desired by Le Corbusier and provided by the glass brick walls. The garages accessed via the corridor to the cellars, as well as the refuse container storeroom, have however conserved their interior access and their metal doors.

The original glass bricks above the two building entrances have all been replaced by new “Nevada“ bricks.

4

5

6

4
2, rue Saint-Laurent, entrance, demolition of the glass brick panel, 30 April 2009.
5
2, rue Saint-Laurent, entrance, installing glass bricks, 2 November 2009.
6
4, rue Saint-Laurent, entrance, installing glass bricks, 11 March 2010.
7
Cross-section showing detail of the exterior glass brick wall, February 2010.
8
Curved glass brick restaurant facade, February 2010.
9–10
Conserved glass brick panel to the right of the restaurant entrance, before and after work.

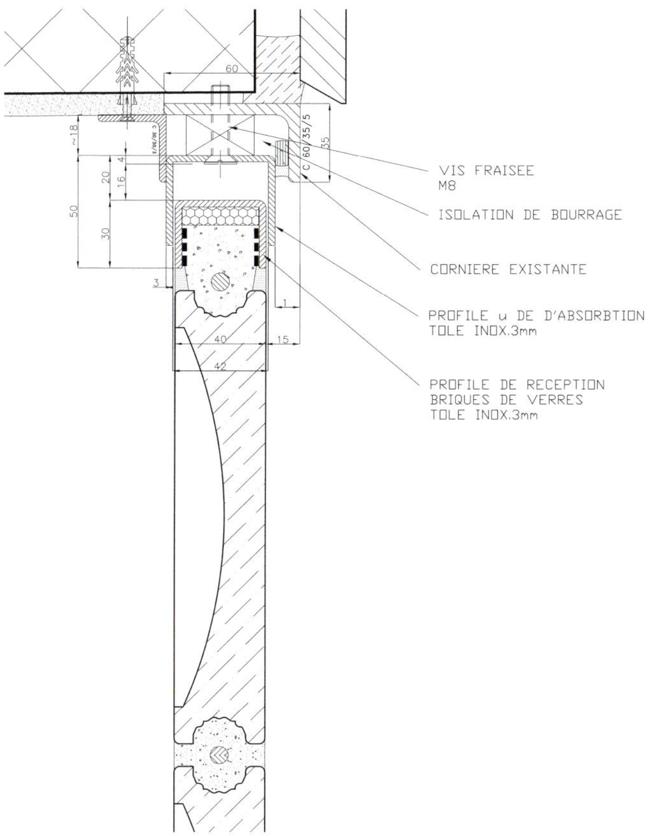
VIS FRAISEE
M8
ISOLATION DE BOURRAGE
CORNIERE EXISTANTE
PROFILE u DE D'ABSORBTION
TOLE INOX.3mm
PROFILE DE RECEPTION
BRIQUES DE VERRES
TOLE INOX.3mm

7

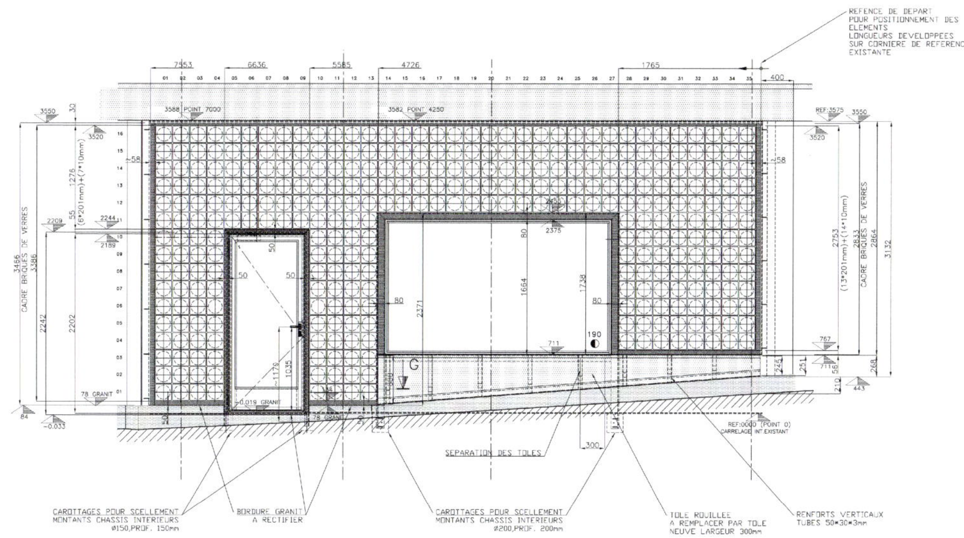
REFENCE DE DEPART
POUR POSITIONNEMENT DES
ELEMENTS
LONGUEURS DEVELOPPEES
SUR CORNIERE DE REFERENCE
EXISTANTE
SEPARATION DES TOLES
CAROTTAGES POUR SCELLEMENT
MONTANTS CHASSIS INTERIEURS
Ø150,PROF. 150mm
BORDURE GRANIT
A RECTIFIER
CAROTTAGES POUR SCELLEMENT
MONTANTS CHASSIS INTERIEURS
Ø200,PROF. 200mm
TOLE ROUILLEE
A REMPLACER PAR TOLE
NEUVE LARGEUR 300mm
RENFORTS VERTICAUX
TUBES 50*30*3mm

8

RESTAURANT

9

10

Sanitation systems

Condition

The sanitation systems (cold water, hot water, waste water) were in a very dilapidated condition.

Intervention

All the sanitation systems (around ten in total) had to be renewed, with partial renewal of the drainage, floor by floor, from the bottom to the top, starting with No. 2, and then No. 4 of rue Saint-Laurent (the waste water and rainwater pipes replaced in 1976 were in perfect condition and hence were conserved; all the hot and cold water pipes were replaced). It was on the occasion of this restoration that water stopcocks were installed for each apartment. In addition, the principal water supply valve, previously located in a dedicated cabinet, was replaced by four principal stopcocks (one each for No. 2 and No. 4, one for the communal areas, and one for the restaurant) installed in the former access room to the water tank. The electricity and water mains were replaced, and a gas main was added.

Heating and electricity

Condition

Originally, the electricity meters were placed in the apartments and the central heating was most probably coal fired. Before the restoration, the boiler was oil fired.

Intervention

In order to adapt to current standards, all electrical panels were centralised in an electrical services room, newly created for the occasion in place of three ground floor storerooms, between the old access room to the water tank and a transverse corridor.

Several intercoms, in actuality "telephonic doorman" systems linked directly to the inhabitant's telephone line, have been installed outside the main entrances. They have the advantage of requiring neither many cables nor the installation of receivers in the apartments.

The apartments' power supplies have all been replaced. The conduits and electric cables were routed through the fire-resistant false ceilings of the entrance lobbies and in the double wall of the stairwell, which had previously been used for the passage of electric distribution cables. The low current (telephone, television, etc.) cables have also been installed there. The television reception system has been renewed, the building having been connected to the cable network.

The old oil tank was dismantled and new cellars created in the space thus recovered. The old oil-fired boilers were replaced by two gas condensing boilers. The main heating valve as well as the distribution to the foot of the risers have been completely renewed. An existing chimney flue was lined (in stainless steel) for the new heating system. All the original cast-iron radiators were left in place and thermostatic valves installed.

Ventilation

Condition

Originally seven small yards, of which one was common to both addresses, served as ventilation shafts for the soil stacks. This was the practice for buildings of the period in Geneva. A system of open grilles provided ventilation. Some of these still existed in 2007 but the majority had gone, thereby preventing the natural ventilation afforded by the shafts. In consequence several soil stacks had no ventilation. Kitchen ventilation was originally provided by the windows; ventilation ducts did not exist at the time.

As for ventilation of the restaurant, installed during the years 1975–1977, a large duct passed through one of the studios to an exhaust vent on the first floor terrace.

Intervention

The ventilation shafts were conserved but a firewall was installed at the level of each floor slab. The inspection hatches were walled up, however their covers were conserved. As a consequence of the firewalls blocking the ventilation shafts, a general system of forced air ventilation has been created. Adjustable round vents have been installed. In order to avoid further installations on the roof terrace, extraction ducts have been incorporated into the existing chimney stacks. Round ventilation grilles were installed in the kitchens, connected to the newly created extraction ducts.

Passages have been created for the restaurant's new ventilation ducts, such that they exit at roof level and not on the terraces. The duct from the restaurant's cooker extractor hood has been bored through to the building's central ventilation shaft, in its turn joined to the old heating flue. The other ventilation duct from the service rooms has been connected to one of the original rubbish chutes, reassigned for ventilation of the apartment kitchens. Automatic fire-protection valves have been installed in the ducts at each passage through a wall delimiting the protected zones (fire-escape routes). In addition the ducts have been wrapped with fire-resistant insulation in order to provide an adequate level of protection.

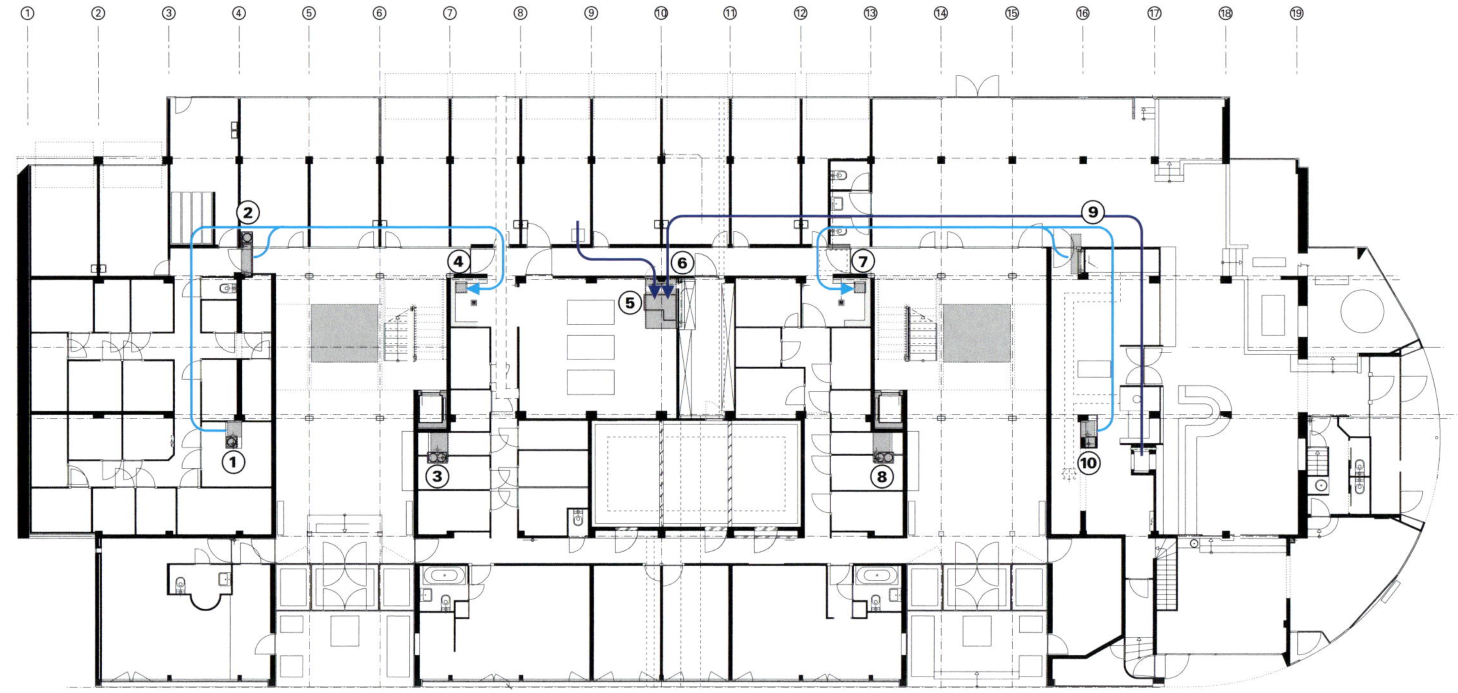

General ventilation schematic,
ground floor plan,
scale 1:300, December 2006.

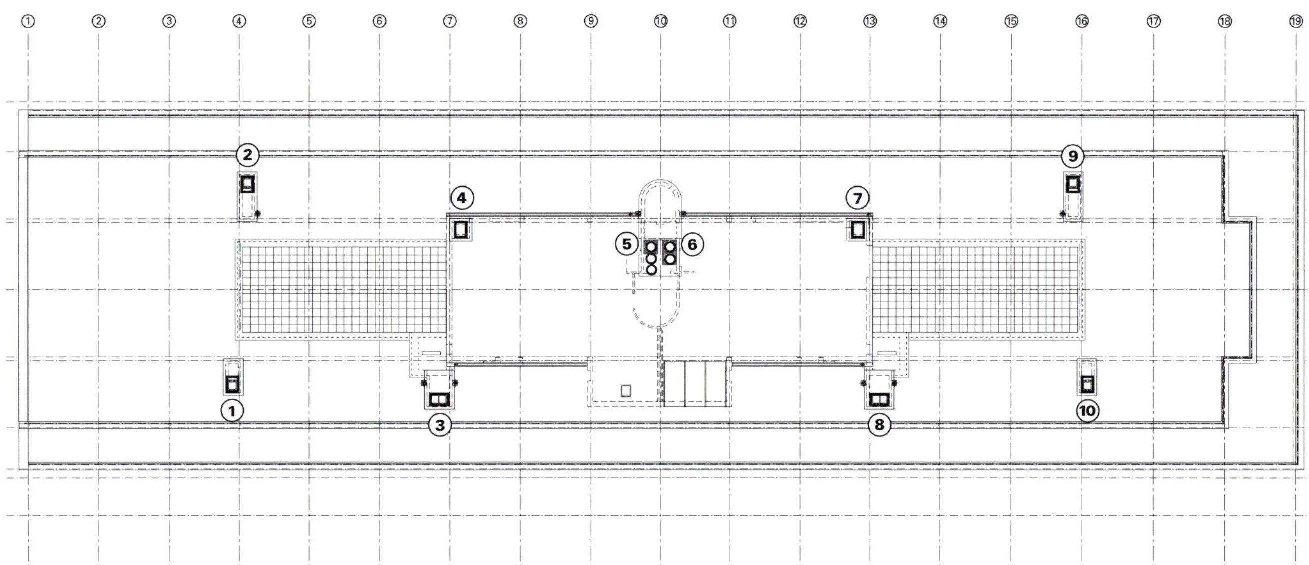

General ventilation schematic,
roof plan, scale 1:300, December 2006.

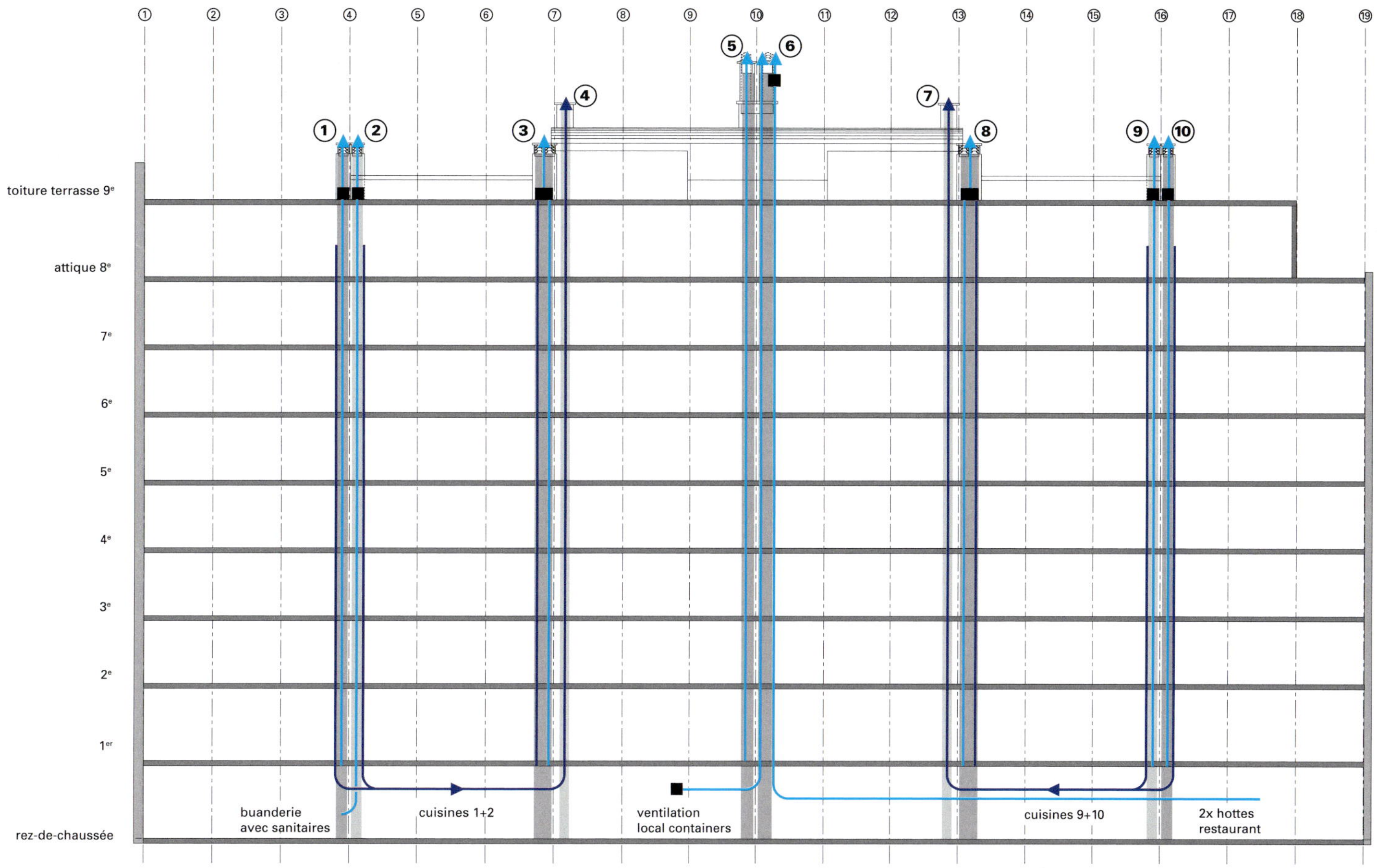

1 Existing vent ø 250mm
Toilet blocks
2 Existing vent ø 250mm
Laundry and toilet blocks
3 Two existing vents ø 250mm
Kitchen and toilet blocks
4 Former brick refuse chute 400×400mm
Kitchen blocks
5 Existing vent ø 350mm
Boiler exhaust, refuse room ventilation,
toilet blocks
6 Two existing vents ø 350mm and ø 240mm
Smoke stack, rooftop ventilation
of restaurant hobs
7 Former brick refuse chute 400×400mm
Kitchen blocks
8 Two existing vents ø 250mm
Kitchen and toilet blocks
9 Existing vent ø 250mm
Toilet blocks
10 Existing vent ø 250mm
Toilet blocks

General ventilation schematic, longitudinal section, scale 1:300, December 2006.

The communal areas

The communal areas had been relatively well maintained and had not undergone any major works, with the exception of painting, renewal of the letter boxes and lighting, and the creation of the restaurant at No. 2.

The entrance halls and stairwells

The entrance halls

Originally the entrance hall's floors and the steps of the building entrances were covered with slabs of Hauteville limestone. These have been preserved. During the 2007–2011 works, the only intervention was their restoration by cleaning and polishing, together with some re-dressing and repair of joints (mastic).

In the soil boxes framing the entrances some of the original plants remained. It was not possible to conserve them and they were replaced.

The original letter boxes had been replaced in the years 1975–1977. At the time of the 2007–2011 restoration, new standardised larger models had been installed. This change had required work to enlarge their alcove, in order that the letter box facings were flush to the wall.

The stairwells

All areas of the stairwells, and particularly the metalwork, were found to be in excellent condition, aside from the paintwork which had been renewed several times. Most of the landing doors had been replaced. Nonetheless, a few original ones remained.

All elements of the stairwells were conserved. The large metal structural elements, as well as the ground floor columns, were coated with an intumescent paint. This fire-resistant paint, applied in several layers, required rubbing down several times in order to obtain a smooth finish, as per the original.

To allow the passage of light, the steps and the landing floors of the stairwells had been constructed from 36 cm square glass slabs, originally manufactured by Saint-Gobain. The few that were broken at the moment of restoration were replaced.

The lifts had probably been replaced during the 1960s and completed by the addition of a sliding interior security door. At the time of the 2007–2011 restoration they were found to be in good working order and only underwent routine servicing.

1
Detail of entrance hall light-fitting by Arthur Rüegg, 2009.
2
4, rue Saint-Laurent, entrance hall, after restoration.
3
Stairwell, after restoration.

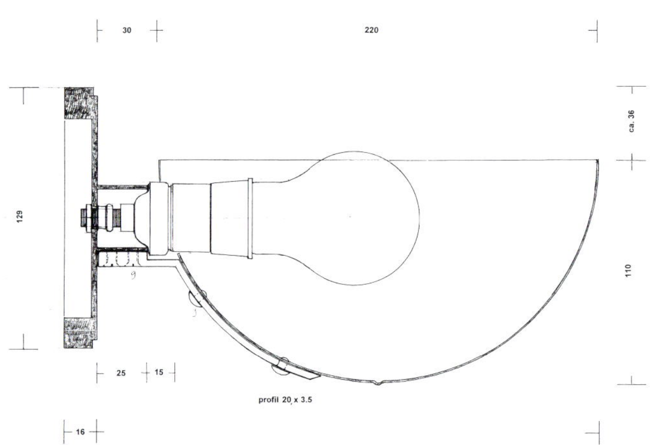

1

2

3

The lighting

At the time of the works, the lighting in the entrance halls was not original.

During restoration, the lighting was reconstituted to closely resemble the initial design. Reproduced as closely as possible from an original model that had been preserved in place (out of the twelve lamps, only one remained) six lamps per entrance hall were fixed to the structural steel columns, in their original positions: one lamp on either side of both columns in the centre of each entrance hall and one lamp behind each of the rear columns (opposite the panels of glass bricks). Adopting the form of spotlights beaming indirect light in the direction of the ceiling, they were remade in stainless steel although originally made from nickel plated brass.

Inside, above the building's entrance doors, lighting was installed behind translucent glass. It was conserved as is.

The stairwell lighting system took the form of a nickel plated metal tube suspended from above by a steel wheel running on a rail. Naked light bulbs were simply fixed to the metal tube providing, at the time, a very original industrial style solution for an apartment building. In order to change a bulb the entire light hanging was simply rolled toward the landings by gently pulling the loop of electrical cable supplying its power. The only intervention consisted of repairing some bushes and of replacing the incandescent bulbs with new energy saving ones.

Ground floor: the plant rooms, the "caves", the garages, and the restaurant

The plant rooms [15] and the "caves [16]"

The original plans for the plant rooms were extremely rational, being centralised in the middle of the building, with services distributed by two longitudinal corridors linking the entrance halls of No. 2 and No. 4. The caretaker lodges were situated to the north, to the side of the building entrances, and the garages, to the south.

During the 1975–1977 restoration, the "caves" had been requisitioned for other uses. However, during the 2007–2011 work, the volumes previously occupied by the "caves" were further modified to create an electricity services room and a room

4
Glass slabs, stairwell, scale 1:10.
5
Stairwell lighting, nickel plated tube, and system of suspension by rail.
6
4, rue Saint-Laurent, stairwell, glass slabs, and lighting.

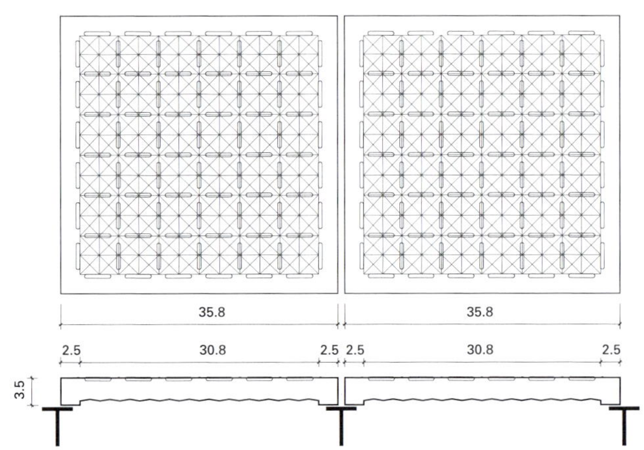

4

5

6

containing the principal service valves (water and gas). Nonetheless, in order to ensure once again that each apartment had a "cave", new ones were created (eight in former utility stores located between two former caretaker lodges, seven in the old water tank room, four in the room that had housed the waste disposal chutes for No. 2, and two more in the one for No. 4). Two bicycle stores were also created in the space previously occupied by the waste disposal chutes. This was achieved without removing any original walls, the new spaces having been fitted within the existing room partitioning.

To meet current fire protection standards, fire-resistant enclosures were installed on the ground floor: A complete barrier was created between the restaurant and the rest of the building as well as between the central core ("caves" area) and the entrance halls. Eight glazed EI30 standard fire doors were put in place to isolate the central core from the rest of the ground floor; five additional unglazed EI30 fire doors were installed; nine original doors have been transformed and lined with fireproof insulation to give the equivalent performance of EI30 standard firewalls. An F60 fire-resistant ceiling has also been installed throughout the entire ground floor, including the entrance halls.

The concrete floors of the service areas were simply cleaned and repainted.

Some original elements were preserved, such as the old wooden milk boxes built into the "cave" access corridors, opposite the former caretaker lodges. Also preserved were the cabinets with sliding doors, in which the main water stopcocks used to be located.

The windows of the plant rooms, the "caves", and the former caretaker lodges were dismantled, then reinstalled after restoration and adaptation in the workshop (fire-resistant glass was installed in place of the old material).

The office of the architects directing the renovation works, which had initially been installed at the heart of the worksite, in one of the vacant second floor apartments at No. 2, was moved to the ground floor of No. 4, occupying an old bicycle store, then utility room, transformed for the occasion.

The garages

Originally, every garage had an individual metal door communicating directly with an entrance hall, or with the connecting corridor.

1
4, rue Saint-Laurent, ground floor, structure with Solomite panels, before the installation of fire-resistant ceilings, 26 January 2009.
2–3
In the hallway of No. 2, door marked "Concierge" which leads to the corridor on the rue Saint-Laurent side.
4
In its extension, the corridor leading to the entrance hall of No. 4; to the right, the milk cabinet with sliding door.

1

2

3

4

The eleven original exterior overhead doors – a model called "Lightning", produced by the Wanner company – in steel sheet (measuring 2.5 by 2.4 metres) with rails, counterweights, and pulleys, were partially glazed (fixed reinforced glass in the upper half). At the time of renovation, two of them had been replaced. The garage doors are within a metal wall, which includes a matching fixed glazed upper half. All the garage doors as well as the door to the laundry room were badly corroded and deformed, in addition the glazing was cracked.

The garage's external doors were conserved and restored on site, undergoing repairs and reconstruction of some bent or missing items. The two doors that had been previously modified had both their opening mechanism and appearance restored to match the original. The reinforced glass of the garage doors and of the metal wall was replaced, as well as that of an outer door and the laundry.

The restaurant

The creation of the restaurant dates back to the 1975–1977 restoration, and had required the demolition of four arcades, five garages, a laundry, a bicycle store, and a dozen apartment "caves". It was at this time that one of the two original laundries (that of No. 2), located at the facade to allow the access of natural light, was suppressed. That of No. 4 was retained, together with its famous drier drawers, as an example of the original realisation (see photo, p. 136).

Various metallic elements of the restaurant's windows were badly corroded and deformed, and there were many panes of cracked glass. The glass in the large restaurant windows was replaced by insulating glass. For the walls of glass brick, refer to the chapter "The glass bricks".

5
The garages, before restoration.
6
Garages, exterior, "Eclair" plate on door.
7
The garages, after restoration.

5

6

7

Utility rooms

1 entrance
2 garage
3 laundry
4 refuse container store
5 “caves”
6 former caretaker rooms
7 boiler room
8 main stopcock room
9 electrical services room

partitions removed
partitions added

Fire-resistant partitioning

modified steel door (double steel +insulation)
existing EI30 door
EI30 glass door
EI60 glass wall

Ground floor, modification of utility rooms and fire-resistant partitioning, scale 1:300.

The door handles

In the communal and service areas, only a few of the original door handles remain (Model No. 2263 of the Arnold Karli catalogue). Many original doors, whether untouched or painted, are equipped with aluminium handles. The doors of the existing apartment caves located off the hallways do not have handles but only simple or combination locks. The old caretaker lodges on the ground floor still have original handles (Model No. 2432 of the Arnold Karli catalogue).

Regarding the handles of the apartment doors on the stairwell landings, many changes have been made over time. Inside the apartments, the original handles have mostly been preserved. The door handles of both of the building's entrances are original.

15 Plant rooms: English terminology for room containing building services, central heating boilers, electrical distribution boards, main gas valves etc.

16 The French term "cave": traditionally a room below ground for storing wine and other items. The term "cave" is also used to describe an apartment storeroom, and in the case of Clarté, these are located on the ground floor.

8
Laundry at No. 4, conserved as an example of the original, together with its famous drier drawers.
9
Model No. 2263 from the Arnold Karli catalogue was originally used as the handle for doors to the communal areas.
10
Model No. 2432 from the Arnold Karli catalogue was originally used for the ground floor doors to the caretaker lodges.
11
Original door handle, Model No. 2263 of the Arnold Karli catalogue.
12
Handle of the door leading to the garages.
13
Stairway landing door handle, Model No. 2432 of the Arnold Karli catalogue.
14
Handle of the main entrance door to the building.

8

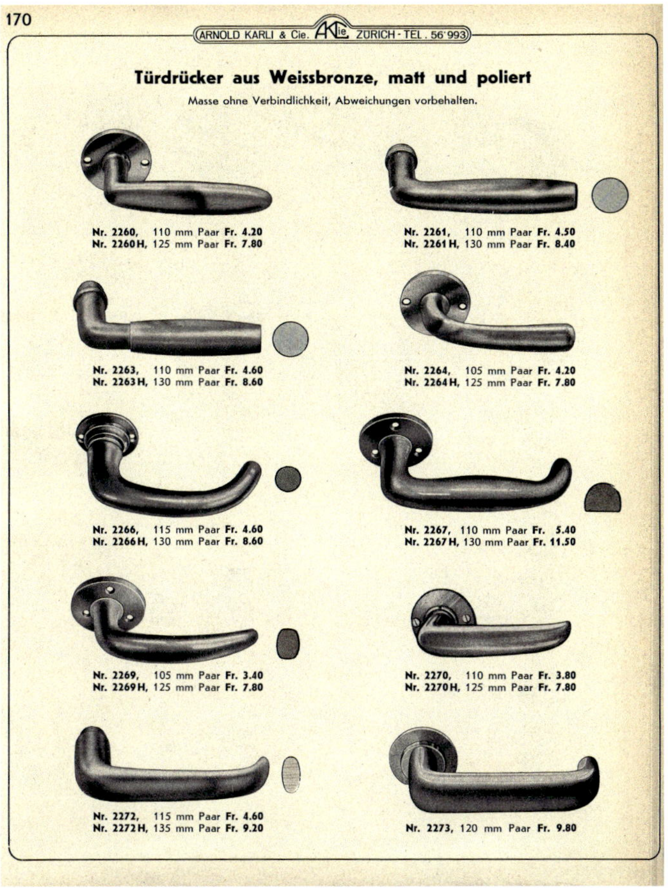

170

(ARNOLD KARLI & Cie. AKCie ZÜRICH - TEL. 56'993)

Türdrücker aus Weissbronze, matt und poliert

Masse ohne Verbindlichkeit, Abweichungen vorbehalten.

Nr. 2260, 110 mm Paar **Fr. 4.20**
Nr. 2260 H, 125 mm Paar **Fr. 7.80**

Nr. 2261, 110 mm Paar **Fr. 4.50**
Nr. 2261 H, 130 mm Paar **Fr. 8.40**

Nr. 2263, 110 mm Paar **Fr. 4.60**
Nr. 2263 H, 130 mm Paar **Fr. 8.60**

Nr. 2264, 105 mm Paar **Fr. 4.20**
Nr. 2264 H, 125 mm Paar **Fr. 7.80**

Nr. 2266, 115 mm Paar **Fr. 4.60**
Nr. 2266 H, 130 mm Paar **Fr. 8.60**

Nr. 2267, 110 mm Paar **Fr. 5.40**
Nr. 2267 H, 130 mm Paar **Fr. 11.50**

Nr. 2269, 105 mm Paar **Fr. 3.40**
Nr. 2269 H, 125 mm Paar **Fr. 7.80**

Nr. 2270, 110 mm Paar **Fr. 3.80**
Nr. 2270 H, 125 mm Paar **Fr. 7.80**

Nr. 2272, 115 mm Paar **Fr. 4.60**
Nr. 2272 H, 135 mm Paar **Fr. 9.20**

Nr. 2273, 120 mm Paar **Fr. 9.80**

9

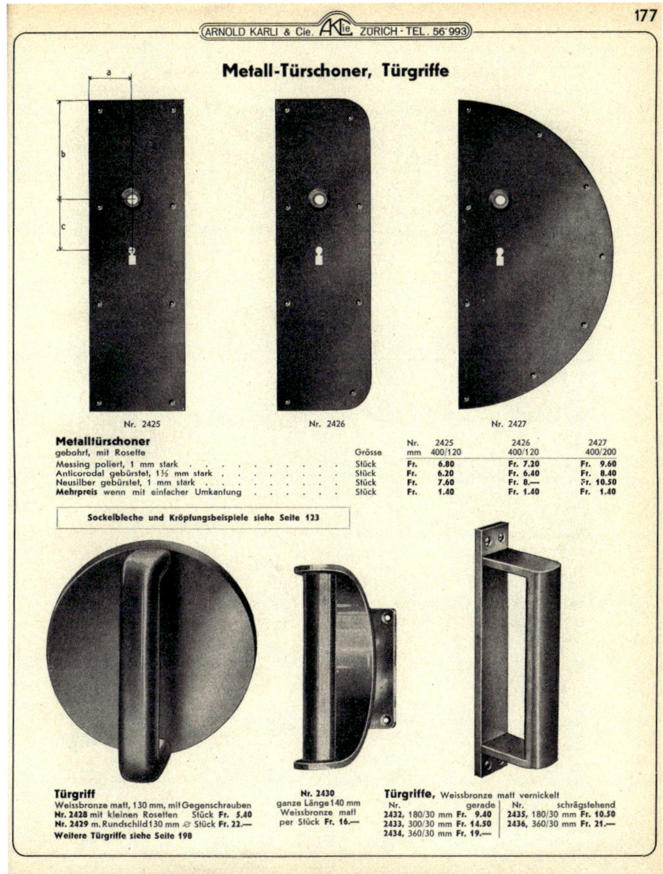

177

(ARNOLD KARLI & Cie. AKCie ZÜRICH - TEL. 56'993)

Metall-Türschoner, Türgriffe

Nr. 2425 Nr. 2426 Nr. 2427

Metalltürschoner gebohrt, mit Rosette	Grösse	Nr. mm	2425 400/120	2426 400/120	2427 400/200
Messing poliert, 1 mm stark	Stück	Fr.	6.80	Fr. 7.20	Fr. 9.60
Anticorodal gebürstet, 1½ mm stark	Stück	Fr.	6.20	Fr. 6.40	Fr. 8.40
Neusilber gebürstet, 1 mm stark	Stück	Fr.	7.60	Fr. 8.—	Fr. 10.50
Mehrpreis wenn mit einfacher Umkantung	Stück	Fr.	1.40	Fr. 1.40	Fr. 1.40

Sockelbleche und Kröpfungsbeispiele siehe Seite 123

Türgriff
Weissbronze matt, 130 mm, mit Gegenschrauben
Nr. 2428 mit kleinen Rosetten Stück **Fr. 5.40**
Nr. 2429 m. Rundschild 130 mm ⌀ Stück **Fr. 22.—**
Weitere Türgriffe siehe Seite 198

Nr. 2430
ganze Länge 140 mm
Weissbronze matt
per Stück **Fr. 16.—**

Türgriffe, Weissbronze matt vernickelt

Nr.	gerade	Nr.	schrägstehend
2432, 180/30 mm	**Fr. 9.40**	**2435,** 180/30 mm	**Fr. 10.50**
2433, 300/30 mm	**Fr. 14.50**	**2436,** 360/30 mm	**Fr. 21.—**
2434, 360/30 mm	**Fr. 19.—**		

10

11

12

13

14

As an architect and painter Le Corbusier attached great importance to colour. He developed a purist chromatic range, which he applied to architecture. In 1931, at the time of the Clarté building's construction, the wallpaper factory Salubra SA had placed an order for a collection of colour samples, thereby offering a commercial outlet for his research. At Clarté, colours play an integral part in the architectural coherence. Outside, the colour of the materials emphasises the architecture: the minerality of travertine, which contrasts with the glass brick panels; the dark railway-green of the metal frame, which blends with the changing reflections from the windows; the wooden blinds. In the lobbies and stairwells, various shades play with space and light: dark brown for the hall's metal fixings and pillars, sea green, light brown, beige, blue for the wall and ceiling panels, grey for the metal structure of the stairs. Inside the apartments, the use of Salubra wallpaper was originally imposed on the tenants, which nonetheless allowed a choice of colours, as given by the catalogue's colour coordination charts [17].

Over the years, the coherence of the original coordinating colours disappeared completely under multiple layers due to successive repainting. Finding the original colours proved difficult, as photographs of the period were in black and white. The only reliable colour information was that concerning the apartments' wallpaper. Regarding the facades and communal areas, the archives contained no information. The questions that arose on the subject of surface appearance led to the launch in 2007 of a campaign of sampling, investigation, and documentation of paint coatings, at the request of the Office of Heritage Buildings and Sites. Given the presence of all the original paint layers, the stratigraphic surveys allowed the recovery and documentation of the building's initial colours. Some sequences were confirmed only after microscope examination at the laboratory of conservation and restoration of paintings of the Geneva museum of art and history. This research project was led by Anne Rinuy, the assistant conservationist.

Outside, details of the first colours applied to metal components were sought in places both less exposed to sunlight and better protected from the weather, notably inside the roller blind enclosures, where the original colours were still visible. These reference shades were documented by taking colour photographs; descriptions and

1
South facade colours, 24 August 2009.
2
Samples of the first Salubra series of wallpapers for the Clarté building apartments, collected in 1976 by Arthur Rüegg.

1

colour codes have been established using the international standard colour system NCS (Natural Color System® ©, of the Scandinavian Colour Institute, Stockholm). This research was conducted by Saint Dismas workshop SA, led by Eric-James Favre-Bulle[18].

The results revealed the richness and subtleties of the colours that previous renovations had destroyed. In the light of this, the decision was made to return to colours, as far as possible, identical to the original.

Arthur Rüegg, the author of *Le Corbusier – Polychromie architecturale*[19], first revision of the Claviers de couleurs Salubra colour keys, contributed to the identification of certain original colours, as well as to the choice of new ones.

The exterior colours

Railway-green

The railway-green is a dark shade, typically used for industrial constructions of the period, as applied to rail wagons and to trams. Originally all the external metal parts of the Clarté building, such as the load-bearing frame, the metalwork of the window units, the external surface of the balcony parapets, the roller blind enclosures and runners, had been covered with railway-green oil based paint.

In 2007, these metal parts were painted dark brown, a principal modification applied at the time of the 1975–1977 restoration. Several samples had to be taken in order to identify the original colour.

For the exterior metal parts, it was decided to reproduce a colour corresponding to the original. By its very dark tone, the railway-green reinforces the smooth nature of the metal and glass facade, and visually restores the coherence and the aesthetic sought by the architects.

To ensure the correct paint application during the works, the different layers of paint were differentiated by their colour; first the red epoxy, then the grey, and, finally, the first coat of polyurethane paint, slightly different from the fourth and final railway-green coat.

Sea green

The sea green is a light green, used for the exterior of the garages (all metalwork, including the lightweight steel doors); this colour was also found on the external sides of the "wagon" (the metalwork and rendered parts). Thence the external surfaces of the "wagon", which had been painted white,

2

rediscovered their original sea green colour. This green was also seen inside, in the entrance halls.

Light blue

The interior face of the facade framework, like the interior surface of the parapets and the balcony consoles, visible from the apartments, was originally painted light blue, as was confirmed by the samples taken from those locations. The light blue was of particular importance as it created a link between the interior (the apartments) and the exterior (the balconies), perhaps to merge with the sky and increase the brightness of the apartments.

In old black and white photographs it was found that the panels forming the balcony ceilings were coated with a glossy light coloured paint. However, these having been removed during the 1953–1954 restoration, there remained no physical evidence to identify the original colour.

At the time of the building's restoration, the visible part of the underside of the balconies comprised the lower face of the wooden slats, producing an aesthetic effect far from that of the original appearance.

Hence to restore the original colours, the interior face of the facade frame within the apartments, as well as the inside parapet surface and the balcony consoles, was repainted light blue. The same colour was also adopted for the balconies' new sheet metal soffit, even though it was not possible to confirm that this corresponds to the original.

Other exterior colours

The wooden frame of the glazed balcony doors (partially glazed in reinforced glass), the fixed frame, as well as the spacers within the insulating glass of the sliding windows were painted brown. A black silicone sealant had been used around the periphery of the glass on the outside, and a grey silicone sealant on the inside.

All the old black and white photos were studied, and based on the shade of grey, it was deduced that the textile awnings were originally of a fairly light colour, perhaps a slightly washed-out pink, a "standard" of the time, which tended toward a natural raw fabric colour. The awning fabrics, a deep yellow before the restoration, have all been replaced to reflect this probable original shade.

As for the roller blinds, they were of varnished natural wood slats. They have been refurbished to maintain the original appearance.

1
The "sea green" of the restored "wagon", south side, 2010.
2
The "light blue" of the window frames, glazed doors, and balcony parapets, seen from inside an apartment.
3
The "sea green" of the garages.

1

2

17 Le Corbusier, *Salubra, colour keys,* Editions Salubra, Basel, 1931; then, *Salubra, colour keys* (2nd series), 1959; revised in 1997, 2002, and 2015: Arthur Rüegg, *Le Corbusier – Polychromie architecturale,* Birkhäuser Verlag, Basel.

18 See the summary tables of colours at the end of this chapter.

19 Arthur Rüegg, *Le Corbusier – Polychromie architecturale,* Birkhäuser Verlag, Basel, 1997 [Le Corbusier, *Claviers de couleurs,* Salubra, 1931].

3

The interior colours

"We continued the search for colours destined to give the intention of light, which is the basis of our architectural research. [...] The colour that characterises the walls according to whether they are in full daylight or darkness can draw the eye through complicated spaces and far extend the impression of space: the red retains its qualities only in full light, the blue vibrates in the shadows, etc.: physics of colour. Physiology of sensations: red, blue, yellow, etc., sensations determined. Shade, shadow, light: ditto. One can compose architecturally on this basis." [20]

Sea green

Sea green was found on the radiators and on the ceilings of the plant cabinets, which were situated to either side of the building entrances, as well as on the entire wall supporting the letter boxes.

The brown, grey, blue, and beige

The dark brown constituted the colour which segments, and which brings contrast. Applied to the metal columns of the entrance hall, this colour highlights the building's principal structure. It is found on the metal frames of the building entrances as well as on the hall radiators and on the two interior doors near to the entrance, which lead to the plant rooms. In the stairwells, the dark brown applied to the flange and to the web inside the steel beam supporting the landings reinforced the linearity of the building's structure. The same colour covered the metal frames of the apartment doors on the landings.

A medium grey paint was found on the metal parts of the stairwells (balustrade and structure, with the exception of the chromed metal handrail), on the front of the lifts, and on the metal doors that are built into the southern glass brick panel, deep in the building's entrance hall. At the stairwell landings, the medium grey highlighted the edge of the floor slab at every alternate floor, it covered the semi-circular wall of the projecting staircase to the small duplex apartments, and continued over the plastered ceilings of the corresponding landings. In the ground floor services area, a slightly lighter grey covered the walls of the east-west transverse corridors, and those of the laundry.

The walls framing the flights of stairs were distinguished by a blue paint, also applied to the south

1

1
The sea green walls of the entrance hall.
2
The stairwell, after restoration, blue, beige, grey, brown.

ceiling of the entrance halls and to the walls of the stairway leading to the "wagon".

A beige colour had been applied in the halls, on the wall opposite the one supporting the mailboxes, thereby extending to the interior the effect of travertine cladding at the base of the building. Upstairs, the beige colour covered all walls bordering the landings and the skylights, including the metal frame of the duplex bathroom's glazing that overlooks the stairwells.

The large north ceilings of the entrance halls, that of the northern corridor of the communal central areas, and the eighth floor ceilings had been painted a light brown colour.

In the communal areas and the stairwells, the original colour scheme was restored.

A medium grey was also applied to the framework of the windows overlooking the stairwells, created in the years 1975–1977, to replace the original glass slabs.

20 Le Corbusier, "Le pavillon de l'Esprit Nouveau", in Charles-Edouard Jeanneret (Le Corbusier), *Almanach d'architecture moderne,* Editions Crès, Paris, 1925; revision by Roberto Gabetti, Bottega d'Erasmo ed., Turin, 1975, p. 146.

2

Summary table of the original aspect (1930–32) – 2 and 4, rue Saint-Laurent, exterior

painted surface	colour ~	description
metal facades, in general from 1st to the 8th storey		railway green
facades, windows, frame, exterior surfaces		railway green
facades, balconies, exterior surfaces		railway green
facades, balcony structures (metal)		railway green
facades, roller blind enclosures and runners		railway green
facades, balconies, handrails		railway green
facades, balconies, separators, upper elements		railway green
edges of glazing frames (see note 1)		railway green
edges of balcony doors and opening windows (see note 2)		railway green
north porch, entrance doors		railway green
north porch, side doors		railway green
north porch, glazing frames, caretaker, etc.		railway green
ground floor, west shop windows		railway green
ground floor, window frame, utility room north		railway green
west commerce, windows, concave niches		railway green
terrace, 9th storey west, balustrade (see note 3)		r.g., then white
north facade, entrance porch canopies 2 and 4		sea green
slab soffits, north-west commerce		sea green
south garages, static door frames		sea green
south garages, tilting metal doors		sea green
south garages, east masonry facade		sea green
laundry, south chest wall		sea green
west facade, 8th storey, side wall		sea green
terrace, 9th storey, parapet wall east plus north and south return		sea green
facades, 9th storey, wagon		sea green
facades, 9th storey, wagon, window frames		sea green
facades, 9th storey, wagon, doors		sea green
facades, 9th storey, wagon, central tower		sea green
facades, 9th storey, wagon, metal staircase		sea green

painted surface	colour ~	description
facades, balconies, interior face parapet walls		light blue
balconies, separations, lower part		light blue
embrasures balcony doors and opening windows (see note 4)		light blue
balcony soffits (painted panels, abolished)	?	light blue ?
garages, the two to the east, masonry		mid grey
garages, the two to the east, static door frames		mid grey
east wall from the 1st to 8th storey, north, south, and west surfaces		mid grey
terrace, 9th storey, facades of the skylights (stairways)		dark grey
terrace, 9th storey, facades of the lift heads		dark grey
terrace, 9th storey, chimney stacks, open parts (see note 5)		dark grey
east facade, from ground floor to 9th storey, render		dark grey
mortar joints of the glass bricks (see note 6)		dark grey
travertine panels, north, west, and south facades (see note 7)		light beige
garages, west facade, travertine panels (see note 7)		light beige
windows, wooden spacers between the panes		light brown
slab edge, behind the reinforced glass		light brown
Nos. 2 and 4 entrance porch canopies, north bases		yellow ochre
terrace, 9th storey, chimneys (see note 8)		white
terrace, 9th storey, TSF framework, west (see note 9)	±, + brillance	grey
factory applied brown anti-rust		red ochre
site applied orange anti-rust		bright orange
axles of the textile awnings		pink beige

Notes

1 exterior surrounds
2 only on the sliding frames
3 overpainted very light shade before 19 October 1932
4 on the static frames
5 in place on 19 October 1932
6 construction mortar not painted
7 natural stone
8 painted white before 19 October 1932
9 metallic paint, aluminium
10 except the chrome handrail
11 colour documented in photographs
12 on the landings
13 in addition to the metallic elements
14 created in 1975/76, initial state not preserved
15 outside of the apartments
16 inside of the apartments
17 in the stairwells
18 right at the top: below the skylights
19 frames of skylights
20 at the centre, over the doormat, in the box
21 not painted, natural mortar colour
22 smooth plaster, not painted
23 not painted, natural plaster colour
24 metal frame
25 except the kitchens of the caretaker lodges
26 in the apartments
27 visible on the photos of 12 June 1933 and February 1934
28 with reserves
29 natural stone with veining
30 not painted, colour of the material

Source: Atelier Saint-Dismas SA

Summary table of the original aspect (1930–32) – 2 and 4, rue Saint-Laurent, communal areas

painted surface	colour ~	description
stairwells, metallic elements (see note 10)		mid grey
lifts, angled metal profile with the north wall		mid grey
lifts, doors, exterior surfaces (see note 11)	replaced 1975	mid grey
from 2nd, 4th, and 6th storey, exterior of the spiral stairways (see note 12)		mid grey
plaster ceilings of storeys 1, 2, 4, and 6		mid grey
intermediate landings, painted plinths, south wall (see note 13)		mid grey
skylights, metal profile, north-south surfaces, upper and lower		mid grey
skylights, south wall, painted slab ends		mid grey
skylights, 8th, upper cornice in wood		mid grey
8th storey, dumb-waiter cross-bar, on upper metal profile		mid grey
8-9th, metallic stairways for wagon access		mid grey
halls, south doors in glass brick panels		mid grey
north ground floor corridor, doors, glazing frame and cabinets		mid grey
eastern caves, east-west corridor, metal doors		mid grey
laundry, back of the communicating door		mid grey
laundry, interior surface of the metal facade		mid grey
garages, back of the tilting metal doors		mid grey
garages, faces of the interior metal doors		mid grey
garages, backs of the interior metal doors		mid grey
skylights, vaults, metal parts (1975) (see note 14)	created 1975	mid grey
north entrances, doors and glazing frame, interiors		dark brown
north entrances, exterior face of internal doors		dark brown
halls, entrance airlock, light box framework		dark brown
halls, metal columns		dark brown
halls, doors to east and west utility rooms		dark brown
halls, radiators		dark brown
stairways, skylights, DIN north-south		dark brown
apartment doors, metal door frames		dark brown
stairwells, repainting of refuse chutes		dark brown
entrance halls, wall opposite letter boxes		beige
storeys, north wall		beige
storeys, No. 2 west wall; No. 4 east wall		beige
lift cages, skylights, south wall		beige
metal glazing frames of bathrooms (see note 15)		beige
caretaker lodges, kitchen glazing frames (see note 16)		beige
door splays of the north, south, and west walls (see note 17)		beige
skylights, 8th storey, exterior walls (see note 18)		beige

painted surface	colour ~	description
stairwells, east, south, and west walls		light blue
8-9th storey, wagon access stairway, walls		light blue
stairway walls, east and west door splays		light blue
skylights, 8th storey, top of the walls of the stairways		light blue
halls, ground floor ceilings, south		light blue
halls, walls, letter box side		sea green
halls, plant enclosures, ceilings		sea green
halls, plant enclosures, ceilings, metal frames (see note 19)		sea green
halls, plant enclosures, radiators		sea green
halls, entrance air-locks, light box ceilings (see note 20)		sea green
laundry walls (trowelled cement mortar) (see note 21)		grey
caves east, interior walls (caves) render (see note 21)		grey
garages, walls (trowelled cement mortar) (see note 21)		grey
garages, floors, cement mortar screed (see note 21)		grey
halls, mortar joints of the south glass brick wall (see note 21)		grey
eastern caves, north-south corridor, smooth walls (see note 22)		white
eastern caves, internal plaster partitions (see note 23)		white
eastern caves, plaster ceilings (in the caves) (see note 23)		white
laundry, smooth plaster ceiling (see note 23)		white
commerces north-west, interior, bays and glazed doors (see note 24)		light blue
ground floor north, apartments and storerooms, glazing frames (see note 25)		light blue
from 1st to 9th storey, metal window frames (see note 26)		light blue
entrance halls, north ceilings		beige
8th storey, ceiling over stairways (to the south)		beige
ground floor, north corridor, ceiling		beige
stairwells, metal handrails	±, + polished	chrome
skylights, tubular metal lights	±, + polished	chrome
central communal, east-west corridor, walls		light grey
caves east, east-west corridors, walls		light grey
caves east, east-west corridors, walls		dark grey
landings, skirtings of grey tile		black
apartment doors, surfaces stained and varnished (see note 27)		brown
hall No. 2, north-east door, inscription *CONCIERGE*		yellow ochre
halls, plant enclosures, water containers, interior walls		blue
caves, cave doors (both faces) (see note 28)		beige
halls, plant enclosures, walls, travertine panels		light beige
ground floor, north corridor, ceiling (see note 29)		beige
caves, cave doors (both faces) (see note 30)		beige

	No.	Sample	Stratigraphy: succession of paint layers from outer to inner (under normal and UV light)	MEB	Original colour
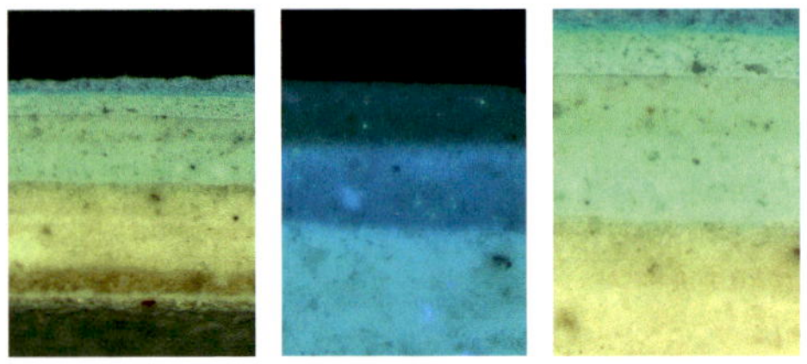	001	Stairwell at No. 2, landing between the 7th and 8th floor, south wall, plasterwork support	Succession of blues (1, 2), then pale greens (3, 4 show different binders under UV) on plaster (5abc, 6), constituted of zones. 5c could contain a primer?	–	4ab
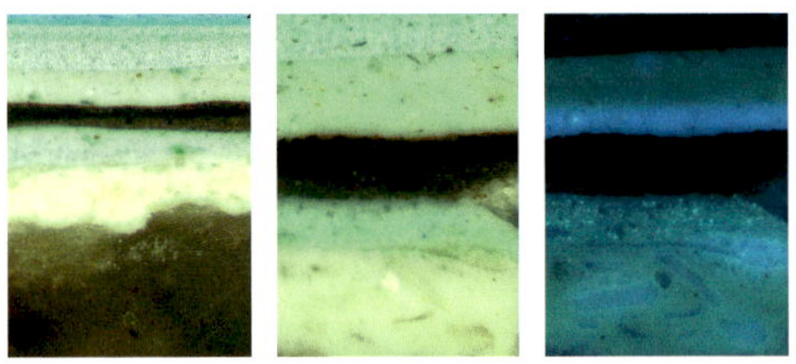	002	Stairwell at No. 2, landing between the 7th and 8th floor, east wall, north side of the waste chute	Succession of blue layers (1, 2, 3), then greens (4, 5), then dark (6 abc), pale turquoise blue (7), plaster (8), on transparent glue (9)?	–	7; 6 for the chute
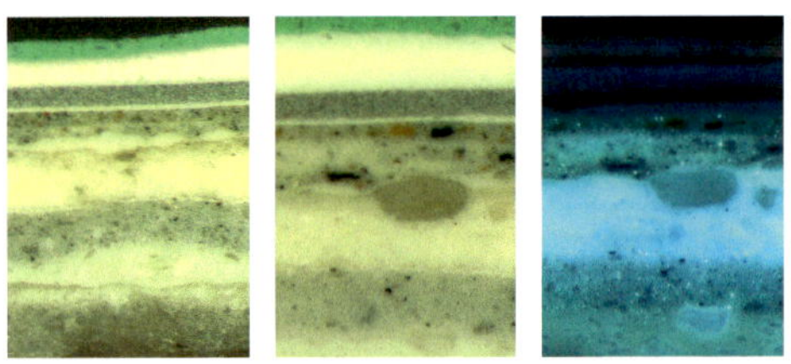	003	Stairwell at No. 2, 6th floor, west side, rounded exterior of the wall to the spiral staircase	Vivid green (1) on beige-white (2), then medium grey (3a, b undercoat same binder under UV), mottled grey-beige (4a), fine beige, undercoat (4b), coarse beige (5), light grey (6), beige (7) on plaster (8)	–	6
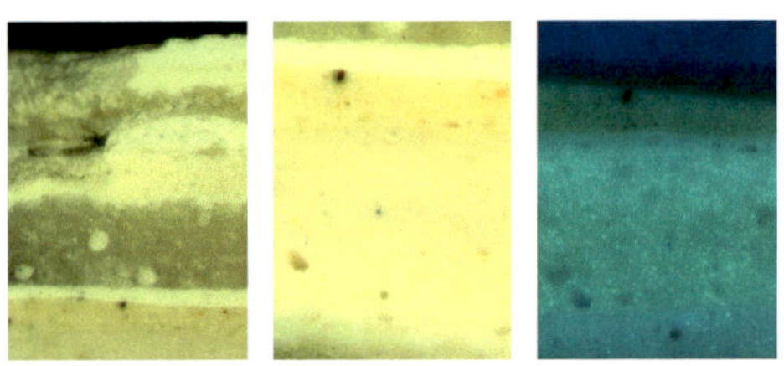	004	Stairwell at No. 2, 1st floor, north side, plasterwork support	Succession of white and beige layers, finally beige on plaster (9, 10)	–	8ab
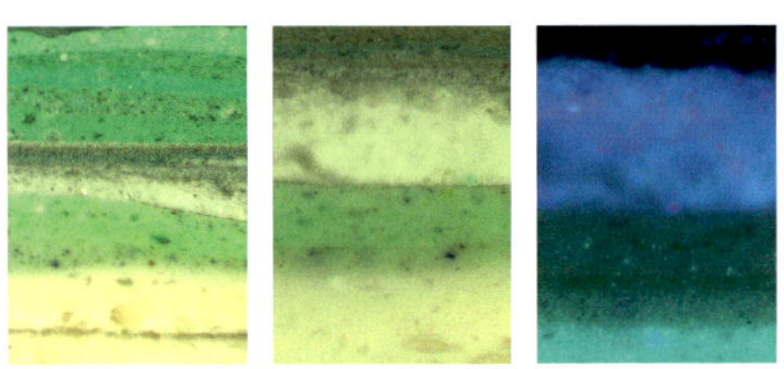	005	Entrance hall at No. 2, east side, plasterwork support	Succession of 4 layers of turquoise and green hues (1 to 5), then grey on coarse white (6, 7, 8, 9), greens (10ab), beige (11ab) on a layer of transparent glue? on plaster (12)	–	10 ab

	No.	Sample	Stratigraphy: succession of paint layers from outer to inner (under normal and UV light)	MEB	Original colour
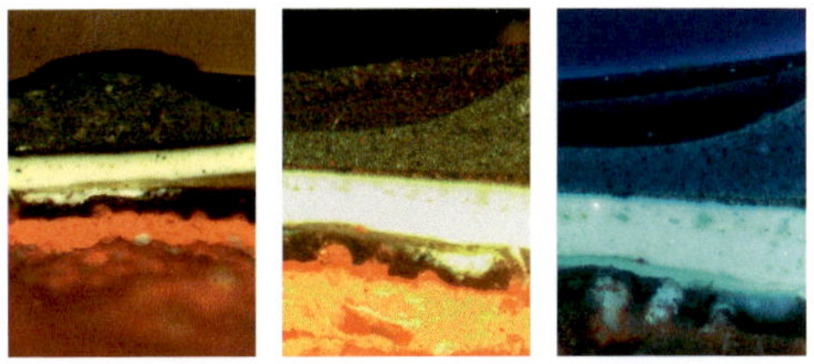	006	Entrance hall at No. 2, central steel column	Black (1), dark grey (2), fine black (3), beige-white (4), transparent primer layer (5), brown (6), Minium (anti-corrosion primer) on the metal	–	6
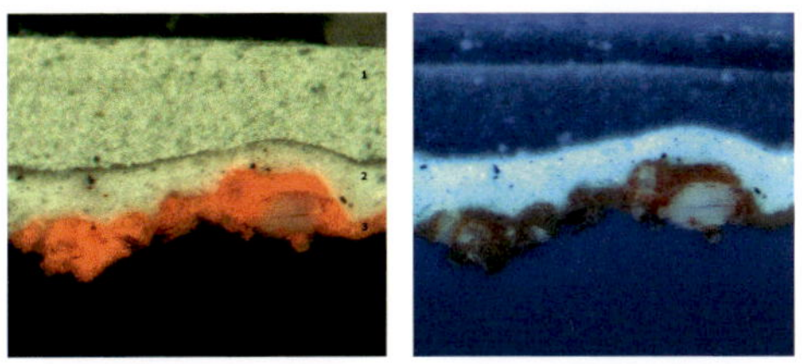	007	Entrance hall at No. 2, metalwork of the staircase to the south of the structure	Metallic grey (1), light grey mat (2), Minium (anti-corrosion primer) on the metal	–	2
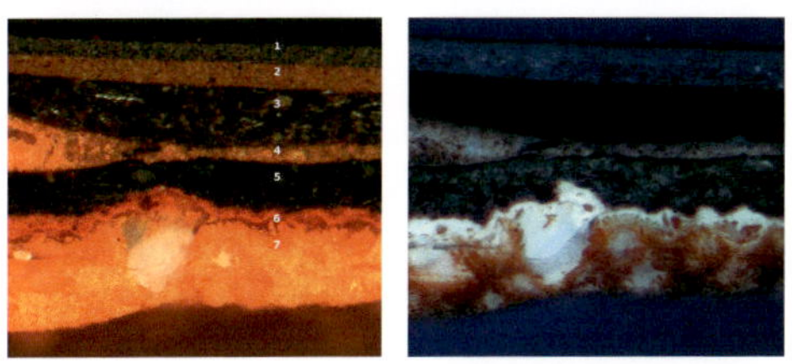	008	North balcony, large duplex at 3rd floor, of No. 2, north facade, metal side	Mat black (1), mat brown (2), coarse black layer (3), minium? (4) dark green (5), quartz, barium sulphate + organic colouring red undercoat (6), minium + iron oxide, Minium (anti-corrosion primer) on metal	(5) Si, Ba, S, (K) (6) Fe, Pb, (7) Pb	5
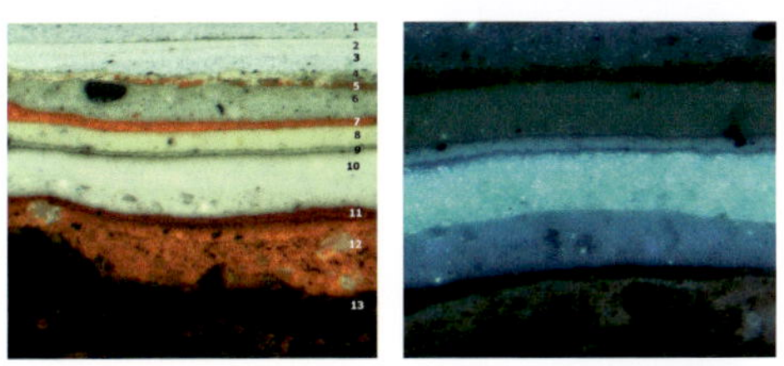	009	North balcony, large duplex at 3rd floor, of No. 2, metal balcony interior, west side	Succession of turquoises (1, 2, 3, 4), minium (anti-corrosion primer) (5) turquoise (6 ab), minium (7) pale green (8), undercoat (9), pale turquoise-green (10a = green2: zinc oxide + organic colouring), (10b = green1: barium sulphate (coarse grains) + zinc oxide + organic colouring turquoise green) minium (11), minium + rust (12), steel and rust (13)	(10b = green1: Zn, S, Ba) 10b white grain: S, Ba) (10a = green2: Zn)	10 ab
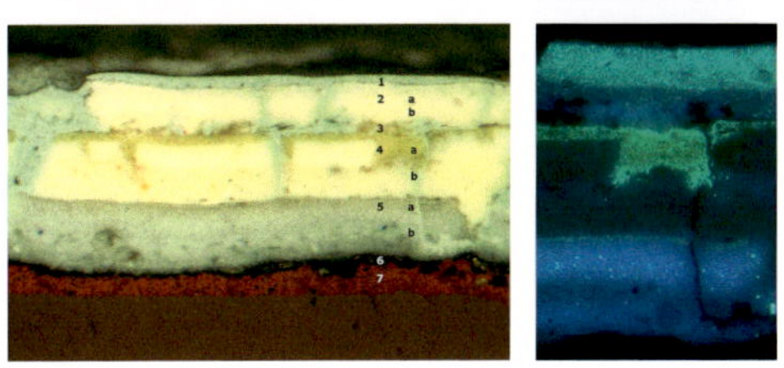	010	Inspection of large duplex at 3rd floor, of No. 2, north interior, window frame	Blue, this layer is bleeding into the crazed underlying layers (1) on white (2), then yellowed transparent layer (3), beige (4 ab) on blue-grey (5 ab) fine black (6), dark red (7) Minium + ochre?	–	5 ab

	No.	Sample	Stratigraphy: succession of paint layers from outer to inner (under normal and UV light)	MEB	Original colour
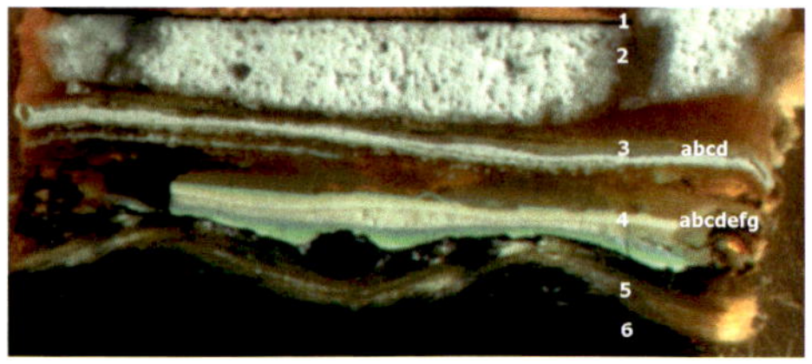	011	Inspection of large duplex at 3rd floor, of No. 2, north-west room, south column	black paint (1), white layer (2), 3 layers coarse paper (3 abc) jute? each one painted white, 7 very fine paint layers: green, beige, two different whites, pale blue, pale green, white (4 abcdefg), g = undercoat of green, hessian? painted dark brown (5), animal hair padding (horse, bull, etc.) black, white, jute, cotton + ? (6). Summary: the column had been wrapped with animal hair padding, horse or bull, assorted fibres, then re-covered with hessian, painted black, then in different colours, covered with white painted wallpaper, and then finally covered with a thick white layer and painted black.	–	hessian painted dark brown (5)
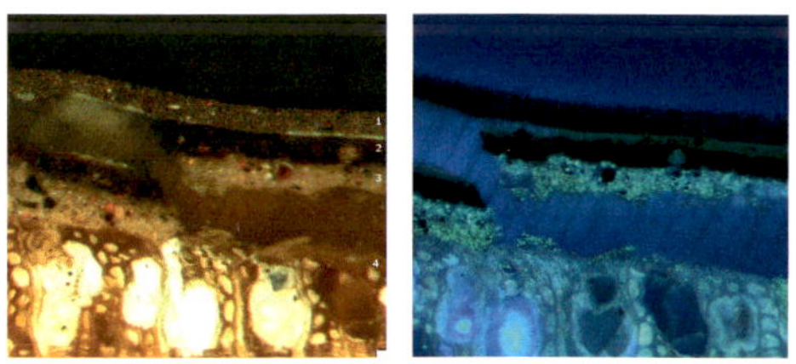	012	Inspection of large duplex, 2nd floor, at No. 2, interior of the wooden door in the recess beneath the staircase to the 3rd floor	Dark brown (1), warm reddish brown (2), beige undercoat (3) (pore-filler?), wood (4)	–	2

Source: Anne Rinuy and Martine Degli Agosti, *Stratigraphic examination of samples 001–012*, Art and History Museum laboratory, Geneva, October 2006, Laboratory file No.: HI 2006–304.

p. 149
No. 2, rue Saint-Laurent, eighth floor, view from the landing, 8 April 2011.

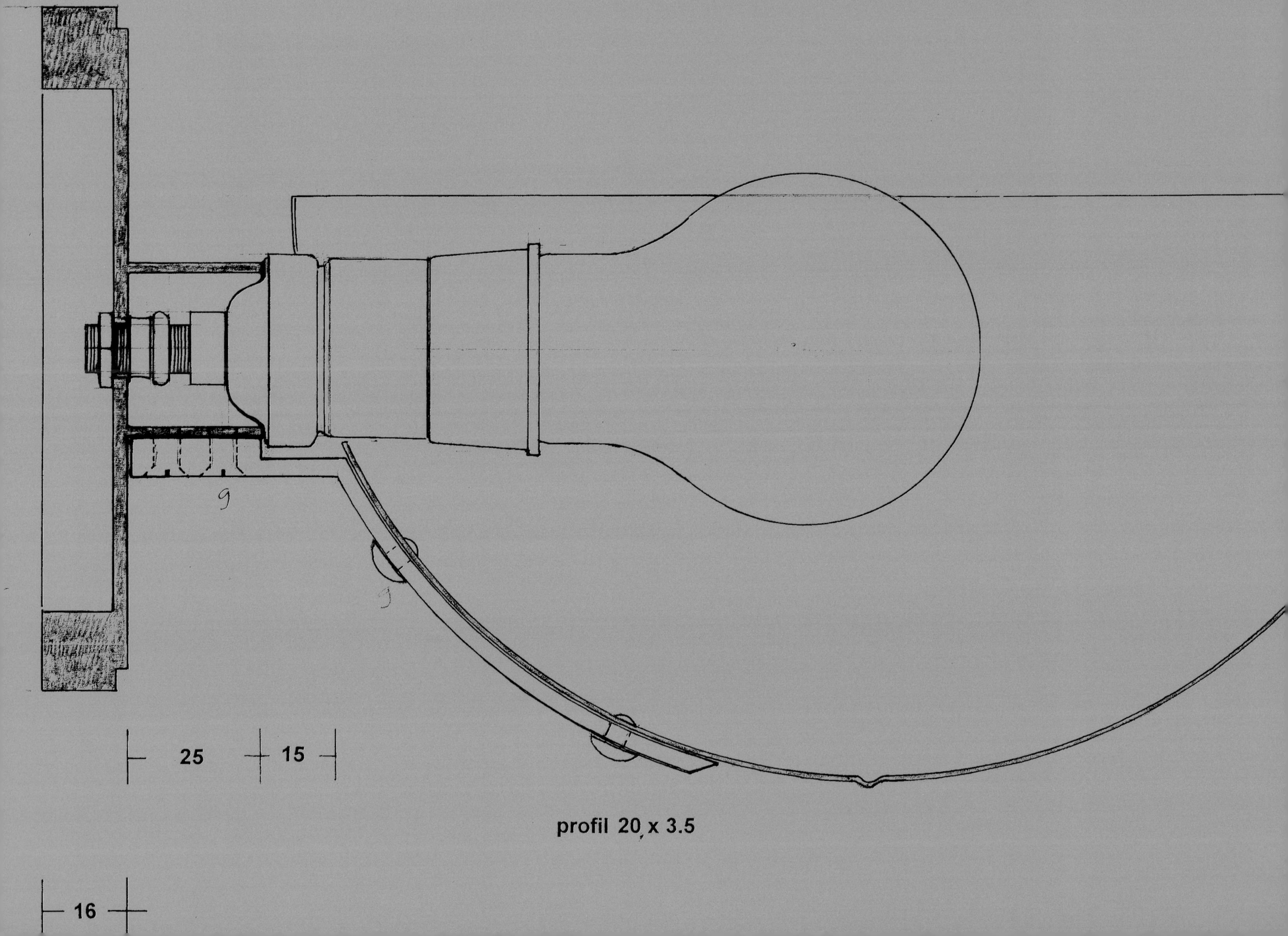

25
15
profil 20 x 3.5
16

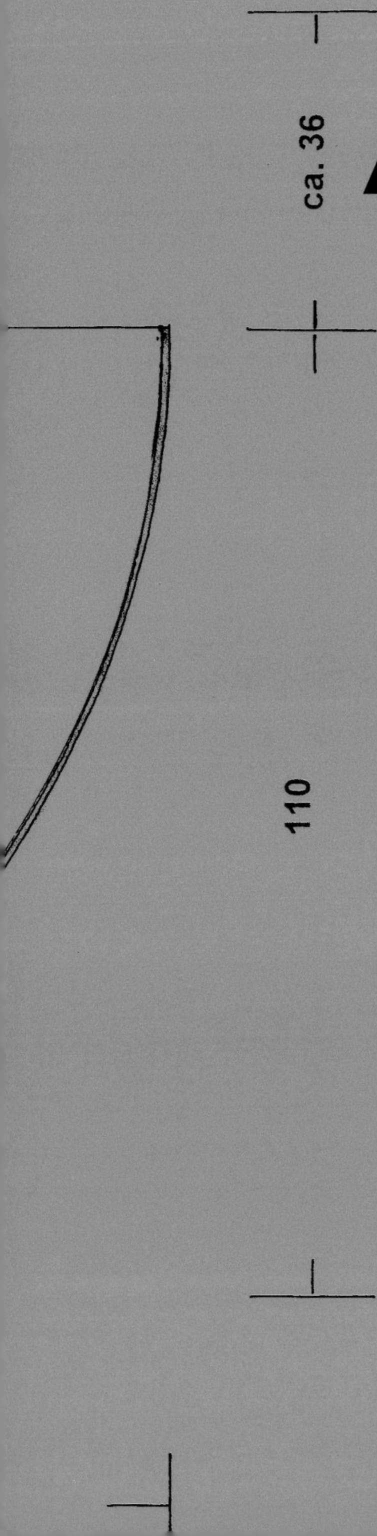

ANNEXES

Chronology
Catherine Courtiau

1925
The Pavillon de l'Esprit Nouveau created by Le Corbusier and Pierre Jeanneret at the International Exhibition of Modern Industrial and Decorative Arts in Paris. An entire "immeuble-villas" unit with hanging garden, a concept foreshadowing the Geneva projects. Perhaps the first meeting with Edmond Wanner, a winning exhibitor.

1926
Le Corbusier's father, Georges-Edouard Jeanneret, died 13 January at Corseaux, in the Villa le Lac, the small house on Lake Geneva that the son had just built for his parents. His mother, Marie-Charlotte-Amélie Jeanneret-Perret, lived there until her death on 15 February 1960, at the age of 100 years. His brother Albert remained there from 1939 to 1971.

1927
Weissenhof City Exhibition (Weissenhofsiedlung) organized by the Deutscher Werkbund in Stuttgart. Le Corbusier and Pierre Jeanneret exhibited two houses there. Edmond Wanner came to visit the exhibition. The "five points of a new architecture" were announced in the exhibition publication.

1928
12 April, signature of the contract between Le Corbusier and the contractor and landowner Edmond Wanner[1]. Le Corbusier and Pierre Jeanneret prepared the first projects for housing on the rue de l'Athénée. Wanner reserved the right to study the detail and submit changes for the architects' approval, manage the site work, and oversee finances.
The aim was to create "immeubles-villas", compact house clusters. The architects proposed an initial building style with a central corridor, a type of indoor street, used subsequently at the "Cité radieuse" in Marseille.
The second proposal was to create buildings with inside walkways, called "open galleries", comprising a succession of small duplex apartments. Wanner foresaw the use of Solomite[2], panels of compressed straw reinforced by galvanised steel wires bound together by cement or plaster, for which he was the manufacturer. Correspondence between Meyfarth[3], one of the directors of the Sécheron Workshops, and Wanner indicates that it was probably the first agreement between these enterprises to proceed with the industrial production of Solomite, and also for the use of Exotherme electrodes for the welding of metal structures, a technique invented by Sécheron.
In June, Wanner informed Le Corbusier of a change of site location, notably for financial reasons. He proposed the land at rue de la Terrassière belonging to his mother[4].
The first projects involved the consolidation of four apartments around a central staircase combined with two levels of hanging gardens, a configuration that could be repeated infinitely, either horizontally or vertically.

1929
Construction of the Villa Ruf at 12, chemin des Manons, Grand-Saconnex, for Jean Ruf, an engineer at the Sécheron Workshops. Francis Quétant was ultimately responsible for its implementation, while Le Corbusier and Pierre Jeanneret had developed the initial sketches and plans. Several protagonists of the Clarté building were involved with it: Edmond Wanner and his employee Quétant, in collaboration with Boris Nazarieff. Several of its construction elements were also applied at Clarté, notably, Solomite panels, long windows, the spiral cast-iron staircase, and the roof terrace.

1930
At Clarté, Le Corbusier and Pierre Jeanneret had initially reused the idea of a central corridor, aligning the balconies of two longitudinal facades at the same level. The project evolved and the galleries were staggered, allowing each dwelling, duplex or single-level, full or partial storey width, to benefit from a balcony. The median corridor was abandoned in favour of a broad central staircase for each corridor of the building. Finally, on 30 August, Wanner filed the application for a building permit (No. 1004).

1931
The building permit was issued on 30 May 1931, subject to some changes, notably the location of storerooms at ground level. The building's size exceeded the height of twenty-one metres authorised in this area, but subtle changes to the plans and the dimensions of the upper storey (setting back the facades to construct an attic) provided a solution. Wanner asked Le Corbusier to fit out the attic as artist studios, to be transformed into apartments once permission had been obtained. Set back from the general facades and thus benefiting from large terraces originally intended for all inhabitants, the attic was rented to Quétant. The illegal habitation of this "penthouse" saddled Wanner with a long legal procedure, which however resulted in a very advantageous arrangement for him[5].
The development plan adopted on 2 June by the city authority foresaw the subdivision of the entire plot of land, including the Clarté building site (see plan pp. 22–23).
The land, known as the Villereuse triangle, consisted of soft ground and hence presented a structural stability problem. It was therefore necessary to hire a specialist to design and construct a raft foundation. The engineer Robert Maillart was employed to undertake this work[6].
Following assembly of the metal frame, Wanner ordered the construction of floor-slabs working from top to bottom, but following an accident, this procedure was reversed.
An initial report by Mauritius Bremond, dated 15 October 1931, of an evaluation carried out at the request of John Torcapel, put into

question the stability of the outer gallery structure.

1932–33

The second expert report by Mauritius Bremond. Responsibility for the defects in the gallery structure was passed from Wanner to Torcapel, then from Torcapel to his subcontractor Toso-Badel.
Peter Scheidegger, architect, manager of the Zurich-based furniture company Wohnbedarf, occupied the arcade on the Adrien-Lachenal side of the building's ground floor, under the name of "Ameublement-Typ" from June 1932 to July 1933. This branch organised an exhibition spread over two floors at 4, rue Saint-Laurent from 25 May to 15 June 1932. Various interior decorators, including Gustavus Adolphus Hufschmid and Else Hamann, took this opportunity to furnish several apartments.
Construction of Clarté was completed in August 1932.
This was followed by photographic sessions undertaken by Paul Boissonnas and Frank-Henri Jullien, at Wanner's request in 1932 and 1933, and by Hans Finsler on behalf of Wohnbedarf in 1933. The following year, Ms. Meyfarth ordered a new series of photos to be taken by Jullien.

1953–54

Clarity renovation by architect Marc-Joseph Saugey. Saugey attended, together with Pascal Häusermann and Bruno Camoletti, a conference chaired by Le Corbusier. He asked him about the colour of the balconies. Le Corbusier answered Saugey saying that he could do as he wished, that the building had simply to live, that it was necessary to ensure freedom in the organisation of apartments and the adjacent floors, which were strong enough to allow the placing of walls where required. It was a question of not mummifying the building[7]. In November 1953, Saugey lodged an application for the fitting out of four shops on the site of the current restaurant.[8]
Saugey changed the glazed roof of a shed for a conventional roof, added metal flashing, because of waterproofing problems, and overlaid the wooden floors of the galleries with asphalt. According to additional information from Eric-James Favre-Bulle of the atelier Saint-Dismas, Saugey commissioned two large murals of abstract expressionist style, by the artist Georges Aubert, a childhood friend of Le Corbusier. These paintings, realised in 1953, in the entrance halls, on the wall opposite the letter boxes[9], disappeared during the 1975–77 restoration work.

1968

Threatened with demolition by real estate speculators, the Clarté building was bought by the Federation of Swiss Architects (FAS), or, in other words, by about sixty architect shareholders.

1975–77

Interventions by Pascal Häusermann and Bruno Camoletti[10] who, in 1975, bought the majority of shares in the Clarté building, through their contacts with the banks, notably with René Weibel, CEO of Rentenanstalt (now Swiss Life).
On 25 August 1975, Bruno Camoletti lodged an application (D68816) for permission to build. This was granted on 15 October of that year. During the restoration work, the architects proceeded with technical renovations (heating, electricity, sanitation system), the replacement of bottle glass tiles in the stairwells by square glass tiles, and the division of the penthouse apartment into two units[11]. They removed the asphalt and asbestos cement over the wooden slats of balconies that Saugey had specified, because lack of air was causing the wood to rot. They replaced the canvas awnings and wooden blinds, and eliminated the waste incinerator. Coal heating was replaced by an oil-fired system. The architects created a restaurant on the ground floor, on the site occupied by the arcades and two garages.
This restoration was successful, and took place without too many constraints. Häusermann and Camoletti had a free hand and could make quick decisions. They benefited from contact with Charlotte Perriand, Wanner, and Torcapel.

1982

First monograph on the Clarté building[12].

1986

12 November: classification of the Clarté building as a historic monument by the State Council of the canton of Geneva (MC-c219).

1987

From 5 to 30 May: exhibition in the Clarté building, "Le Corbusier in Geneva 1922–1932", accompanied by a publication.

2003

9 December: Authorisation by the Foundation for Asset Valuation of the Cantonal Bank of Geneva to study the restoration of the building envelope.
16 December: report of the Federal Commission for historical monuments, with its recommendations.

2004

7 September: The General Assembly of the Clarté building's residents' association decides to accept the recommendations of the architects funded by the Valuation Foundation and to accede to the mandate for a definitive study with a view to applying for a building permit.
17 December: Building permit requested.

2005

24 June: building permit approved.

2006

January: facade restoration prototype (second storey south duplex at No. 4).

From 2003 to 2006, the architect Laurent Chenu undertakes an exhaustive inventory of surveys and plans of Clarté, by mandate of the Office of Heritage Buildings and Sites, State of Geneva.

2007

January: balcony restoration prototype.

4 June: Restoration work begun by installation of scaffolding.

2010

In summer, completion of the external restoration work.

2011

Partitioning for fire protection on the ground floor in accordance with the safety standards.

2012

Warranty work on roller blinds of the duplex apartments; replacement of the slides.

2016

Inclusion on the UNESCO World Heritage list.

1 12 April 1928 – Contract between Edmond Wanner, and Le Corbusier and Pierre Jeanneret (FLC Paris, H2-18-25): Construction of 75,000 m^3 of buildings until the end of 1929. Payment fr. 5,000 to launch the undertaking and enable talks with financiers.

2 27 February 1928 – Edmond Wanner to Le Corbusier (FLC Paris, H2-18-6): Construction of buildings through separate companies for each of them. "The two principals shall be the Solomite Production Company, which for the moment I am solely responsible for, and Wanner & Co. a business I own with my uncle [Felix Wanner], who does not share my interests from an architectural point of view. ... The construction is done by myself, as owner and general building contractor. The constructions are ordered from me by a client or by an architect, myself operating as a general contractor and building in accordance with your plans. ... I am seeking a well located plot of land."

3 9 March 1928 – Meyfarth to Wanner (Archives of the City of Geneva, ongoing series, SD 4.44), "rental to Wanner of a plot of land, with access to the SBB railway connection, avenue Blanc [Sécheron Workshops] for building a small Solomite building for the treatment of straw allowing the fabrication of so-called Solomite panels." Information kindly sent by Philippe Velay. – In February 1934, Ms. Meyfarth ordered multiple shots of the building by Geneva photographer Frank-Henri Jullien.

4 19 June 1928 – Edmond Wanner to Le Corbusier (FLC Paris, H2-18-29): "The construction of all planned developments would be of great interest, but the cost of the operation, which would be about 6 million Swiss francs, for the moment seems to me impractical, since I do not have the means available to undertake this scale of construction. Alternatively, as I've said, I have land at my disposal where I would like to construct relatively low-cost dwellings, each on the order of four to five rooms. My idea, I wish this year to put in place a group of four luxury buildings and a set of small groups of apartments (the latter on the land of which I spoke)."

5 Initially, he had anticipated a fine of fr. 500, together with an annual payment of fr. 4000, from the year 1931, and this over a thirty year period, together with the demolition of the buildings in question. Finally, this penalty was reduced to a fine of fr. 100 – and a payment of fr. 1000 – for 1932 only, the buildings in question being allowed to remain!

6 Plans dating from 18 March and modified on 30 April and 30 June 1931.

7 Meeting with Pascal Häusermann on 10 April 2008.

8 Information from Philippe Velay.

9 Information from Maurice Besset. – Stéphanie Pallini, "Georges Aubert, un relais de purisme en Suisse romande", in *Le Corbusier – La Suisse, les Suisses*, Paris: 2006, p. 144. Editions de la Villette.

10 Meeting with Pascal Häusermann and Bruno Camoletti, 21 May 2008.

11 Subsequently, these penthouse dwellings were gradually abandoned. Their condition became alarming, particularly due to the deterioration of the waterproofing and the structure of the roof.

12 Published under the auspices of the Société d'histoire de l'art en Suisse in the series *Les Guides de monuments suisses*, série 32, no. 319: Catherine Courtiau, *L'immeuble Clarté Genève. Le Corbusier – 1931/32*, Berne: 1982.

Regulations for co-owners 2008

Extracts: articles concerning maintenance and conservation

1997 Edition, developed by the Association of apartment owners (GPA) of the Geneva association for property owners (CGI) and the Society of Geneva property managers (SR)

(...)

Article 4 – Private Areas

Exclusive right applies in general to any component or facility located inside the premises, which can be modified or removed without compromising the existence, strength, structure or appearance inside or outside the building, without damaging public areas, or restricting the exercise of the same rights of other owners. It shall include:

a) the floor, screed, parquet, tiles or other coverings with the exclusion of the slab , its insulation and its embedded floor heating coils;

b) the ceiling and its coating, excluding insulation and the supporting elements of the upper slab;

c) the partitions and other separations, excluding facade walls, load-bearing walls that cross communal areas, partition walls and courtyards of the units and various ducts that pass through the entire building;

d) all interior and exterior carpentry, including access doors to private areas, windows and glazed doors, as well as coatings and balustrades of terraces and balconies;

e) the blinds, shutters, textile awnings, and their mechanisms;

f) the sanitary fixtures and fittings;

g) the electrical installations: radio, television, telephone, intercom, network, etc.;

h) the individual heating meters, the valves and coatings, including the painting of heating installations;

i) the kitchen fixtures and fittings;

j) the pipes, ducts, conduits, and services of any kind from their principal connection, allocated for the exclusive use of the premises, excluding those that transit the premises;

k) the individual fireplaces, their ducts, stacks and associated metalwork.

Article 5 – Communal areas

In general, the communal areas comprise all elements of the building including all installations and accessories that equip them and to which are not assigned an exclusive right. These include:

a) all of the land or the property: the walls, fences, railings and gates that delimit the property; the external fixtures and fittings;

b) in general, the fabric of the building (i.e., including balconies and terraces that are not for the exclusive use of another residential unit, slabs, roof, etc.) including its waterproofing and insulation;

c) the foundations, the facades, and their accessories, as well as the load-bearing walls and walls separating the individual residential units;

d) the entrances and hallways of buildings, the staircases, stairwells, the staircase landings;

e) the utility rooms, courtyards, ventilation and chimney ducts and pipes that are not reserved for the exclusive use of one individual residential unit;

f) the facilities and pipes providing heating, cooling and hot water for the entire building;

g) the pipes, ducts, conduits, mains and services of any kind from and including their connection to the public network to the junction box serving the networks of the individual residential units;

h) the lifts, lift shafts and their accessories;

i) the waste disposal facilities and the areas reserved for their use, the garages for bicycles and baby carriages, the laundries and their equipment, the collective meters and antennas of any kind, the plant rooms of service installations, the blast protection shelter and their accessories, the electrical installations, plumbing, metalwork, carpentry, glazing, mailboxes and the other equipment and accessories of the communal areas;

j) the caretaker's lodges and its annexes, if they are stated in the property association's specification.

Chapter III – Rights and obligations of the co-owners

A. Private areas

Article 6 – Usage

Each owner is free to use, as intended, the utility areas upon which he has an exclusive right, but only to the extent where it affects neither the same rights of other co-owners nor the interests of the condominium.

Notwithstanding, they must not:

a) change the destination of the utility areas on which they have an exclusive right, without the consent of a double majority of the General Assembly of co-owners as stipulated in Article 37 of the current regulations;

b) overload the floor of the utility areas;

c) store inflammable or explosive materials in the building;

d) cause humidity or flooding (in particular, by washing using large quantities of water);

e) display any poster or banner of any kind whatsoever at windows, balconies, or external parts of the buildings;

f) changing the external appearance of the premises;

g) install anything on the balconies and loggias likely to exceed the height of the safety barrier, including parabolic antenna.

He may, under the same conditions, equip his premises as he pleases, except for all that is located in the visible external parts, such as loggias, terraces, canvas awnings, etc., which must be maintained in their initial configuration and location.

The co-owners having exclusive rights to the roof dwellings must:

h) not undertake work or carry out installations that can harm the waterproofing of the roof slab or overload it;

i) cultivate plants only in containers with anti-root protection and ensure that vegetation does not exceed a height of four metres and does not extend beyond the facade.

The co-owners having exclusive rights to the ground floor gardens must:
j) refrain from any misuse of the garden causing significant inconvenience to the other co-owners;
k) for the gardens located above the common garage, not plant species other than small shrubs whose roots shall not damage the waterproofing of the garage structure.

The doors leading to private areas, the windows, blinds, shutters, etc., shall be maintained in good condition by their respective owners.

However, repainting of the exterior woodwork or replacement of any of these elements may be included in a general maintenance operation decided by a simple majority under Article 36 of this Regulation.

The owners and beneficiaries of cellars, garages and various utility rooms located in shelters that can be requisitioned by the competent authorities must strictly comply with their respective requirements and injunctions.

Article 7 – Fittings and fixings
Subject to the reservations set out in this Regulation, each co-owner is free to install fittings and fixings in his or her private areas, under his or her responsibility.

The co-owner who intends to undertake work other than that of routine maintenance is required to submit prior notification in writing to the administrator stating the nature and programme of the works, in order to obtain authorisation. He must also take all necessary measures to avoid and minimize the nuisance and damage to public areas and to the units of other co-owners. In case of any damage caused, he assumes responsibility for reinstatement.

The administrator must grant an authorisation, provided that the proposed work will not affect the common areas, the exclusive rights of other owners and do not involve any increase in building service fees. If deemed necessary, the administrator can consult the Council, or the Assembly, of co-owners to determine whether these conditions are met.

The work must be performed during the official hours of work, in accordance with the current Regulations of the Public Works Department. The administrator may grant authorisation, subject to payment of a security deposit. The co-owner concerned must also obtain all necessary regulatory approvals before starting their works.

Article 8 – Maintenance and repairs
Each owner shall, at his expense, maintain and repair his private areas to ensure the good condition of the building.

The owners of the balconies, terraces, gardens, etc. shall, at their expense, ensure that these are maintained in a good and orderly condition at all times.

The same obligation applies to those who have exclusive use, or the right to use, the roof terraces, who shall pay particular attention not to damage the waterproof coating on the roof slab, while ensuring, at their expense, regular maintenance, notably of the roof drains, including weeding.

Special provisions and exemptions – detail
(...)
Special provisions for the maintenance of the building, and for works on it, together with safety requirements:
The building was listed as a historic monument by decree of the Geneva State Council on 12 November 1986, and any intervention, even maintenance, is subject to Article 10 and the following, of the regulations regarding the protection of monuments, of nature and of sites.

As part of the restoration of the building carried out during the years 2007 to 2009 special undertakings were necessary to ensure its longevity.

Article 57 – Specific Maintenance of the building ensured and supported by the co-owners' association, this in derogation of certain private prerogatives:
a) Work to be done on an annual basis:
— checking the balconies with cleaning of the support surfaces beneath the gratings,
— checking the rainwater run-off areas and the gutters, with cleaning and rehabilitation if needed, of the roof, 8th and 1st floor terraces,
— checking of wooden shutters and the textile awnings, including maintenance and repair of the motors, mechanisms and runners if required.
Replacement of the roller blinds and the textile awnings remains the responsibility of the owner according to Article 4 para. e) but must comply with the building's existing colours and materials.
b) Work to be carried out on a five-year cycle or less:
— thorough check of the facade's waterproofing seals and their renewal if necessary,
— check the condition of the paint on the facade, particularly in the exposed areas such as all load-bearing elements of the balconies and their bases, at each storey level.

Article 58 – Work done by owners

a) affecting the facade:

It is restated that the entire facade is a central element of the building's design.

All work on the facade (drilling, window vents – modification of openings in particular) is subject to authorisation by the building's administrators, subject to the legal provisions applicable to its listed status.

In as far as the restrictions allow, any approval will be conditional on the works maintaining the facade waterproofing, the longevity of the building and its heritage value.

b) in the communal areas:

All interior installations close to the facade must be movable or removable to allow access to it for any maintenance and or replacement of windows.

The principles of conservation of the interior spaces – Rules of Intervention applicable to the owners – issued by the Department of Construction and Information Technologies – Office of Heritage Buildings and Sites dated 18 January 2008 and approved by the Commission monuments and landmarks 29 January 2008 is an integral part of the regulation governing administration and use.

The co-owners must comply with its requirements regarding any operations in the private areas, subject to the legal provisions applicable to the building's listed status.

Article 59 – Safety requirements – national standards

a) maximum loads to balconies, terraces and interiors:

The installation of any special items such as flower pots, jacuzzi, aquarium or other heavy item shall not exceed the load of two hundred kilos per square metre.

b) fire safety:

The communal areas shall be equipped with fire extinguishers in order to meet the fire protection requirements given by the building permit issued for the restoration works of 2007–2009. This equipment shall be permanently maintained in operating condition.

In the case of restoration works within the private areas, visible supporting columns shall be coated with intumescent fire-resistant paint having a fire resistance of 60 minutes.

During work, the necessary precautions shall be taken to avoid damage to wooden structures and the existing insulation material.

The building's electrical installation was completely renewed during the 2007/2009 restoration in accordance with the applicable standards with regard to all electricity supply to the distribution panel at the interior of each privately owned area. The upgrading of the electrical installation within each privately owned area is the responsibility of each owner.

Excerpts from the Inventory undertaken by the firm of architects Laurent Chenu

Office of Heritage Buildings and Sites, State of Geneva, March 2006

Presentation of the Inventory, by Sabine Nemec-Piguet

Saving the Clarté building, classified as a historical monument in 1986, is as much about its interior spaces, both the communal and private, as its outer shell. Since its construction in 1932, Clarté has suffered multiple interventions. If works to the facades and roofs were fairly well documented, those to the various apartments within the building have been ignored. Various transformations have been made, mainly under the description of routine maintenance: renovations to kitchens and bathrooms, redecorating, together with some cases of important layout changes. The work permits were granted on a case by case basis, without rules for preservation of the building. It was therefore impossible to estimate the impact of those interventions on the architectural value of the building. To remedy this situation, a complete inventory of the interior work has been prepared, apartment by apartment, to assess the state of conservation of typologies and of the original materials. The objective is to precisely determine the applicable rules for protection of a historical monument of international importance, of which the residential function imposes constraints of use.

The study began in 2003 and ended in 2006. It took place in two phases. Initially, the familiarisation and the consultation of archival documents enabled the preparation of a survey "consistent with the original state". Secondly, a systematic tour of the apartments was conducted in the presence of the tenant or owner to record the changes since construction. The visits took place between May 20 and August 11, 2003. Of a total of forty-seven apartments, forty could be visited, nonetheless each type of apartment has been visited and surveyed. This systematic and rigorous work was only possible thanks to the welcome and availability of the residents, both tenants and owners.

The inventory includes the documents described below:

1) A complete list of available archive plans. They include, in particular, references of the John Torcapel collection kept at the gta Institute of ETH Zurich.

2) A record of floor plans "in accordance with the original state" at the time of construction of the building in 1932. These plans have been recreated to scale 1:100, based on archived documents.

3) An account of the apartment visits, including a fact sheet on each visited apartment, an overview, a description, and photographs (as of 2003).

4) A layout plan of each apartment visited, 1:50 scale, with a description of materials (status 2003).

5) An apartment plan (scale 1:50) and a floor plan (scale 1:100) on which are recorded all works that have taken place between 1932 and 2003, with reference to the original plan, according to the colour convention (red: added, yellow: removed). This documentation exists only for those apartments that were visited.

This rigorously documented condition survey has allowed an estimate of the degree of change and preservation of the interior heritage assets. From this analysis it has been possible to draw up rules governing applicable future interventions within the apartments of the Clarté building.

This inventory documentation constitutes an indispensable monitoring tool for the conservation of a listed building. It is available to the building owners and their agents. The restoration specification has been included in the co-owner regulation document, bringing to the attention of each owner the detail of works allowed.

Left: 4, rue Saint-Laurent, third floor and second floor. Right: 2, rue Saint-Laurent, third floor and second floor. Selection of plans showing apartment modifications and transformations by floor, drawn to scale 1:100, January 2004. In black, unchanged original state; in red, transformation by addition; in yellow, transformation by removal.

Principles for conservation of interior areas – rules of intervention for the owner's attention

Appendix to the 2008 regulations for co-owners

Office of Heritage Buildings and Sites of the State of Geneva, 18 January 2008 – Approved by the CMNS, 29 January 2008

Preservation

The Clarté building is a unique achievement in the works of Le Corbusier. In Europe, it is one of the most representative buildings of the Modern Movement, which revolutionised architecture, urbanism and decorative arts after World War II. It is being placed on the UNESCO World Heritage list.

The building, which had suffered from a severe lack of maintenance, underwent a state-of-the-art restoration in 2007–2009 through the efforts of the co-owners and with substantial financial assistance from the Canton of Geneva and from the Confederation under whose protection it is placed.

To sustain these efforts and to preserve the building in the condition which constitute its heritage and cultural identity, a conservation specification has been established, in addition to the legal provisions safeguarding its preservation in accordance with its listed status.

Preservation Conditions

The value of the different apartments that make up the building lies in their diversity (eight different types) and their qualities of: volume, orientation, material, and colour, as well as in the use of each type and the interfaces between them.

While, based on the recognition of these values, one can accept some minor changes or isolated replacements, including sanitary and kitchen equipment, enlargements by modification of room partitions is not desirable.

Comparison between the state of conservation of the apartments that have not undergone this type of transformation and those which have been sometimes extensively transformed shows that ever-changing demands of lifestyle and comfort generally result in irreversible changes of types and of the qualities outlined above, giving rise to an irreversible loss of stylistic, architectural and heritage qualities.

The rules set out below are intended to preserve the authenticity of the building while ensuring the sustainability of the original unique character of each apartment type. They are intended to guide the owner who wishes to make changes within his apartment.

Each of the preservation requirements must be considered holistically. It is not a question of simply giving a list of points to respect, but to offer co-owners the principal elements of a dynamic and coherent conservation philosophy.

The principles are based on a detailed analysis of all the apartments, completed in March 2006 by Laurent Chenu architecture workshop on behalf of the Office of Heritage Buildings and Sites. They are based on the architectural properties of the building components identified through the characteristics of this type of work for the period of the Modern Movement.

Rules Governing Interventions

a) The building's defining outline

Constraints: The Clarté building's layout is not strictly speaking "open plan". The structure of the apartments, the arrangement of the spans, the choice of the different size and positioning of the apartments, heavily influence the building's interior and exterior architecture. The arrangement of three distinct spans around the stairwells provides the distinct and clear definition of the building.

Conditions: Maintenance of divisions per span. No interlinking of habitable spaces shall be allowed between spans or between the apartments.

b) Apartment types and internal circulation

Constraints: The layout of each apartment is based around a clear distinction between day, and night, areas. This distinction structures circulation within the apartment thereby encouraging movement.

Conditions: Maintenance of the distinction between day, and night, areas, maintenance of the expected people movement within each apartment type.

c) Partitioning

Constraints: The size of living spaces is founded on a clear relationship between apartment subdivision and the internal facade structure. Changes to the internal wall partitions are not possible as their positions correspond to the relationship between the internal layout of each apartment type and each functional group of rooms (day-night).

Conditions: Maintenance of the interior partitioning of each functional set of rooms. Maintenance of the rapport between the partitions, the structure and the facades.

d) Storage

Constraints: Each type of apartment generates storage space that is specific to it. Alcoves, fitted wardrobes, "mobile" cupboards, constitute the diversity, the particularity of use and the housing function. They structure each dwelling type.

Conditions: Maintenance of the diversity and the position of storage spaces.

e) Sanitary facilities

Constraints: These are frequently changed elements during the lifetime of a home and the target for many of the interventions undertaken. A change of taps, replacement of tiles and earthenware, enlargement of the "bathroom" surface; these pieces and associated equipment are subject to constant updating due to changing standards of comfort.

Conditions: Possibility to replace and remove sanitary fixings, tiles and earthenware (as long as they are not original, or are original but not in good condition) after prior consultation with the services of the Office of Heritage Buildings and Sites.

f) Kitchens
Constraints: Similarly as for sanitary facilities, the kitchens constitute an area where numerous changes have been made: creation or suppression of partitioning, replacing kitchen furniture, adding equipment, responding to concerns about modernising the home's fixtures and fittings.
Conditions: Possibility to replace kitchen furniture, tiles and earthenware (as long as they are not original, or are original but not in good condition) after prior consultation with the services of the Office of Heritage Buildings and Sites. Maintenance of the kitchen area with the possibility of installing a doorway to the living room for certain types of apartments.

g) Facades, woodwork, metalwork, interior finishes, colours
Constraints: Fortunately the successive renovation and transformation works have allowed the conservation of a significant proportion of the woodwork, interior metalwork and original coatings, together with their restoration or identical replacement. All types of doors (landing, solid, glazed, sliding), cabinets, stairs, parquet floors (patterns and wood), tiles and earthenware (types, colours and materials), wallpapers (texture and colour) and paintings (characteristics and colours) are present in most apartments. However, many fixed lower glazed surfaces had been painted or hidden from view from within the apartments.
Conditions: Maintenance of and, if necessary, restoration of woodwork interiors, metalwork and finishings (as long as they are not original, or are original but not in good condition) after prior consultation with the services of the Office of Heritage Buildings and Sites or with the architect responsible for restoration.

Take particular note of the following conditions:
1) Works to the facade are the responsibility of the co-owners' association. In case of accident requiring replacement of transparent glass it is imperative to use clear insulating glass with brown coloured spacer strip in accordance with the specifications of the architect responsible for restoration or administration of the condominium.

The old original armoured glass in good condition should always be kept as it is of a type becoming unobtainable. If replacement is necessary, one should check whether any of the broken armoured glass pane can be reused, for example for kitchen splash-backs or for balcony doors. Replacement shall be made with the grade or armoured glass specified by the architect responsible for the restoration or administration of the building.

All glazing: facade, interior, mobile or fixed, may in no circumstances be obscured by signs, linings, wall coverings, reflective glass (even added reflective sheets). Fixed furniture shall not be placed against the glass facade in a way that would prevent maintenance. The system adopted for the restoration of facades during the 2007–2008 works must be strictly observed.

The application of paints and sealants to the facade must be made according to the colours and specifications given by the architect responsible for the restoration or the administration of the building. The facade's original metal fittings, handles, counters, latches, sash, roller-blind pulleys, ropes, etc., must be conserved and maintained.

2) All modification or replacement of landing doors shall conform to the model provided by the architect responsible for the restoration or the administration of the building.

3) The original radiators are an integral part of the building's characteristic fixtures and are to be preserved.
In the case of unavoidable replacement due to a defect, or to replace an already modified device, preference will be given to a model whose references will be provided by the architect responsible for the restoration or the administration of the building.

4) The choice of colours (colour combination) plays a key role in the work of Le Corbusier, for the Clarté building as for his other works. The colours of the facade and communal areas were carefully and attentively restored during the restoration of 2007–2009. Their conservation is imperative. The interior facade colour (grey – sky blue) is a part of that and shall therefore be maintained.
The same consideration applies to the "Salubra" wallpaper used by Le Corbusier. The architect responsible for the restoration or the administration of the building retains, for the use of the co-owners, the file of colour analyses as well as the range of suitable colours and wallpapers for any interior redecorations.

5) All original interior design elements (sinks, taps, woodwork, cabinets, curtain rails, skirting-boards, including those against the facade, etc.) must be conserved and maintained according to best practice. Elements that are obsolete to the point of requiring replacement will be recovered by the administration of the building with a view to their eventual restoration and reuse. To this end, the administration

of the condominium must always be contacted before any removal of any original interior design elements.

6) Any localised installation of air conditioning elements must remain invisible from the street. To this end it is recommended to locate the devices on the balcony floor, laterally against the separations (consoles).

h) Original plans

Constraints: Some apartments have been heavily modified. These changes do not justify new interventions that will further distance the apartment from its original condition. *Conditions:* In the case where significant works are planned in a modified apartment, every endeavour shall be made to restore the original elements of spatial distribution, and of interior design.

A document and photographic bibliography, together with a detailed inventory of all the apartments, may be consulted at the Office of Heritage Buildings and Sites, State of Geneva.

Construction of 1931–1932

Technical data

Address
2–4, rue Saint-Laurent,
5, rue Adrien-Lachenal, Geneva
Development plan
plan No. 1137-68, accepted by the State Council 2 June 1931
Plot surface
1,501 m^2
Plan surface
1,187 m^2
Number of storeys
8 storeys + roof apartments and roof terrace with "wagon"
Building permit
No. 1004, authorisation of 30 May 1931
Owner: SI La Clarté
Applicant: Edmond Wanner

List of collaborators

Le Corbusier and Pierre Jeanneret
Designers
Edmond Wanner
Property owner, landowner, entrepreneur and inventor of diverse construction elements
Robert Maillart
Engineer of the foundations and ground slab
John Torcapel
Supervising architect
Francis Quétant
Architect, employed by Edmond Wanner, responsible for design and cost control
Boris Nazarieff
Site foreman
Delessert & Mouchet
Setting out engineers

Enterprises

Badel
Geneva electrical contractor founded in 1903 by Felix Badel, today Badel & Cie: electricity, telephone, motive power
Drivet
Reinforced foundation piles
Alfred Eypper
Tiles, parquet floors
Geneux-Dancet
Waterproofing, "wagon"
H.Grandchamp & Co.
(formerly Maison Buscarlet)
hanging of Salubra wallpaper
"Kernerator"
Waste disposal company, Paris, Licensee of Kerner Incinerator Co. and for the Establishments Ch. Blanc
A duct was provided for waste destined for incineration, of which a waste chute was located on each staircase landing. This installation was condemned during the 1977 works, following a tragic accident, brought to the Geneva court of assises.
W.Krebs & Co. Bern
"Spezialgeschäft für modernen Küchenbedarf" or "Specialist shop for modern kitchenware"
Cabinets, racks, kitchen units of model "Simple" proposed by Edmond Wanner in February 1928
Louis Magnin
Metal flashings, gutterings
Louis Meid
Glazing, installer of windows, sliding windows, Saint-Gobain glass tiles and slabs
Salubra, Grenzach (Germany)
Wallpapers, colour charts created by Le Corbusier in 1931 and from 1957 to 1959
SA des Ateliers de Sécheron
Autogenous electric arc welding with the "Exotherme" system
Solomite SA (Edmond Wanner)
Supply of composite compressed straw panels for partitioning and insulation
F.P. Soudan
Timber frames, beams, cabinet making, "wagon", goods lifts, stairways
B. Toso-Badel
Gallery floors
Vaucher & Cie
Masonry, reinforced concrete
(Edmond) Wanner & Cie
Metal framework, ironwork, steelwork, Solomite, Arki
Société française des ateliers Wanner (Neuilly-sur-Seine)
"Eclair" model tilting doors, built especially for the garage doors of the south side of the Clarté building as well as for the buildings in the rue des Tourelles and the rue Nungesser et Coli
Charles Zanello
Plasterwork

Restoration project of 2007–2011

Technical data

Land registry data
Building C95 and 928, plot 727, sheet 13, Geneva district, Eaux-Vives

Building status
Building classified, by order of the State Council dated 12 November 1986, MS-c 219; under federal protection from 14 May 2007, PF No. 2014; Inclusion on the UNESCO World Heritage list in July 2016.

Owners
Clarté building co-owners' association

Management
Jean Simonin SA, Property management, Geneva

Condition survey – facades
Initial survey allowing concepts of conservation and restoration, 1992–1993. Scale: 1:20. Architects: Inès Lamunière and Patrick Devanthéry. Mandate from the Office of Heritage Buildings and Sites

Condition survey – apartments
Inventory and survey of the apartments, March 2006. Scale: 1:100. Architect: Laurent Chenu. Mandate from the Office of Heritage Buildings and Sites

Restoration design
Office of Heritage Buildings and Sites, Fondation Le Corbusier, Arthur Rüegg, Jacques-Louis de Chambrier

Restoration Architects
Site manager: Jacques-Louis de Chambrier, architect EPFZ-SIA
Assistants: Michael Palffy, architect; Elsa Desaire, designer HES; Emma Read, architect HES
Finance manager: Alain Dutheil, architect

Civil engineer (structure and balconies)
Bureau Pierre Moser, project manager: Igor Berger, civil engineer

Cantonal control
Office of Heritage Buildings and Sites, Sabine Nemec-Piguet, Bernard Zumthor
Service of Heritage Buildings and Sites, Yves Peçon

Consultants
Michel Richard, Fondation Le Corbusier
Arthur Rüegg, Federal expert
Eric Favre-Bulle, Alain Besse (Saint-Dismas workshop), study of colours

Photographic record of the works
Claudio Merlini, Geneva

Building permit
DD 99'620, authorisation of 24 June 2005. Preliminary approval by the Cantonal commission of monuments, nature and sites of 2 February 2005

Cantonal financial aid
1,556,200 CHF

Federal financial aid
1,200,000 CHF

Cost of the works
13'887'365 CHF

List of principal consultants and contractors Preliminary studies / Consultants and engineers

Thermal review
BuRoTeC

Security report
Securiconsult SA

Heating and ventilation engineering
Balestra Galiotto TCC SA

Sanitary engineering
A. Schneider SA

Electrical engineering
Coelec SA

Facade prototype study
EDFM Sàrl

Balcony and facade prototype Consultants and engineers

Provisional electrical installation
Coelec SA

Stone / reinforced concrete investigation – blast cleaning
THR SA

Provisional waterproofing
Cerutti Toitures SA

Temporary scaffolding
Implenia SA

Windows – wood and metal
AAV Contractors SA

Balcony wood coatings
Dasta Charpentes SA

Heating
Balestra Galiotto TCC SA

List of principal contractors

Scaffolding
Von Ro Echafaudages SA

Stonework, reinforced concrete, blast cleaning
THR SA

Metalwork, metal facade elements
Batimétal SA

Natural stone facades
Harry Baerlocher SA

Glass brick walls
Jean-Pierre Conti SA

Balcony wood coatings
Dasta Charpentes SA

Rolling shutters and fabric blinds
Senn SA

Waterproofing – flashing
Dentan Etanchéité SA

Plasterwork and fire-resistant ceilings
Matamoros SA

Interior and exterior paintwork
Matamoros SA

Fire-resistant coatings
Bâti-Rénov. SA

Heating installations
Multi + Therme SA

Ventilation installations
Ventil-Energies Sàrl

Sanitary installations
A. Schneider SA

Electrical installations
Piazzolla Electricité Sàrl

Biographical notes

Catherine Courtiau

The actors of the original construction

Charles-Edouard Jeanneret, alias Le Corbusier (1887–1965)

Charles-Edouard Jeanneret was born in La Chaux-de-Fond, where he attended Charles L'Eplattenier's classes in ornamental composition at art school from 1901. There he met Georges Aubert and Léon Perrin, with whom he remained friends. His father, George-Edouard, was a modest enameller, and his mother, Marie-Charlotte-Amélie Perret, was a pianist. His brother Albert, one year his senior, became a violinist. After his study tours from 1907 to 1911 and internships with the Perret brothers in Paris and with Peter Behrens in Berlin, he taught at the new department of the art school in his hometown and opened his architectural practice.

In 1917, he moved to Paris where he met the painter Amédée Ozenfant. From 1920, the "Esprit Nouveau" era, he was always seeking solutions in the fields of construction and urbanism as well as a synthesis of the major arts: architecture, painting, and sculpture. Under the pseudonym Le Corbusier, his writings ensured the dissemination of his theories and explained his work. He presented it as a "diary" in his eight-volume *Œuvre complète* issued through the course of his career, the first appearing in 1929, the last in 1965, shortly after his death.

He was one of the main initiators of the CIAM (International Congress of Modern Architecture), first held in 1928 at La Sarraz Castle, the home of his admirer, the patron Hélène de Mandrot.

Pierre Jeanneret, his third cousin, joined the agency in 1922 and remained until their temporary separation in 1940. Their collaboration continued in 1950 with the construction of Chandigarh, the new capital of Punjab.

Naturalised a French citizen in 1930, he married Yvonne Gallis (1892–1957), with whom he had no children. On 27 August 1965, a fatal swimming accident in front of his cottage in Roquebrune at Cap Martin brutally interrupted the activity of one of the greatest architects and theorists of the XX century.

Pierre (André) Jeanneret (1896–1967)

Pierre Jeanneret, a native of Geneva, where he lived until 1921, was a brilliant student at the Geneva School of Fine Arts, where in 1915 he won first prizes in architecture, sculpture, and painting. After a period at the studio of the Perret brothers in Paris, he joined his third cousin Le Corbusier in 1922 and became head of the agency until their separation in 1940. They had a great-grandfather in common. The home of his parents in the avenue Calas, Champel, Geneva, remained his pied-à-terre. After the separation – Le Corbusier moved to Vichy – Jeanneret worked initially with Jean Prouvé, then Georges Blanchon and finally Dominique Escorsat. He continued to research lightweight prefabricated transportable housing, and social housing. At the outset he designed furniture, notably with Charlotte Perriand, and then he produced household elements with Denise Varela-Cresswell, marketed under the name "Home equipment".

The collaboration between Le Corbusier and Jeanneret resumed in 1950, thanks to Eugène Claudius-Petit, the French Minister for Reconstruction and Urbanism. The following year, Jeanneret moved to India to concretize the master plan for the new capital of Punjab, Chandigarh, developed by Le Corbusier at the request of Prime Minister Nehru. Jeanneret also designed his own buildings there, in austere conditions, and had furniture by a self-taught workforce, using local materials. He was appointed director of the Chandigarh School of Architecture as well as Architect-Urbanist to the State of Punjab. He returned from India in August 1965 to live in Geneva, where he died on 4 December 1967. His ashes were transported to Chandigarh in April 1970.

All the construction projects, before and after their breakup, were the fruit of a close collaboration between Le Corbusier, who was authoritative and emotional, theoretical and analytic, preoccupied above all by form and by innovation, and Jeanneret, who was a "hands-on" man, sensitive and reserved, concerned with practical, simple, and economical solutions to everyday problems. Through dialogue and the complementarity of their interests, their collaboration was mutually enriching and made their agency one of the most innovative of the XX century.

Edmond Wanner (1898–1965)

The company of this family of entrepreneurs was established in Eaux-Vives, Geneva, in 1853 by Jean Samuel Eugene Wanner (1826–1889) under the name "Serrurerie du bâtiment et Ferronnerie d'art" [1]. His sons Louis (1859–1916) and Felix (1861–1936) took over the workshops in 1889 and formed a partnership to found "Wanner Frères Serrurerie d'art", which by 1900 had more than a hundred employees. The company received the gold medal at the Swiss National Exhibition in Geneva in 1896 and the World Exhibition in Paris in 1900, and the Grand Prix at the Swiss National Exhibition in Berne in 1914.

After Louis's death, his son (Max) Edmond – wrought iron craftsman and entrepreneur with landholdings in Geneva and Algeria – replaced his father as manager alongside his uncle Felix, commercial director, and Jeanne, the latter's sister. The firm took the name of "Wanner & Cie – Ferronnerie d'art" and was awarded the first prize by the jury at the International Exhibition of Modern Industrial and Decorative Arts in 1925 in Paris. In 1945, following the death of his aunt Jeanne, Edmond single-handedly directed this modern enterprise for the production of prefabricated elements (besides the structural metalwork, manufacturing composite compressed straw

Solomite panels, and overhead "Eclair" doors for garages), a business that came to an end after his death.

Wanner created many important metalwork, notably in Geneva in the early 1930s, at the Palais des Nations, the main station, and the Clarté building, for which he was the promoter and project owner. In 1928/29, three years before major construction began at the Clarté site, he had had built, by Quétant in collaboration with Boris Nazarieff, the Villa Ruf at 12, chemin des Manons in Grand-Saconnex, from sketches by Le Corbusier and Jeanneret, who had withdrawn for financial reasons. There, one already finds: sliding windows, a flat roof, Solomite panels, and a spiral staircase.

Wanner founded a subsidiary in Madrid, then another in Algeria, where activity was suddenly interrupted by the war of independence. After two years in prison and the murder in 1959 of two of his sons, Marcel and Jean-Jacques, Wanner returned to Geneva, where he focused on the construction of lightweight aluminium facades. His relationship with Le Corbusier was intense and fruitful, and also tumultuous.

Robert Maillart (1872–1940)

This engineer of Belgian origin, born in Berne, was educated at the ETH Zurich under Karl Wilhelm Ritter between 1890 and 1894[2]. Employed in Berne (1894–96) by the firm Pümpin & Herzog, he designed bridges for the Bière-Apples-Morges railway line. He worked for the Zurich Department of Roads and Bridges (Tiefbauamt) from 1897 to 1899, where he was in charge of the Stauffach bridge project (Stauffacherbrücke) on the Sihl, constructed between 1899 and 1901. His last major project as an employee was the bridge over the Inn at Zuoz, for the reinforced concrete company Froté & Westermann.

In 1902, Maillart moved to Zurich, where he founded his own company, "Maillart & Cie", specialising in building bridges and reinforced concrete elements. From 1908, he developed "mushroom slab construction", and erected halls and industrial buildings in Spain, France, Italy, and, from 1914 to 1918, Russia.

Maillart settled in Geneva in 1919, opened his engineering consultancy, and founded branches in Berne (1924) and Zurich (1929); the headquarters and his family home remained in Geneva. His most notable construction project was the bridge over the Salgina gorge near Schiers in 1930, the first true reinforced concrete bridge in Switzerland, a structure that earned him an international reputation. His expertise prompted John Torcape and Edmond Wanner to call upon him to solve problems posed by the soft ground where the future Clarté building was to be built, for which he designed the reinforced concrete base. In 1936, Maillart built the bridge over the river Arve at Vessy. In 1937 he was elected honorary member of the Royal Institute of British Architects, together with Eugene Freyssinet, the first engineers to receive this high distinction. Then in 1940 he became an honorary member of the Focus Group on Bridges and Structures of the Swiss Society of Engineers and Architects (SIA). At the 1939 national exposition in Zurich, he executed the elegant and ephemeral Zementhalle, a shell structure built with reinforced sprayed concrete.

John Torcapel (1881–1965)

This architect, born in Geneva of French origin, spent two years at the Geneva Schools of Art, according to the application form addressed to the Federation of Swiss Architects (FAS). This is probably a reference to the School of Industrial Arts, which became in 1909 a section of the School of Arts and Crafts. He then worked with various architectural practices. A competition to build a garden city in the district of Mervelet was launched in 1912; the chosen project was that submitted by John Torcapel and his employer, the architect Adolphe Guyonnet. After several further architectural successes he established his own architectural practice in 1925 at 59, rue du Stand, Geneva, and designed a number of detached homes and rental properties, most notably at the corner of rue Henri-Mussard and avenue de Malagnou. In 1926, he became a member of the FAS and the Society of Engineers and Architects (SIA).

From 1930 to 1932, during the construction of Clarté, Torcapel was the supervising architect. He also figured among the building's first residents.

In 1932, he collaborated with Guyonnet on the Saint-Gervais development plan, which led to further projects by Le Corbusier.

Following the 1942 founding of the Geneva School of Architecture, he was named director of one of the studios, where he distinguished himself as a teacher, particularly appreciated for his knowledge and teaching skills.

Finally, his last architectural work, in 1964/65, was the building of the temple of Onex.

Torcapel also devoted himself to painting, printmaking, and drawing. As such, he joined the Swiss Society of Painters, Sculptors and Architects (SPSAS) and the Gottfried Keller Foundation (FGK). In 1908, the Geneva-based Editions d'art et d'architecture published his drawings in *Clochers Savoyards, 25 dessins de John Torcapel,* with a foreword by Henry Baudin. Then, in 1926, Payot published other drawings in the book *Vieilles Maisons, 30 dessins autour de Genève.* His copious work was shown in numerous exhibitions.

Sarkissoff Maurice (1882–1946), Georgian artist and teacher at the School of Industrial Arts, sculpted a portrait of Torcapel, a bronze head now displayed at the Art and History Museum in Geneva.

Francis Quétant (1905–1953)

From 1920 to 1924, Francis Quétant studied at the Geneva School of Fine Arts while, in parallel, being apprenticed to the architects Amedeo Henchoz and Henry Baudin. From 1928 to 1929 this Geneva-based architect-artist of French origin, together with his employer Wanne, and in collaboration with his brother Boris Nazarieff, worked on the Villa Ruf at 12, chemin des Manons in Grand-Saconnex. It was designed according to the sketches of Le Corbusier and Pierre Jeanneret, who had abandoned the project for financial reasons. In 1931 he became a founding member of the Groupe pour l'Architecture Nouvelle in Geneva (GANG), the headquarters of which was his office at 10, rue du Prince, before being transferred to the address of another Geneva architect, Marc-Joseph Saugey. He was also a member of the International Congress of Modern Architecture (CIAM) and the Federation of Swiss Architects (FAS).

During construction of the Clarté building, Quétant was employed by Wanner to carry out detailed studies and cost estimates. He redrew most of the dimensionless sketches and established the construction plans. He was one of the first tenants, renting the attic "penthouse" illegally because the rooms were not intended for habitation but as artist studios (see chapter "Chronology").

During the construction of Clarté, Quétant designed a decidedly avant-garde villa near to the chemin de Ruth. In 1936, he won the second prize for large buildings for his recently completed structure located at 1 and 3, chemin de Roches. Two years later, permission to build an apartment building at 9–11, avenue Théodore-Weber was granted to Adolphe Guyonnet, Boris Nazarieff, and Quétant. The latter had been interested in city planning from the start when, in 1945, together with Jean-Jacques Honegger, he conceived projects for the development of the Malagnou and Villereuse neighbourhoods, presented in the *Rapport de la commission d'étude pour le développement de Genève.* In 1949 he worked with engineer Peter Honegger on the tramway kiosk at the Place des Nations. Finally, in 1949–1950, Quétant finalized the design of the Eglise néo-apostolique in Servette, working with plans drawn up by the architects Moser, Haefeli and Steiger.

Boris Nazarieff (1908–1979)

Born in Saint Petersburg, Russia (1914 Petrograd, Leningrad 1924, now Saint Petersburg) and arriving in Geneva in 1918, Nazarieff studied architecture at the Technicum de Geneva. Employed by Wanner, from 1928 to 1929 he took part in the construction of the Villa Ruf at 12, chemin des Manons in Grand-Saconnex, under the direction of his brother-in-law Quétant and Wanner. Then he was hired as site foreman for the construction of the Clarté building.

After the completion of Clarté and leaving Wanner's employment, together with Quétant he opened an architectural practice at 10, Prince Street, Geneva. From 1938, Nazarieff worked with Adolphe Guyonnet and Francis Quétant on the construction of the apartment buildings at 9–11, avenue Théodore-Weber.

He was a founding member of the Groupe pour l'Architecture Nouvelle in Geneva (GANG) in 1931 and fought for the defence of modern architecture through his articles published in the Bulletin of the Association of Technicians of Geneva (ATG).

The first Clarté residents

The Clarté building was intended for the better-off classes, professionals and senior public servants. Most of the main figures involved in its construction and interior decoration lived there in the early years: Pierre Scheidegger and his publicity adviser René Chevalley, Gustavus Adolphus Hufschmid, Else Hamann, Robert Jeanneret (brother of Pierre and father of Jacqueline Jeanneret, who since the building's construction has lived in a nine-room duplex at 2, rue Saint-Laurent), Theo Divorne, painter and decorator (draughtsman from April 1900 for the brothers Louis and Felix Wanner), and the architects Torcapel and Quétant.

Until 1939, Clarté also lodged several senior officials of the League of Nations and the International Labour Office, including Ernest Charrère, as well as various painters, architects, doctors, lawyers, attorneys, banking executives, teachers, and journalists, including the director of Radio-Genève SA, Felix Pommier. It also housed the pharmaceutical company Plastiform SA, a beauty salon, and a physical education institute.

Pascal Häusermann lived in the building with his parents in the nine-room duplex at No. 2 from 1939. In 1940, the young architect Pierre Braillard, son of Maurice, came to settle there. Finally, Wanner lived there for twenty years or so.

Subsequently, numerous personalities from various professions lived at Clarté. We cannot list them all but mention two architects with close ties to the property, Bruno Camoletti and Jean-Jacques Oberson, and finally the eminent art historian and executor of Le Corbusier's will, Maurice Besset, who sadly passed away in 2008.

The executor of Le Corbusier's will

Maurice Besset (1921–2008)

Art historian, museum curator, university professor, and the author of major studies, including on Le Corbusier, Maurice Besset was from Mouthe, in the French Jura. He studied at the Ecole Normale Supérieure in rue d'Ulm in Paris, where he obtained an aggregate in German. His career began in Austria, at the French Institute of Innsbruck (1947–1958), and continued at the Maison de France in Berlin.

He was then appointed curator at the Musée National d'Art Moderne in Paris (1960–65) and became director of the Grenoble museum, a position he held between 1969 and 1975, while teaching the history of contemporary art at the universities of Besançon, Grenoble, and Geneva (1972–1991), succeeding another great personality, Jean Leymarie. Besset shaped a generation of students with his multidisciplinary teaching combining literature, theatre, philosophy, music, painting, photography, sculpture, architecture, and urbanism. His curious mind was open to all the fields of the creative arts, and he was able to transmit his polymorphous cultural knowledge to his students. Starting in 1963, at the request of André Malraux, he participated in the cataloguing of XX century French architectural heritage buildings, and published, in 1967, one of the first synoptic studies of contemporary architecture, *La nouvelle architecture française.*
Soon after the war, Maurice Besset met Le Corbusier and wrote the masterful survey of his work, *Qui était Le Corbusier?,* published in 1968 in the Skira series edited by Jean Leymarie. He contributed to the publication in 1981 of *Carnets de Le Corbusier (Le Corbusier Sketchbooks),* co-published by MIT Press, Cambridge, and the Le Corbusier Foundation in Paris. He had become a close friend to Le Corbusier, who made him executor of his will. Besset lived in the Clarté building from 1978 until his death in a five-room apartment at No. 4.

Clarté photographers

Photographers of the Clarté's construction

The construction and outfitting of the Clarté building were photographed by well-known professionals like Paul Boissonnas, Frank-Henri Jullien, Hans Finsler[3], and Sigfried Giedion. Most of their work was commissioned by Wanner and Geneva interior designers, particularly Gustavus Adolphus Hufschmid and Peter Scheidegger[4]. The latter was the Geneva representative of the Zurich-based Wohnbedarf furnishings company, which had a showroom in an arcade on the Clarté's ground floor. This company had furnished several Clarté apartments between 1932 and 1933. These were immortalised by photographs, valuable evidence that clarify the various stages of construction and fitting-out, since the Boissonnas photographs bear the date of delivery, and those of Jullien the order date. Boissonnas, who illustrated the text on the Clarté building in *L'Œuvre complète*[5], was also sought to catalogue the Wohnbedarf furnishing range in June 1933.
As for the art historian Sigfried Giedion[6], enlightened amateur photographer and friend of Finsler – co-owner of the Wohnbedarf company founded in 1931 – he took several snapshots. Most notably, he documented the flight of the Zeppelin over Geneva with a photograph in which the airship is visible between the elements of the Clarté building's structural frame.

The attribution of certain photographs to Lucien Hervé is erroneous. In reality this eminent photographer only started working for Le Corbusier in 1949.

Paul Boissonnas (1902–1983)

The Boissonnas[7] dynasty of photographers was founded in 1864 in Geneva by Henri-Antoine (1833–89). The studio was taken over on his death by his eldest son, Fred (1858–1946), in 1920, and then for four years by Fred's eldest son, Edmond-Edouard (1891–1924), who was succeeded by Fred's third son, Paul-Henri (1894–1966) from 1924 to 1927. Paul Boissonnas (1902–1983), Fred's seventh child, directed the workshop from 1927 to 1969. These photographers enjoyed international fame and established various studios abroad, notably in Lyon in 1902, Marseille, Petrograd (today, Saint Petersburg), and in Paris in 1923.

Frank-Henri Jullien (1882–1938)

Born into a dynasty of Geneva photographers, Frank-Henri Jullien had collaborated with "one of the best Geneva photography studios"[8] before taking over the company Fueslin-Rigaud in 1912–13. He made many portraits, notably of people who gravitated around the international organisations such as the League of Nations and the International Labour Office, many of whom lived in the Clarté building. He was a sports photographer, an active member of the Société nautique de Genève, as was his contemporary Felix Wanner, brother of Edmond, and also a photographer of industry and architecture. He was a founder of the photojournalists' union of the Geneva press association.

Hans Finsler (1891–1972)

A Swiss from Heilbronn[9], Hans Finsler studied architecture in Stuttgart and Munich, where he completed his art history courses, notably under Heinrich Wölfflin, and also befriended Sigfried Giedion. He continued his education in Berlin and studied under Paul Frankl at the Kunstgewerbeschule in Halle. He was an active member of the Swiss Werkbund from 1932, and initiated the photography class at the Kunstgewerbeschule in Zurich, where he taught. Among his many students were the photographers Werner Bischof and René Burri.

Sigfried Giedion (1888–1968)

Born in Prague, Sigfried Giedion studied engineering at the Technical University of Vienna (Austria) and then art history in Zurich and Munich, where he obtained his doctorate in 1922 under Heinrich Wölfflin, influenced by the ideas of Jakob Burckhardt and Alois Riegl. At the first Bauhaus exhibition in Weimar in 1923, he met Walter Gropius. After his meeting with Le Corbusier the same year in Paris, shortly after the publication of the book *Vers une architecture,* Giedion became co-founder and secretary general of the International Congresses of Modern Architecture (CIAM) from 1928 to 1956. Professor at the ETH School in Zurich and then Harvard University, he published his lectures in 1940 in the work *Espace, temps, architecture,* which remains a work of reference to this day.

The photographer of the Clarté restoration (2007–2011)

Claudio Merlini

A graduate of the Geneva fine arts school in 1987, Claudio Merlini was an assistant teacher in the school's photography workshop and a member of the photography jury. A freelance photographer from 1989, he focuses on architecture and architectural heritage. He undertakes public and private commissions while pursuing personal research on photography of Switzerland, its cityscapes, suburbs, and industrial sites. Between 2007 and 2010 he was commissioned by the Office of Heritage Buildings and Sites to make a photographic record of the actual condition and the restoration of the Clarté building. Then in 2012 he was commissioned by the Société d'histoire de l'art en Suisse to provide illustrations of the building for the book *Le Corbusier. Formation, projets et constructions en Suisse,* published in 2012.

The architect and engineer of the Clarté restoration (2007–2011)

Jacques-Louis de Chambrier (*1951)

An architect who graduated from the Federal Institute of Technology in Zurich (ETH) in 1976, Jacques-Louis de Chambrier has made numerous architectural voyages. He participated in the architectural inventory of the Canton of Geneva of the Service des monuments et des sites in coordination with the office of Monique Bory. Then he opened his own architectural practice in 1978. Until 2006, his practice involved several partnerships in Neuchâtel and Geneva. His many activities include architecture and construction, building construction, real estate promotion, conversions, and restorations. Following a competition, he designed the N5 highway maintenance service centre at Boudry with Jean-Louis Rivier in 1994. He was responsible for the restoration of Le Corbusier and Pierre Jeanneret's Clarté building; the architectural studies and construction lasted from 2004 to 2011. He was a committee member of the Art History Society in Switzerland from 2000 to 2012 and helped redefine the publication series *Monuments d'art et d'histoire de la Suisse (MAH).*

Igor Berger (*1969)

A civil engineer who graduated from the Federal Polytechnic School of Lausanne (EPFL) in 1994, Igor Berger has been working at Peter Moser's firm of civil engineers, based in Geneva. During his career, he has notably specialised in wood construction. He was responsible for the engineering work during the restoration of Le Corbusier and Pierre Jeanneret's Clarté building; the studies and restoration lasted from 2004 to 2011.

The authors

(in alphabetical order)

Igor Berger (*1969)

See above.

Catherine Courtiau (*1950)

An independent art and architecture historian, Catherine Courtiau is a Master of Arts graduate in art history and Russian from the Faculty of Arts of the University of Geneva in 1980. She was employed part-time by the Swiss art history society, in Berne, from 1980 to 2014, for its Romande branch in Geneva, and as a science writer. She undertakes publishing work and translations from German into French. She has been a member of the committee of the International Council of Monuments and of Sites (ICOMOS) for Switzerland since 2015.

She writes for many publications and undertakes research commissions on buildings of the XIX and XX centuries at the request of public and private organisations.

Author of the first monograph on the Clarté building in 1982, published in the series *Guides de Monuments Suisses,* she has also penned texts for the catalogue of the exhibition *Le Corbusier à Genève 1922–1932,* which took place in the Clarté building in May 1987, as well as the catalogue for the exhibition *La construction de l'immeuble Clarté* organised by the Accademia di architettura dell'Università della Svizzera italiana at Mendrisio in 1999. She devoted an entire chapter to this building in the same series of *Guides de Monuments Suisses,* published in 2012 under the title *Le Corbusier. Formation, projets et constructions en Suisse.*

Jacques-Louis de Chambrier (*1951)

See above.

Jean-Pierre Duport (*1942)

Jean-Pierre Duport, honorary prefect, graduated from the Institute of Political Studies in Paris and the National School of Administration (promotion "Marcel Proust"). He held various positions in high public office: Director of Architecture at the Department of Urban Planning and Housing (1981–1987), delegate for regional planning and regional action (1989–1993), prefect of Seine-Saint-Denis (1993–1998), prefect of Paris, prefect of the Ile-de-France region (1998–2002), President of the French national railway network (2002–2005), he was then appointed an extraordinary board member. He is a Grand Officer of the Légion d'honneur. Jean-Pierre Duport was President of the Le Corbusier Foundation in 2003–2012.

Sabine Nemec-Piguet (*1954)

Graduate of the Federal Polytechnic School of Lausanne in 1978, Sabine Nemec-Piguet, Architect dip., is director of the Office of Heritage Buildings and Sites of the canton of Geneva, and cantonal conservationist of monuments. Within the administration, she led numerous studies and publications on the protection of older neighbourhoods and the preservation of construction heritage. From 1999 to 2010 she was a member of the Federal Commission for the Protection of Nature and Landscape. Since 2012 she is a member of the Federal Commission of Historic Monuments, of which she is Vice President since 2016. She is also a member of the board of the foundation of St Peter's Cathedral in Geneva and a member of the scientific committee of the MAS "Heritage protection and museum studies" at the University of Geneva.

Arthur Rüegg (*1942)

Independent architect and emeritus professor, Arthur Rüegg is a graduate of the Zurich Polytechnic School (1967, Alfred Roth). He practised as an architect in Zurich, Paris, and Boston before opening his own architectural studio in Zurich in 1971, where he practised until 1988 as part of the ARCOOP with his partner Ueli Marbach. They did public and residential building construction and restorations (Werkbundsiedlung Neubühl, Doldertal, Villa Bleuler, Kunstmuseum Winterthur). Arthur Rüegg is also sought as an expert in the restoration of historic monuments (the Jeanneret-Perret house (1997, 2006, 2015); the "white house" in La Chaux-de-Fonds; Villa La Roche, Paris; the Clarté Building, Geneva; Villa Tugendhat, Brno).

He was a professor at Zurich Polytechnic from 1991 to 2007. He is the author of numerous publications and initiator of exhibitions on Swiss architecture, and construction, colour, and design in modern architecture: *Le Corbusier – Polychromie architecturale. Le Corbusier – Photographies de René Burri/Magnum* (1999). *Le Corbusier before Le Corbusier* (editor with von Moos, 2002). *René Burri : Pour Le Corbusier* (2006). *Le Corbusier – Art in Architecture* (editor with von Moos and Kries, 2007). *Le Corbusier – Meubles et Intérieurs 1905–1965* (2012). *La cellule – L'unité d'habitation de Marseille* (editor, with Bonillo, Drut, Tropeano, 2013).

Marielle Savoyat (*1977)

Architect graduate from the Ecole polytechnique fédérale de Lausanne (EPFL) in 2004, Marielle Savoyat worked since 2001 in several architect/urbanism offices in western Switzerland and Paris. As an expert assistant, she collaborated with Professor Bruno Marchand from 2005 to 2013 at the laboratory of the theory and history of architecture at the EPFL (LTH2), then with Professor Yves Weinand from 2013 to 2015 at the laboratory for construction in wood (IBOIS). She has contributed to several books on architecture in Switzerland.

In 2010, she founded the office *marielle savoyat – communiquer l'architecture* in Lausanne, whose core business is the valuation of architecture in western Switzerland.

Bernard Zumthor (*1943)

With a degree in the history of art and architecture from the University of Geneva and a doctorate from the University of London (UCL) in the history of urbanism, Bernard Zumthor wrote the thesis "Urban Theory in Nineteenth-century Europe" in 1975. Then, until 1984, he was professor of the history of architecture and urbanism at the University of London. Thereafter, and until 1993, he held the post of Consultant in Heritage Conservation for the City of Geneva. In 1993 he was appointed director of the former Ecole supérieure des beaux-arts of Geneva (HEAD – Genève), a position he held until 2002. From 2002 to 2008 he was director of the Directorate of Heritage and Sites of the State of Geneva, and in 2007, Cantonal Monuments Conservationist. Since 1985, he has also worked as a federal expert for heritage conservation with the Federal Office of Culture, and is a member of the Federal Commission for Historic Monuments. From 2013 to 2015, he held the role of vice president of the Federal Commission for Historical Monuments.

1 *Wanner & Cie Genève Vous présentent…*, n.d. [after 1932]. – *Théo Divorne, Centenaire Wanner et Cie*, Geneva 1853–1953, Geneva 1953; Théo Divorne was a painter-decorator and draughtsman at the firm of the brothers Louis and Félix Wanner from 1900. – Armand Brulhart, Catherine Courtiau, *Le Corbusier – une encyclopédie*, Paris, 1987, pp. 477–478.

2 David P. Billington, "Robert Maillart (1872–1940)", in *Schweizer Pioniere der Wirtschaft und Technik*. Fünf Schweizer Brückenbauer, Verein für wirtschaftshistorische Studien, Zurich, 1985. – Peter Marti, Emil Honegger (dir.), *Robert Maillart. Beton-Virtuose*, exhibition catalogue, Gesellschaft für Ingenieurbaukunst, Zurich, 1996.

3 Lists of Boissonnas with the delivery date, and Finsler's record books with the date of the order, documents held at the Geneva Library (CIG).

4 Le Corbusier and Pierre Jeanneret, Pierre Scheidegger, "La maison de verre. Immeubles 'Clarté'", in *L'art en Suisse*, Geneva, April-May 1933. – *Allgemeines Lexikon der bildenden Künstler des XX. Jahrhunderts*, Leipzig, 1953–1962. – *Künstlerlexikon der Schweiz. XX. Jahrhundert*, Frauenfeld, 1958–1967.

5 A series of books in which the photographic credits are hugely absent!

6 The series Sigfried Giedion und die Fotografie. *Bildinszenierungen der Moderne, Werner Oechslin and Gregor Harbusch*, ed., Zurich: gta Verlag, 2010.

7 Nicolas Bouvier, *Un siècle de photographie à Genève. Les Boissonnas*, exhibition cat. Rath museum, Geneva, 8 October to 29 November 1981. – Nicolas Bouvier, *Boissonnas, une dynastie de photographes 1864–1983*, Payot, Lausanne, 1983.

8 Obituary of Frank-Henri Jullien in the *Tribune de Genève* of 20 October 1938.

9 Hans Finsler. *Neue Wege der Photographie series*, Leipzig, 1991.

Select bibliography and sources

Catherine Courtiau

(in chronological order)

L'immeuble Clarté

— M.P., "Clarté, la maison de verre. Rue Adrien-Lachenal, Genève", in *Bâtir,* II / 1, january 1932, pp. 1–4.

— Sigfried Giedion, "Ein Mietsblock Le Corbusier in Genf", in *Bauwelt,* issue 37, 15 September 1932, pp. 1–8.

— Christian Zervos, "Immeuble 'Clarté' à Genève, par Le Corbusier et Pierre Jeanneret", in *Cahiers d'art,* 6–7, Paris 1932, pp. 289–294.

— Sigfried Giedion, "Le Corbusiers Miethaus 'Clarté' in Genf 1932/33", in *Das ideale Heim,* VII/2, February 1933, pp. 45–59.

— Le Corbusier, Pierre Jeanneret, Pierre Scheidegger, "La Maison de verre, immeubles 'Clarté'", in *L'Art en Suisse,* Geneva, April-May 1933.

— Ms [Herbert J. von Moos?], " 'Clarté', Le Corbusier et P. Jeanneret, architectes", in *Architecture – Art appliqué,* May 1933, pp. 15–22.

— R[ené] Lhote, "Des maisons de verre", in *L'Architecture d'Aujourd'hui* (volume dedicated to Le Corbusier et à Pierre Jeanneret), 10, 1933, pp. 93–99.

— Peter Meyer, "Diskussion um Le Corbusier. 'La Maison de Verre', von Le Corbusier and Pierre Jeanneret, Paris", in *Das Werk,* September 1934, pp. 257–269.

— Le Corbusier and Pierre Jeanneret, "Immeuble 'Clarté', à Genève, 1930/32", in *Œuvre complète de 1929–1934,* published by Willy Boesiger, Editions Girsberger, Les Editions d'Architecture (Artemis), Zurich 1964 (1st édition 1935), pp. 66–71.

— *aujourd'hui, art et architecture* (volume dedicated to the œuvre of Le Corbusier and Pierre Jeanneret published by *L'Architecture d'Aujourd'hui),* 9/51, November 1965, pp. 22, 32.

— Maurice Besset, *Qui était Le Corbusier?,* Skira, Geneva 1968, pp. 84, 154, 209.

— Jacques Gubler, "SOS. Le sort de l'immeuble 'Clarté' de Le Corbusier & Pierre Jeanneret", in *Werk,* Winterthour, No. 5, May 1969, pp. 293–295.

— André Corboz, Jacques Gubler, Jean-Marc Lamunière, *Guide d'architecture moderne de Genève,* Payot, Lausanne 1969, pp. 9, 11, 65.

— Jean Petit, *Le Corbusier lui-même,* Editions Rousseau, Geneva 1970, pp. 71, 200, 204.

— Florian Adler, Hans Girsberger, Olinde Riege (ed.), *Guide d'architecture suisse,* Artemis, Zurich 1978 (2e éd.), No. 101, pp. 13, 17.

— Christian Sumi, "Il progetto Wanner", in *Rassegna (I clienti di Le Corbusier),* II, No. 3, July 1980, pp. 39–46.

— Catherine Courtiau, *L'Immeuble Clarté Genève. Le Corbusier – 1931/32,* Guides de Monuments suisses SHAS, volume 32, No. 319, Berne 1982.

— Bruno Reichlin, "The Pros and Cons of the Horizontal Window. The Perret-Le Corbusier Controversy", in *Daidalos, Berlin Architectural Journal,* 13, 15 September 1984, pp. 65–78.

— Christian Sumi, "Clarté (immeuble)", in *Le Corbusier, une encyclopédie, monographie,* Centre Georges-Pompidou / CCI, Paris 1987, p. 100.

— Christian Sumi, "L'immeuble Clarté et la conception de la 'maison à sec' ", in *Le Corbusier à Genève, 1922–1932, projets et réalisations,* catalogue de l'exposition à l'immeuble Clarté, Payot, Lausanne 1987, p. 93–112.

— "La réception: Le Corbusier dans 'Das Werk' ", in *Werk. Bauen + Wohnen* (Le Corbusiers Erbe), No. 7/8, July/August 1987, pp. 50–60.

— Maurice Besset, "Im Glashaus leben", in *Bauwelt,* issue 38/39, 9 October 1987, pp. 1456–1458.

— Catherine Courtiau, "L'immeuble Clarté, Genève, 1930–1932, de Le Corbusier et Pierre Jeanneret", in *Habitation,* 5, 1987, pp. 43–48.

— Christian Sumi, *Immeuble CLARTÉ Genf 1932, von Le Corbusier & Pierre Jeanneret,* gta/ Ammann, Zurich 1989.

— Christian Sumi, "Treppenhaus als Lichtquelle. Das Treppenhaus des Immeuble Clarté in Genf, 1932, von Le Corbusier und Pierre Jeanneret", in *Werk, Bauen + Wohnen,* 6/1989, pp. 62–66, 69.

— Armand Brulhart et Erica Deuber-Pauli, *Ville et canton de Genève, Arts et monuments,* Société d'Histoire de l'Art en Suisse, Catherine Courtiau (dir.), Berne 1993 (2nd ed.), pp. 161–162.

— Inès Lamunière and Patrick Devanthéry, "L'immeuble 'Clarté' à Genève (1930–1932)", in *Le Moniteur, AMC Architecture,* 65, October 1995, pp. 68–72.

— Paul Marti Jr, "Immeuble résidentiel Clarté 1931–32", in *Guide d'architecture suisse,*

1920–1995, Christa Zeller (réd.), Werk Verlag, Zurich 1996, vol. 3, No. 408, pp. 140, 159.

— Catherine Courtiau, Inès Lamunière, Arthur Rüegg; Luca Bellinelli (dir.), *La costruzione dell'Immeuble Clarté / La construction de l'immeuble Clarté,* Cataloghi dell'Accademia di architettura, Mendrisio 1999.

— Laurence Carducci, "La Clarté sur les traces de Le Corbusier", in *Tendance Déco,* 6, Décember 2001 – February 2002, pp. 36–46.

— Inès Lamunière and Patrick Devanthéry, "La 'Clarté', le fer, le verre et l'immeuble d'habitation urbain", in *Massilia, Annuaire d'études corbuséennes,* 21, Barcelona 2003, pp. 110–117.

— Naïma Jornod and Jean-Pierre Jornod, *Le Corbusier (Charles Edouard Jeanneret), Catalogue raisonné de l'œuvre peint,* 2 volumes, Skira, Milan 2005, t. I, p. 132.

— Laurent Chenu, "Inventaire intérieur de l'Immeuble Clarté, 1207 Genève (GE)", in *Architecture suisse,* 161/2, 2006, pp. 15–18.

— Isabelle Claden, "Inkunabel", in *Tec21,* No. 7, February 2006, pp. 14–17.

— Jacques-Louis de Chambrier, "La restauration des fenêtres de l'immeuble Clarté à Genève", in *Patrimoine et architecture. Les fenêtres, vues sur un patrimoine,* Office du patrimoine et des sites, journal No. 16, Geneva, May 2008, pp. 52–54.

— Catherine Courtiau (dir. and co-author), *XXe. Un siècle d'architectures à Genève, promenades,* Infolio, Patrimoine suisse Genève PsG, Gollion, Geneva 2009, pp. 48–49.

— Catherine Courtiau, "L'immeuble Clarté", in *Patrimoine et architecture. Chantiers 2005–2010,* Office du patrimoine et des sites, No. 19–20, Geneva, January 2012, pp. 48–49.

— Catherine Courtiau, *Le Corbusier. Formation, projets et constructions en Suisse,* Guides d'art et d'histoire de la Suisse SHAS, series 91, No. 908, Berne 2012.

Archives, raports, records, plans

— Fondation Le Corbusier FLC, Paris (founded 1966 for public use).

— Archives d'Etat de Genève AEG.

— Bibliothèque de Genève BGE / Centre d'iconographie genevoise CIG.

— Ecole polytechnique fédérale de Zurich EPFZ, Institut gta, Fonds John Torcapel: copies of the original plans 1931/32.

— Dominique Gampert, Janez Hacin, Jean-Jacques Oberson, architectes: plans, records and transformations, Geneva 1966–1970.

— Jean-Pierre Grand, Roger Praplan et associés SA, plans, records, transformations, Carouge 1971/72.

— Bruno Camoletti, Pascal Häusermann, architectes: plans, records and transformations, Geneva 1975/76.

— Inès Lamunière and Patrick Devanthéry, architectes: section of the facade, state of reconstruction at the end of 1932 and changes, scale 1:20, mandate of the Service des monuments et des sites, Geneva 1992.

— Jacques-Louis de Chambrier, Alain Dutheil, Pietro Carlo Sartorio, *Descriptif sommaire de la construction et points remarquables,* Geneva, 11 March 2004.

— Laurent Chenu, "Immeuble Clarté, cahier d'inventaire", mandate of the Direction du patrimoine et des sites, Geneva March 2006.

— Atelier Saint-Dismas (Eric James Favre-Bulle, Alain Besse), "Rapport sur les couleurs d'origine (d'après sondages sur place)", mandate of the Direction du patrimoine et des sites (Geneva), Lausanne 2006.

— Pierre Moser, civil engineer, "Rapport sur l'examen de l'enveloppe concernant l'immeuble La Clarté", Geneva, February 2004. – "Immeuble La Clarté. Rapport sur l'examen des balcons après travaux de sablage", Geneva, 12 December 2005. – "Immeuble La Clarté. Rapport sur l'examen des balcons et méthodes de réparation. Compléments et synthèse de nos rapports de février 2004 et du 12 décembre 2005", Geneva, 13 February 2006.

— Pierre Moser, civil engineer, "Immeuble La Clarté, rue Saint-Laurent 2–4,1207 Genève. Réfection des balcons et parapets. Descriptif des travaux de serrurerie pour les éléments porteurs des balcons, dossier photos en annexe à la soumission", Geneva, 20 July 2006.

— Anne Rinuy, Martine Degli Agosti, "Examens stratigraphiques des prélèvements 001–012", laboratoire des Musées d'art et d'histoire, dossier du laboratoire No. HI 2006–304, Geneva, October 2006.

— Jacques-Louis de Chambrier, Alain Dutheil, "Immeuble Clarté, descriptif restauration façade métallique", Geneva, 30 January 2007.

— Catherine Courtiau, "Structure de l'immeuble Clarté, Genève, Le Corbusier / Pierre Jeanneret, 1931/32. La structure des balcons. 1er rapport", juin 2006. – "Etat d'origine de certains éléments de l'enveloppe extérieure et des communs. Rapport de synthèse", 20 mars + complément du 24 avril 2007, mandats de la Direction du patrimoine et des sites, Geneva 2006 and 2007.

— Claude Félix, "Rapport No. UCP/FX/2007/712. Plaques minces agrafées de travertin dans un revêtement extérieur de façades – état de conservation", Ecublens, 30 July 2007.

— République et canton de Genève, Communauté des copropriétaires de l'immeuble Clarté, "Restauration de l'immeuble Clarté de Le Corbusier", press kit of 24 August, 2007, Geneva.

— Jacques-Louis de Chambrier, "Clarté, chantier de restauration", ICOMOS conference, Geneva, 2 November, 2007.

— Dossier for the application for the inclusion to the list of UNESCO World Heritage sites "L'Œuvre architecturale de Le Corbusier. Une contribution exceptionnelle au *Mouvement Moderne*", Immeuble Clarté, Geneva:
Volume I, chapter I, pp. 20, 21, 24, 31, 48–49; chapter II, pp. 80, 83, 85–89, 98, 99, 135–137; chapter III, pp. 185, 227; chapter IV, pp. 245, 253; chapter V, pp. 286, 315; chapter VI, p. 335;

chapter VII, pp. 344, 346, 353; chapter VIII, pp. 362, 364.
Volume II, Immeuble Clarté, pp. 19–24.
Confédération suisse, Département fédéral de l'intérieur, Office de la culture, "Plan de gestion, de communication et de développement durable", Villa Jeanneret-Perret, Petite villa au bord du lac Léman, Immeuble Clarté, January 2011, pp. 1–14.

— Atelier Saint-Dismas (Eric James Favre-Bulle, Alain Besse), "Tableau synoptique des couleurs – investigations, sondages et examens – intérieur cage d'escalier – immeuble Clarté – rue Saint-Laurent No. 2, Genève", Geneva, 13 octobre 2008.

— Jacques-Louis de Chambrier, Alain Dutheil, verbal report, on 17 April, 2007 and 6 July, 2011.

— Atelier Saint-Dismas (Eric James Favre-Bulle, Alain Besse), "Rapport. Investigations, sondages et examens. Appartement ouest, 7e étage immeuble 'Clarté', rue Saint-Laurent No. 4, Genève", rapport provisoire, mandat de la Direction du patrimoine et des sites, 28 novembre 2011.

Select bibliography on Le Corbusier

— Alfred Roth, *Zwei Wohnhäuser von Le Corbusier und Pierre Jeanneret. Fünf Punkte zu einer neuen Architektur,* Akadem. Verlag Dr. Fr. Wedekind & Co., Stuttgart 1927.

— *L'Architecture d'Aujourd'hui* (special volume in the series dedicated to Le Corbusier), April 1948.

— *aujourd'hui, art et architecture* (special volume dedicated to the oeuvre of Le Corbusier and Pierre Jeanneret) published by *L'Architecture d'Aujourd'hui),* 9/51, November 1965, pp. 22, 32.

— Maurice Besset, *Qui était Le Corbusier,* Skira, Geneva 1968.

— Jean Petit, *Le Corbusier lui-même,* Editions Rousseau, Geneva 1970.

— Giuliano Gresleri, *Le Corbusier,* Viaggio in Oriente, Marsilio Editori, Venise, and Fondation Le Corbusier, Paris 1984.

— H. Allen Brooks (dir.), *The Le Corbusier Archive,* edited by Garland Architectural Archives, New York 1982–1984, 32 volumes.

— Gérard Monnier, *Le Corbusier. Qui suis-je?,* La Manufacture, Lyon 1986.

— Jean-Louis Cohen, Bruno Reichlin (scientific adviser), Jacques Lucan (dir.), *Le Corbusier, une encyclopédie,* Centre Georges Pompidou/CCI, Paris 1987.

— Different authors; Isabelle Charollais, André Ducret (coord. of the work), Patrick Devanthéry, Inès Lamunière (commissioner of the exhibition), *Le Corbusier à Genève 1922–1932, projets et réalisations,* catalogue d'exposition à l'immeuble Clarté, Payot, Lausanne 1987.

— "Du 5 au 30 mai. Le Corbusier à Genève dans l'immeuble Clarté", in *Habitat & Architecture,* off-print by the *Journal de Genève,* 7 May 1987.

— Arthur Rüegg (ed. and author), *Polychromie architecturale. Color Keyboards from 1931 and 1959 (3 vol. with 2 color keyboards Salubra),* Birkhäuser, Basel, Boston, Berlin 1997; 2nd revised edition, 2006; 3rd édition, with a new postscript by Arthur Rüegg, 2015.

— H. Allen Brooks, *Le Corbusier's Formative Years,* The University of Chicago Press, Chicago, London 1997.

— Kenneth Frampton, *Le Corbusier (World of Art),* Thames & Hudson, London 2001.

— Stanislaus von Moos, Arthur Rüegg (ed. and author), *Le Corbusier before Le Corbusier,* The Bard Graduate Center for Studies in the Decorative Arts, Design, and Culture, New York; Langmatt Museum, Baden; Yale University Press, New Haven, London 2002.

— Different authors, *Le Corbusier. La Suisse, les Suisses,* XIIIe Rencontre de la Fondation Le Corbusier, Editions de la Villette, Paris 2006.

Selection of publications by Le Corbusier

— Charles-Edouard Jeanneret, *Etude sur le mouvement d'art décoratif en Allemagne,* Haefeli & Cie, La Chaux-de-Fonds 1912.

— Amédée Ozenfant, Charles-Edouard Jeanneret, *Après le cubisme,* Editions des Commentaires, Paris 1918.

— Le Corbusier, *Vers une architecture,* Editions G. Crès et Cie, Collection de l'Esprit Nouveau, Paris 1923.

— Le Corbusier, *Almanach d'architecture moderne,* Editions G. Crès et Cie, Collection de l'Esprit Nouveau, Paris 1925.

— Le Corbusier, *L'art décoratif d'aujourd'hui,* Editions G. Crès et Cie, Paris 1925.

— Le Corbusier, Pierre Jeanneret, *Une maison – un palais. A la recherche d'une unité architecturale,* Editions G. Crès et Cie, Collection de l'Esprit Nouveau, Paris 1928.

— Paul Otlet, Le Corbusier, Pierre Jeanneret, *Mundaneum,* publication No. 28 de l'UIA, Bruxelles, August 1928.

— Paul Otlet, Le Corbusier, Pierre Jeanneret, *Cité mondiale. Geneva: World Civic Center: Mundaneum,* publication No. 133 de l'UIA, Bruxelles, February 1929.

— *L'Œuvre complète,* 8 volumes, by Le Corbusier, the first three by Le Corbusier and Pierre Jeanneret, the sixth by Le Corbusier and his studio rue de Sèvres 35, published by Editions d'Architecture Zurich (Artemis), Hans Girsberger:

1) *1910–1929,* published by Willy Boesiger et Oscar Stonorov, Erlenbach 1929

2) *1929–1934,* published by Willy Boesiger, Erlenbach 1935

3) *1934–1938,* published by Max Bill, Erlenbach 1935 (+ projects from 1935 to 1938)

4) *1938–1946* (1st part, 1938–1940, with Pierre Jeanneret), published by Willy Boesiger, Erlenbach 1946

5) *1946–1952,* published by Willy Boesiger, Zurich 1953

6) *1952–1957,* published by Willy Boesiger, Zurich 1958

7) *1957–1965,* published by Willy Boesiger, Zurich 1965

8) publication posthumous, *Les dernières Œuvres,* by Willy Boesiger, Zurich 1970

— Le Corbusier, *Précisions sur un état présent de l'architecture et de l'urbanisme,* Editions G. Crès et Cie, Collection de l'Esprit Nouveau, Paris 1930.

— Le Corbusier, *Quand les cathédrales étaient blanches,* Librairie Plon, Paris 1937.

— Le Corbusier, *Sur les 4 routes,* nrf Gallimard, Paris 1941.

— Le groupe CIAM-France [Le Corbusier], avec un discours liminaire de Jean Giraudoux, *La charte d'Athènes,* Plon, Paris, April 1943.

— Le Corbusier, *Manière de penser l'urbanisme,* Editions de L'Architecture d'Aujourd'hui, Paris 1946.

— Le Corbusier, *Le Modulor,* Editions de L'Architecture d'Aujourd'hui, Paris 1950.

— Le Corbusier, *Une petite maison, Les carnets de la recherche patiente,* Editions Girsberger, carnet No. 1, Zurich, August 1954.

— Le Corbusier, *Le Modulor 2,* Editions de L'Architecture d'Aujourd'hui, Paris 1955.

Sketchbooks and correspondences published

(avec transcriptions)

— Françoise de Franclieu (commentary), *Le Corbusier – Carnets:* complete publication of 73 skechtbooks in 4 volumes, Fondation Le Corbusier, Paris; The Architectural History Foundation, New York; Editions Herscher/Dessain et Tolra, Paris:

Volume 1, 1914–1948, André Wogensky (preface), Maurice Besset (introduction), Paris 1981

Volume 2, 1950–1954, Paris 1981

Volume 3, 1954–1957, Paris 1982

Volume 4, 1957–1964, published with the support of the Centre national des Lettres, Paris 1982

— Le Corbusier (Charles-Edouard Jeanneret), *Voyage d'Orient. Carnets,* Electa, Fondation L.C., Milan and Paris 1987.

— Le Corbusier (Charles-Edouard Jeanneret), *Voyage d'Allemagne. Carnets,* Electa, Fondation L.C., Milan and Paris 1994.

— Jean Jenger (sélection, introduction and notes), *Le Corbusier. Choix de lettres,* Birkhäuser, Basel, Boston, Berlin 2002.

— Marie-Jeanne Dumont (presentation and annotations), *Le Corbusier. Lettres à ses maîtres. Lettres à Auguste Perret,* tome I, Editions du Linteau, Paris 2002.

— Marie-Jeanne Dumont (presentation and annotations), *Le Corbusier. Lettres à ses maîtres. Lettres à L'Eplattenier,* volume II, Editions du Linteau, Paris 2006.

— Mathilde Tieleman (presentation and annotations), *Le Corbusier – José Luis Sert. Correspondance,* Editions du Linteau, Paris, 2009.

— Rémi Baudouï and Arnaud Dercelles, *Le Corbusier. Correspondance. Lettres à la famille 1900–1925,* volume I, FLC, Infolio, Paris, Gollion 2011.

— Rémi Baudouï and Arnaud Dercelles, *Le Corbusier. Correspondance. Lettres à la famille 1926–1946,* volume II, FLC, Infolio, Paris, Gollion 2013.

— Marie-Jeanne Dumont (presentation and annotations), *Le Corbusier – William Ritter, correspondance croisée 1910–1955,* volume III, Editions du Linteau, Paris 2015.

— Rémi Baudouï and Arnaud Dercelles, *Le Corbusier. Correspondance. Lettres à la famille 1947–1965,* volume III, FLC, Infolio, Paris, Gollion 2016.

Acknowledgements

This book would not have been possible without the initiative of Bernard Zumthor, former cantonal conservator, and Sabine Nemec-Piguet, the incumbent. We are grateful to Elisabeth Alberici and Sonia Augusto Benavente, the secretariat of the Office of Heritage Buildings and Sites, and to the librarian Anaïs Lemoussu.

Our gratitude extends to all those who participated in the production of this book, the authors Catherine Courtiau, Arthur Rüegg, Bernard Zumthor, Sabine Nemec-Piguet, and Marielle Savoyat, Jacques-Louis de Chambrier for the 2007–2011 plans of the site, the photographer Claudio Merlini, the architect Michael Palffy for his re-reading of the chapter "The restoration of 2007–2011: at the heart of the works" for his technical additions and corrections of the plans, not to mention the various reviewers of all texts.

We thank the institutions that have provided support for this work and who have made available to, their iconographic collections:

— La Fondation Le Corbusier, Paris: Jean-Pierre Duport, president from January 2003 to December 2012; Antoine Picon, president; Michel Richard, director; Delphine Studer, librarian.

— Le Centre d'iconographie genevoise de la Bibliothèque de Genève: Nicolas Schätti, conservator; Cécile Dobler, scientific assistant.

— The Geneva museum of history and art: Martine Degli Agosti, technical assistant; Angelo Lui, manager of photographic records.

— The archives of the gta at EPF Zurich: Daniel Weiss, director, Muriel Pérez and Filine Wagner, assistants.

The building's co-owners have shown great interest in this publication project and we are very grateful to them for their support. They received a grant from the Loterie romande destined to support this publication.

Birkhäuser, Basel, who took over the Girsberger publishing house, were inspired by their publication of "The complete works of Le Corbusier" that they had revised in 1995. Birkhäuser's Alexander Felix and Katharina Kulke have thrown themselves into production of this book with enormous enthusiasm, and engaged the Geneva-based graphic designers Séverine Mailler and Marion Wyss to ensure and assist, by close collaboration, the book's production.

Finally we wish to acknowledge the generous support of the Confederation in the realisation of this publication.

Birkhäuser, Basel
Office of Heritage Buildings and Sites
The State of Geneva

Photo Credits

Photographies, plans and sketches

Archives Catherine Courtiau: pp. 25 (3), 30, 33 (2), 54–55, 56–57.
Archives of the state of Geneva: pp. 22/23.
Archives gta/EPFZurich, collection John Torcapel: pp. 42–43, 52–53, 58–63, 74–75, 150–151.
Archives Arthur Rüegg: pp. 38 (9), 39, 40 (12), 128 (1), 137 (10, 11), 139.
Bibliothèque de Genève/Centre d'iconographie genevoise: pp. 5, 6, 7, 24, 25 (2, 4), 28 (7), 29, 40 (13).
Architectural studio Jacques-Louis de Chambrier: pp. 64–73, 87 (6).
Fondation Le Corbusier, Paris : pp. 26, 28 (6), 33 (3).
Hans-Finsler-Nachlass, Moritzburg, Halle (Germany): p. 34
Igor Berger, civil engineer: pp. 87 (4, 5), 92, 93 (9), 95 (14, 15, 16), 116, 117 (4).
Laurent Chenu, architect: p. 159.
Serge Fruehauf, photographer: pp. 82 (1), 88 (1).
Claudio Merlini, photographer: pp. 1, 2, 3, 4, 8, 9, 10–11, 79, 81 (4, 5), 82 (2), 83, 84, 85, 86, 87 (6, 7, 8), 88 (2, 3), 89, 90 (2), 91, 93 (7, 8), 94, 95 (13), 96, 97, 98, 99, 100, 101, 102, 103, 106, 107, 110, 115, 117 (5, 6), 118, 119, 122, 123 (8, 9), 128 (2), 129, 130 (5), 131, 132, 133, 134, 136, 137 (12 à 15), 138, 140, 141, 142, 143, 149.

All the plans in the chapter "At the heart of the works" (pp. 76–143) as well the plans of the roof are provided by the studio of Jacques-Louis de Chambrier and from Bâti-métal. The preparation of the files for the publication were done by Michael Palffy.

Tables

Atelier Saint-Dismas (Eric-James Favre-Bulle): pp. 144–145.
Laboratoire des Musées d'art et d'histoire, Geneva (Anne Rinuy, Martine Degli Agosti): pp. 146–148.

Reproductions taken from the works

— Max Bill (ed.), *Le Corbusier & Pierre Jeanneret, OEuvre complète 1934–1938,* Girsberger, Zurich 1939: p. 32.
— Le Corbusier and Pierre Jeanneret, *Almanach d'architecture moderne,* Crès, Paris 1926: p. 33 (3).
— Arthur Rüegg, Charlotte Perriand. *Livre de bord 1928–1933,* Infolio, Gollion 2004: p. 33 (4).
— Brian Brace Taylor, *Le Corbusier et Pessac, 1914–1928,* Fondation Le Corbusier/Harvard University, 1972: pp. 36, 37.
— *Schweizerische Bauzeitung,* 1931: p. 38 (10).

Editor
Sabine Nemec-Piguet
Editorial assistants
Marielle Savoyat, Catherine Courtiau
Proofreading and iconographic research
Aurélie Buisson, Catherine Courtiau
Proofreading of the chapter "The restoration of 2007–2011 – At the heart of the works"
Igor Berger (The structure), Eric-James Favre-Bulle (The colours), Catherine Courtiau, Michael Palffy (and for reprocessing the plans)
Translation from French into English
Richard Palmer, Palmer Consulting, Divonne-les-Bains, France
Current photographs
Claudio Merlini, photographer
Graphic design
Séverine Mailler, Marion Wyss
Paper
Hello Fat matt, 150g/m^2
Printing and binding
DZA Druckerei zu Altenburg GmbH

REPUBLIQUE ET CANTON DE GENEVE
POST TENEBRAS LUX

Schweizerische Eidgenossenschaft
Confédération suisse
Confederazione Svizzera
Confederaziun svizra
Swiss Confederation
Federal Department of Home Affairs FDHA
Federal Office of Culture FOC

Organisation des Nations Unies pour l'éducation, la science et la culture
L'œuvre architecturale de Le Corbusier, une contribution exceptionnelle au Mouvement Moderne
inscrite sur la Liste du patrimoine mondial en 2016

This publication is also available as an e-book (ISBN PDF 978-3-0356-0759-8; ISBN EPUB 978-3-0356-0758-1) and in a French language edition (ISBN 978-3-0356-0960-8).

Library of Congress Cataloging-in-Publication data: A CIP catalog record for this book has been applied for at the Library of Congress.

Bibliographic information published by the German National Library: The German National Library lists this publication in the Deutsche Nationalbibliografie; detailed bibliographic data are available on the Internet at http://dnb.dnb.de.

Printed on acid-free paper produced from chlorine-free pulp. TCF ∞

Printed in Germany
ISBN 978-3-0356-0961-5

P.O. Box 44, 4009 Basel, Switzerland
Part of Walter de Gruyter GmbH, Berlin/Boston

987654321

www.birkhauser.com